BEER LOVER'S
COMPANION

BEER LOVER'S COMPANION

A guide to
producing,
brewing, tasting,
rating and
drinking
around the
world

By Josh Leventhal

BLACK DOG
& LEVENTHAL
PUBLISHERS
NEW YORK

Published by
Black Dog & Leventhal Publishers, Inc.
151 West 19th Street
New York, NY 10011

Distributed by
Workman Publishing Company
708 Broadway
New York, NY 10003

Beer ratings by Michael Jackson
Copyright © Michael Jackson
The Beer Hunter ® 1996, 1999

Product photographs by George Wieser

Manufactured in the United States of America

ISBN 1-57912-062-8

Library of congress Cataloging-in-Publication Data

Leventhal, Josh (Joshua), 1971–
    Beer lover's companion / by Josh Leventhal.
            p.   cm.
    Includes index.
    ISBN   1-57912-062-8
    1. Beer. I. Title.

    TP577.L482   1999
    641.2'3—dc21
                    98-50119

                    CIP

Design by Jonette Jakobson

TABLE OF CONTENTS

I. Preface and Acknowledgments.........7

II. The History of Beer 11

III. What is Beer? From Raw Ingredients
to the Finished Product...................16
Ingredients 17
The Brewing Process 24
From the Brewery to You...................30
Microbreweries, Brewpubs and a
    Word About Home-Brewing..........32
Beer Tasting: The Sights, the Smells,
    the Taste 34

IV. Beer Styles 39

V. Beer and Food....................................51
Matching Beer with Food...................51
Cooking with Beer 54
    Food Recipes.................................56
    Drink Recipes................................61

VI. Table of Beer Style Definitions 64

VII. The Beers of the World:
An Introduction 67
England, Scotland and Wales 69
Ireland..83
France 85
Belgium..87
Luxembourg......................................95
The Netherlands 95
Germany...98
Switzerland.......................................107
Austria 108
Czech Republic 110
Eastern Europe
    and the Baltic Region.................113
Scandinavia......................................116
    Denmark.......................................116

Finland 118
Norway 119
Sweden 120
Iceland 120
Southern Europe............................120
Asia..123
Japan..124
China 126
South & Southeast Asia 128
Australia & New Zealand 130
Australia......................................130
New Zealand................................134
Africa & the Middle East 136
United States 138
Northeast 140
Midwest 148
South 155
West...161
Canada 171
Latin America & the Caribbean 176

Index 181

PREFACE AND ACKNOWLEDGMENTS

As recently as a decade ago, ordering a beer in a bar, or selecting one from the beer aisle at the liquor store or supermarket, was a simple task: You generally had the choice of a few pale, bland lagers, plus their "lite" versions. They were intended to be consumed quickly and in large quantities, without concern for any depth of flavor, aroma or texture. This was particularly true in the United States, where Budweiser, Miller and Coors, plus a handful of regional breweries, held a firm grip on the market. But even in such storied beer-producing nations as England, Belgium and Germany, the flavorless American-style beers had pushed aside the classic ale and lager styles. Today, although light, pilsner-style lagers are still the leading beer worldwide, and the "Big Three" mass-market breweries still control more than 90 percent of the American domestic beer market, we are currently witnessing a veritable beer revolution, as an ever-growing number of small breweries and pubs are offering traditional and innovative beers. Generally referred to as craftbrewers, these companies are emphasizing quality over cost-efficiency in their handcrafted beers. In the United States, this renaissance is mostly characterized by new ventures—breweries dating from the 1980s are considered "established"—but across Europe the old breweries are finding new markets for their traditional beers, both at home and abroad.

This book celebrates that newfound (or re-found) emphasis on brewing flavorful, even innovative beer styles. We begin with a brief overview of the history of beer in human civilization, followed by a look at the many ingredients and processes that go into its production. Most beer drinkers are fully aware that their tasty brew contains some form of malted grain and hops, but understanding how these and other elements come together in brewing allows for a greater appreciation of beer's many assets. Another key to penetrating the now-overwhelming array of beers flowing from taps and filling the shelves is being able to recognize the different styles: What is the difference between a pale ale and a brown ale? How does a stout differ from a porter, or a bock from a dark lager? Or most basic, what's the difference between an ale and a lager? Getting a clear grasp of the terms used to define beers will allow you to more easily approach the choices and decide what aspects of a beer give you most enjoyment. Finally, we examine the question of matching the beer with food. A lot of attention is given to serving the right wine with a meal, but beer too can accentuate, or mask, the flavors of your food, and vice-versa. Many delicious meals even incorporate beer in the recipe, and several are offered here. The bulk of this book, however, looks at the variety of beers currently being brewed throughout the world. We explore local brewing traditions developed over centuries, as well as new ones currently evolving. From North America to Europe to Africa and Asia, a tremendous number of beers are available for the beer lover, and we invite you to experiment with and investigate those presented here.

My own appreciation for beer took a giant leap forward when I moved to Portland, Oregon, "America's Microbrew Capital," in the early 1990s. Exposure to such tasty beers as the McMenamins Brothers' Hammerhead Ale and the Deschutes brewery's Black Butte Porter, to name just two, was a most welcome treat—particularly after spending four years in the Midwest where Schaeffer, among others, was a beer of choice. With a special nod to the local microbreweries and brewpubs of the Pacific Northwest, I would like to thank the numerous breweries across the globe who are producing an always exciting selection of flavorful beers, and I also wish to acknowledge the helpful information provided by breweries and brewer's associations in the compiling of this book—unfortunately, too many to identify individually. The Oregon Brewer's Guild, in Portland, and the Association of Brewers, in Boulder, Colorado, offered vital assistance and materials, and JV Northwest of Canby, Oregon, was most helpful in providing both images for the book and valuable information about brewing processes and equipment.

Thanks to

Pam and everybody at BD&L

for their assistance throughout the project,

and especially to J.P. and Ellen,

without whom none of this

would have been possible.

I owe Tess and Zora a debt of gratitude

for the joy and encouragement they

have provided over the years.

And finally, many thanks to Jenny,

not only for writing

the chapter on beer and food

(and for testing out the recipes,

including many that didn't make the cut),

but also for reading the manuscript

and providing helpful guidance

for improving it,

and most importantly for

being patient and

supportive throughout.

Some historians and archaeologists argue that the shift from wandering, hunting-and-gathering societies to agricultural settlements was a direct result of the desire to grow barley specifically for beer, attributing to beer a central role in the development of permanent human communities.

THE HISTORY OF BEER

It isn't known exactly how or when beer was first brewed, but it's easy to see how it might have been accidentally discovered: barley harvested for bread-making is left out in the rain; left out a few days longer to dry out in the sun, the barley becomes malted; this sweeter malted barley is itself used to make bread, which is in turn allowed to get wet; as the sugars and starches in the bread dissolve, wild yeast in the air is blown into the mixture, and the fermentation process is underway. The farmer who originally thought that his barley harvest had been ruined by these unfortunate accidents soon realized that the resulting malted barley beverage was in fact a tasty and intoxicating brew. And the first beer was born.

However this concoction was initially happened upon, beer is believed to be one of the oldest alcoholic beverages. Archaeological evidence from hieroglyphics, pictograms, and other written records shows that the making and consumption of beer goes back at least six thousand to nine thousand years. Barley and other grains that are key ingredients in beer were important dietary staples in the early civilizations of the Mediterranean region and elsewhere. Whether it was using barley or wheat in the Middle East, corn in the Americas, rice in Asia, or millet or sorghum in Africa, the great ancient civilizations from all corners of the globe created some type of brewed beverage that is related to what we today know as beer.

Statuette of Ancient Egyptian pressing barley

The Sumerians and Egyptians were among the most knowledgeable of the ancient brewers. A Sumerian clay tablet dating from about 6000 b.c. offers the first recorded beer recipe, and other evidence suggests that the Sumerians developed more than a dozen different kinds of beer. Generally made from partially baked bread mixed with water, these early beers were flavored with such spices as cumin, ginger, nutmeg, honey, juniper, fruits or berries and even flowers. The Egyptians introduced date sugars into brewing, which acted as a preservative, increasing the beer's "shelf-life." As a result, the first commercial brewing enterprises emerged, and it became possible to brew larger quantities of beer to sell.

Ninkasi, known as "the lady who fills the mouth," was the Sumerian goddess of beer, and she held a prominent place among the gods. It was believed that Ninkasi gave barley to women, and as a result, not only were the various deities associated with beer female, but so were the brewers and tavern owners.

Beer took on a spiritual role in many ancient cultures. Priests and priestesses often acted as the brewers, and beer was included in the tombs of Egypt to aid the dead in their passage to the afterworld. Beer was consumed by all social classes, though each level of society drank a different quality of beer. So central was beer's place in these societies that it was often used as payment for services. The first beer tax was implemented in ancient Sumeria.

During the era of the Greek and Roman Empires, beer took a backseat to wine in the lore and culture, since grapes could be grown more easily in the southern European climate, and as a general rule wine is easier to make than beer. Brewing did continue to advance, however, especially in the northern plains of Europe, in what is now Germany and Belgium, and in Gaul, Britain and Scandinavia.

The thirteenth-century Belgian duke Jean I of Brabant is honored in several countries in Europe as the "King of Beer." He is credited as being the first royal patron of brewing as well as with founding the first brewers' guild, the Knights of the Mashing Fork.

Brewing in medieval Europe was largely the purview of

monastic orders. Monks introduced the idea of cold-storing, or "lagering," beer in cool mountain caves, which allowed the beer to last longer and also mellowed the flavors and improved the taste. Not only was beer an important nutritious element in a monk's often meager diet (it was even allowed during times of fasting), but beer was often safer to drink than the polluted water, and weak "table" beer was consumed as an everyday drink among the larger community. As brewing spread beyond the monastery walls, it was undertaken by the women of the household as part of the domestic cooking chores.

Hops likely were used in brewing by the eighth or ninth centuries, but the first recorded use came in the twelfth century by the Benedictine nun Hildegarde in Germany. Despite initial resistance to this new ingredient, hops gradually replaced a variety of spices, herbs, honey, molasses, flowers, fruits and berries, roots and even some vegetables as the preferred flavoring. Another vital development in brewing history was the

German fraulein with beer steins

establishment of the Bavarian "Rein-heitsgebot," or beer purity law, of 1516, which stated that the only ingredients allowed in beer were water, malted barley or wheat, and hops; yeast was added to the list later. (Although the law was recently abolished in Germany, many brewers in Germany and elsewhere voluntarily adhere to the old purity code, proudly stating that fact on their labels.)

The specifics of the brewing process changed little until the late eighteenth and early nineteenth centuries. With the invention of the steam engine, improved transportation systems, refrigeration, and other developments of the Industrial

Authorities spilling confiscated beer during Prohibition (above); Men guarding Prohibition-era illegal brewery (left)

14

Revolution, beer-making shifted from being largely a domestic activity to a large-scale commercial industry. The work of Louis Pasteur improved the general understanding of yeast's role in brewing, and brewers were soon able to isolate specific strains. The more stable, cold-stored lager style of beer gained in popularity in Germany and central Europe, and in the 1840s the introduction of a clear, golden lager from the Bohemian town of Plzen (or Pilsen, in German) revolutionized beer drinking. Improvements in glass-making technology further contributed to the popularity of that style, as the old ceramic mugs were replaced by glass mugs and bottles that highlighted the clarity and color of pilsner lagers.

Beer production and consumption increased rapidly in the latter part of the nineteenth century, although the emergence of temperance movements and the coming of the First World War soon crippled the brewing industry. Even after the anti-alcohol laws were lifted, most breweries were unable to restart their businesses in the midst of a global economic depression and then the rationing and shortages during the Second World War.

In the decades following the war, the beer industry experienced a period of consolidation, as many of the smaller breweries either were bought out by larger breweries or were forced to close. The number of breweries was dramatically reduced compared to the numbers around 1900, and by the 1960s a handful of international giants controlled most of the world's beer production. Led by the large American breweries, these corporate giants focused on making cost-efficient, pasteurized lagers, which were light in both color and flavor to appeal to the broadest market. Many of the classic ale styles all but disappeared.

Led by the Campaign for Real Ale (CAMRA) in England, a backlash to these mass-market brews emerged in the early 1970s, and over the next decades an ever-growing number of small new breweries returned to brewing the more flavorful traditional beer styles. Today, although the large international conglomerates still control a huge piece of the pie, microbreweries and brewpubs are popping up all over the globe, and home-brewing is an increasingly popular vocation. A beer revolution is upon us, and the result is a wide range of high-quality craft brews.

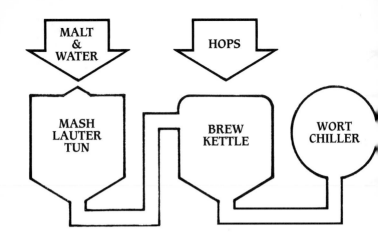

The Brewery Works

WHAT IS BEER?
From Raw Ingredients
to the Finished Product

Malted grains, water, and yeast have been used since as far back as the ancient civilizations of Mesopotamia to create brewed beverages that form a direct line to the beers that we know today, and although a wide variety of spices, herbs and fruits were used for centuries as flavorings for beer, hops has been the standard for the last several hundred years. The sixteenth-century German beer purity law may no longer dictate what brewers can put in their beer, but the majority of brewers the world over remain faithful to the basic ingredients of barley, hops, water and yeast in creating the successful brew. From these few components, a tremendous variety of beer styles can be made, with each style itself encompassing a range of distinct flavors.

16

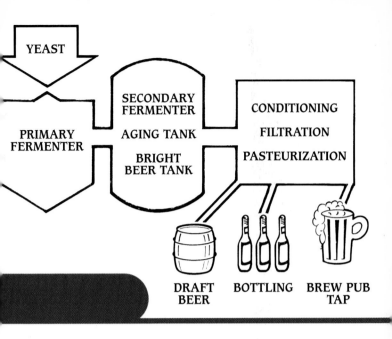

YEAST

PRIMARY FERMENTER

SECONDARY FERMENTER

AGING TANK

BRIGHT BEER TANK

CONDITIONING

FILTRATION

PASTEURIZATION

DRAFT BEER

BOTTLING

BREW PUB TAP

INGREDIENTS

MALT

The primary component of beer is the malt. Malt is barley or other grain that has been steeped in water, allowed to germinate for several days, and then dried out in a kiln. In the malting process, the starches found in the grains are converted to sugar (maltose), giving the grain a sweeter, crunchier element. The malted grains

The eight leading malt producers generate about 75 percent of the world's malt: USA, Germany, Britain, France, China, Canada, Belgium, and Austria.

also provide the sugar, protein and amino acids that the yeast needs to carry out fermentation.

The first component of malt, then, is the barley. A tall, brownish-yellow grass that looks similar to wheat stalks, barley offers a somewhat sweet, clean flavor and a high-starch and low-protein content that make it well suited to beer-making. The barley varieties used by brewers are grown primarily in the Pacific Northwest of the United States, Canada, Australia and central Europe.

Although it is the one most conducive to malting, barley is not the only grain used in beers. Wheat, which is used in the increasingly popular wheat beers, provides for a lighter but tarter brew; oats, used in small amounts in oatmeal stouts, offer a smooth and sweet flavor; and rye, which is less frequently used, has a spicier element. Rice and corn (maize) are used fairly extensively as additives, particularly among the larger breweries, in the United States, where the crops are widely grown. Most brewers will combine these or other grains with malted barley to create distinctive beer flavors.

There are many different types of malt, varying in color, flavor, and sugar content, depending on how it is made. After it is harvested and then screened to remove straw and dirt, the barley is steeped in water for two or three days to make the starches more accessible; most commercial maltsters (as one who produces malt is called) soak the grains in large metal tanks. The grain is then dried out for several days, during which time germination gets underway and the starches are converted to sugars by the plant's natural enzymes. Traditionally, the damp grain is emptied onto large stone germination floors, and some breweries still employ this method, although floor-malting has gradually been replaced by the use of revolving metal drums or by forcing air through large ventilated boxes. After the germination process is halted and the sprouts are removed, the "green malt" is baked in a kiln for about two days at high temperatures.

The various components of the malting process can have subtle impacts on the type of malt that is produced, but the exact temperatures and duration of the kilning is the primary determining factor. The higher the kilning temperature, the darker the beer and the deeper the flavor. Some of the more common malts, used alone or in various combinations, are listed here:

- **Lager or pilsner malt** is cooked at low kiln temperatures and has a slight cereal flavor. It is the lightest colored malt, widely used in the production of lagers, pilsners and light-colored ales.

- **Pale ale malt** is used in many English-style beers. It is cooked at slightly higher temperatures than lager malt, imparting a deeper color and more toasted, biscuity flavor.

- **Mild ale or Vienna malt**, kilned at higher temperatures still, gives beer toffee or caramel flavors.

- **Wheat malt**, used in wheat-based beers, is light in color and gives the beer a strong head and thick mouthfeel or body. Unfiltered wheat beers have a light cloudiness as well.

- **Caramel or crystal malt** is kilned at rapidly rising temperatures and has a reddish color and a rich, sweet flavor. It is commonly used in specialty beers such as bocks or amber lagers.

- **Brown malt** is used in many "winter beers" and brown ales. It gives beer a baked flavor and a rich brown color. Brown malt is traditionally heated over wood fires.

- **Chocolate malt** imparts a dark, chocolate-brown color and a coffee-like or burnt flavor to many brown ales, porters, and stouts. It is roasted at high temperatures.

- **Black or black patent malt** is roasted to a very dark, blackish color and provides the sharp "bite," as well as the color, to many stouts.

- **Roasted barley** is unmalted barley that is roasted to a dark red-brown color. It is often used in dry Irish stouts, giving the creamy head as well as the bitter, burnt-coffee flavor associated with those stouts.

The ability to combine these various types of malt (and many other variations not listed here) into a vast array of beer flavors and colors is in many ways the ultimate stage of the brewer's art. It requires a certain creativity as well as an intimate knowledge of the subtle qualities of malt.

HOPS

After malt, the most noticeable ingredient in beer is the hops. Hops are a crucial component in offering a bitterness to balance the sweetness of the malt, in providing the floral bouquet or aroma, and in acting as a

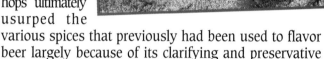

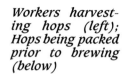

Workers harvesting hops (left); Hops being packed prior to brewing (below)

natural preservative. Although the path to acceptance was a rocky one, hops ultimately usurped the various spices that previously had been used to flavor beer largely because of its clarifying and preservative qualities, in addition to the bitterness.

A perennial vine, the hop plant (*Humulus lupulus*) produces green, cone-shaped flowers that are dried in kilns for use in brewing. Although some breweries use whole hop flowers—which provide the strongest aroma but require additional work to remove the excess straw and petals—most often the hops are packaged in bales or processed into pellets; hop extracts are also available, but these offer a weaker product. The oils and resins in the hops contribute to a beer's flavor and degree of bitterness, and they also determine the aroma or perfume of the beer. Because the delicate aromatic qualities of hops are lost with the boiling process, hops that are being used to provide aroma or flavor are added to the brew kettle late in the boiling stage, whereas those that are included for their bittering traits are added at the beginning. "Dry hopping" refers to the practice of adding hops after the boiling process, during aging, which results in a highly aromatic product.

As with malt, different varieties of hops are used in different regions and in different beers to create diverse effects. Hop production is centered in Germany, the United States and central Europe, and the crop is increasingly being grown in Australia and New

Zealand, as well as China and Japan. The North American Cascade hops, grown in the region of the Pacific Northwest, were introduced into brewing in the early 1970s and are widely used by American craft breweries. Cluster hops are another popular American bittering hop. The Saaz hop from Bohemia is the most popular variety in pilsners and other lagers and is particularly valued for its strong aroma. Hallertau and Tettnang are two aromatic hops that are used in many German lagers. The Northern Brewer variety is a very strong bittering hop grown in both Britain and Germany, while Goldings and Fuggles (named for the farmers who first cultivated the strains) from Kent are the most popular in English ales. There are, of course, many other varieties of hops that provide different levels and qualities of bitterness and aroma, and each brewer will have his or her preferences. American brewers tend to be more "hop happy" than their European counterparts.

Hops, a member of the cannabis family, were traditionally used as a sedative, and the hop flower was often used in pillows for this reason.

WATER

People generally don't think about the water used in brewing when considering the flavor or quality of the beer they're drinking, but since water—or "liquor," in brewing parlance—constitutes more than 90 percent of beer, its importance cannot be overestimated by brewers. In fact, the earliest breweries often established their reputations on the quality of the water available to them. The Bohemian town of Plzen and its pilsner lager were renowned for the "softness" of its water source, while the high-mineral content of the water running through Burton-on-Trent in England helped shape the pale ale style of beer and made Burton ales, such as Bass Ale, famous. So coveted was the Burton water that the process of adding minerals to water came to be known as "Burtonizing." Today, water is easily available and can be manipulated by filtering out unwanted minerals and adding more desirable ones, allowing breweries to produce whatever style of beer they wish. Calcium, chloride, magnesium and sulfate are the minerals found in water that have the greatest impact on the quality of the beer.

YEAST

The combination of malt, hops, and water would be nothing more than that were it not for the yeast. This single-celled fungus is responsible for fermentation, as it consumes the sugars in the mixture to produce the byproducts of alcohol and carbon dioxide (carbonation). The yeast also contributes flavors and aromas to the brew. Individual breweries may use the same strain of yeast for centuries in creating their unique products.

Skimming yeast at the Guinness brewery

Although only two species of yeast are used for brewing beer, there are more than five hundred different recognized strains, not to mention the hundreds of species of yeast that offer negative effects, or none at all, to brewing.

Yeast is invisible to the naked eye, and until just a few centuries ago, the function, or even the existence, of yeast was not fully understood. Before then, the mixture of malt and water was simply allowed to spontaneously ferment, left out in the cask for wild airborne yeast to come and work its magic—and it was indeed considered a magical or mystical process. The only brewers today who stand by the old method of spontaneous fermentation by wild yeast are the producers of the lambic beers of Belgium.

In medieval England, the brown, cakey foam that formed on fermenting brews was known as "godisgood."

22

The species of yeast used for fermenting ales (*Saccharomyces cerevisiae*), also known as top-fermenting yeast since it works at the top of the brew, works quickly but is somewhat inefficient in converting the sugars of the malt. As a result, the sugars that are left behind give ales their sweeter, fruitier, more complex flavors. In addition, ales generally are ready to be consumed sooner than lagers since less time is needed for fermentation.

In 1883, scientist Emil Hansen, working for the Carlsberg Brewery in Copenhagen, was able to isolate a pure culture of lager yeast, and the species was given the name *Saccharomyces carlsbergensis* (though it was later changed to *S. uvarum*).

By contrast, lager or bottom-fermenting yeast encourages a slower and less tumultuous fermentation, and it is more efficient, resulting in the cleaner, drier flavor of lagers. Lager yeast functions at cooler temperatures than ale yeast as well.

OTHER ADDITIVES

Although the four basic ingredients of malt, hops, water and yeast are all that are needed to brew beer—and a vast range of tasty beers at that—many brewers choose to include other additives, or adjuncts, to their brews to influence the flavor, aroma or color and thus create a unique and individual recipe. The most common adjunct is probably sugar in its various forms, including cane sugar, brown sugar, maple sugar or candy sugar. Sugar ferments easily and thus can increase the alcohol content of the beer, while lightening the body. Rice and corn are often used as a partial substitute for barley to give beer a lighter, drier quality. Before hops came on the scene, a variety of fruits and spices were used to flavor beer, and many brewers hang on to that tradition. Belgium is renowned for its fruit beers, such as the cherry-flavored kriek and the raspberry frambozen or framboise. Traditionally, fruit was added to spark a second fermentation in

Processing tanks at an Oregon microbrewery

addition to contributing new flavors, though today brewers often simply add fruit juices or extracts. Cherries, raspberries, apples, oranges, lemons and bananas are just a few of the fruit flavors that have been tried. Honey is another ancient flavor enhancer that is still used. Licorice, ginger, vanilla, molasses, chocolate and even chilies are just a few of the other flavor adjuncts found in beer.

THE BREWING PROCESS

Although science and industry have taken over an activity that was once largely a domestic one where much was left to fate, the process of getting from raw ingredients to finished beer has not changed very dramatically over the centuries. The tools may have changed, and the efficiency and consistency of production may improve with ad-vances in computer and other technologies, but the ultimate success and quality of the beer lies in the brewer's skill. And a certain amount of unpredictability remains.

Most breweries obtain their malt from independent maltsters, although a few of the larger breweries do have malting facilities on the premises. Once the brewer obtains the malt, the first step is to mill it, whereby the malted barley kernels are cracked or broken up to better expose the sugars within. This milled malt is called grist. The grist is transferred to a large wood, copper, or stainless-steel vessel known as the mash tun, where it is mixed with hot water to form the mash. This thick mash concoction is heated for between one and four hours, during which time the enzymes in the malted grain are activated by the hot water and begin to extract the sugars. Because enzymes work differently according to temperature, the temperature employed to heat the mash is critical.

Worker using computers to control brewing specifications

A slight variation on this process of extracting sugar is the decoction method, in which portions of the mash are removed in stages from the mash tun and transferred to a second cooking vessel. In the mash cooker, the mash is brought to a boil and then returned to the mash tun. This method maximizes the amount of sugar extracted from the malt and is therefore used by some lager brewers, since the lighter lager malts generally contain less sugar and so require more effort to extract a sufficient amount.

After the mashing stage, the mixture is strained to remove the grain husks (which are then usually sold off for livestock feed). The syrupy liquid that is drained off is the wort. The straining is done either through a screen in the bottom of the mash tun or in a separate vessel: the lauter. After straining, the grains are sprayed with warm water to rinse out any remaining sugar from the mash; this is known as sparging. Some very heavy, strong beers use only the initial, undiluted liquid runoff

Guinness worker cleaning the hops chute

and do not include any secondary sugar runoff from the sparging.

Once the wort is drained from the mash tun or lauter, it is heated in the brew kettle, also known as a copper. This is the actual brewing stage. Hops are added to the wort and the mixture is brought to a rolling boil. Boiling not only kills the bacteria in the wort but is essential for the extraction of hop resins. After one to three hours of boiling, the hops and unwanted proteins (which coagulate during boiling) are removed, either by a screen known as a hop extractor or hopback or by centrifugal force in a whirlpool. The clean wort is then rapidly cooled in the wort chiller to prepare it for fermentation and also to reduce the chances of bacteria developing. The wort is chilled further as it is pumped into the fermentation tank, and the yeast is added, or "pitched." Wort that is to be used to make ale generally needs to be chilled to between 60° and 75°F (16°–24°C) to allow the ale yeast to do its work; lager yeast requires cooler temperatures around 40° to 55°F (4°–13°C). Fermenters originally were simple wooden barrels, though today huge, conical, enclosed metal fermenters are used.

Within a day or even a matter of hours, a thick foam develops on the mixture, indicating that the yeast is doing its work; this foam is more apparent with the top-fermenting ale yeast. Traditionally, the fermenting wort is kept in a primary fermenter for a relatively

Worker taking measurements at a German brewery (above); Brewing tuns at a Texan brewery (below)

Bottled beer ready for sale (top); Kegged beer on its way to the pub (center); Guinness workers hosing down barrels (bottom)

Beer arriving at a British stadium for a sporting event

short period—ales for five to ten days, and lagers for about two weeks—and then the young or "green" beer is run into secondary fermenters, also known as conditioning or aging tanks. Many breweries today use a single vessel, or uni-tank, for all stages of fermentation and conditioning.

The amount of time spent aging or conditioning at the brewery depends on the beer. In ales, it can be a fairly short process, as little as a few days, and most ales require no more than a month; the stronger ales may age for as much as a year. The bottom-fermenting lagers require more time to smooth out the flavors and aromas sufficiently. With lagers, the temperature of the tank is lowered to just above freezing during conditioning, as the yeast slowly completes the fermentation. Most lagers are conditioned for anywhere from a month to six months or even a year, although the larger mass-market American lager beers may age for only a few weeks. Carbonation in the beer builds up during fermentation, and some brewers add a small amount of still-fermenting beer, or sometimes raw sugar or yeast, to the tank in order to stimulate a secondary fermentation. This method, known as kräusening, wakes up the dormant yeast floating in the beer and adds natural carbonation. A modern alternative to this is simply forcing additional carbon dioxide into the beer.

FROM THE BREWERY TO YOU

Once the fermentation and conditioning stages are completed at the brewery, most beers are filtered before being bottled, canned or kegged. Filtration removes unwanted yeast and proteins, which cause haziness and reduce the shelf-life of the beer, although too much filtering can remove flavor, aroma or body. Certain beers are also pasteurized—heated to high temperatures to kill off any remaining yeast or bacteria—to improve the stability and sanitation of the beer. Although pasteurization increases the shelf-life, it takes away much of the flavor and character of the beer, and as a result many brewers shun the idea. After any filtration or pasteurization, the beer is transferred into "bright beer" tanks for storing before packaging or for serving direct to the customer, as in a brewpub.

More traditional beers are transferred directly from the conditioning tanks at the brewery into wood or metal casks or into bottles, without pasteurization and in some cases without filtration. The beer may be given an additional dose of sugar, yeast, or sometimes more hops (dry hopping) in the cask. Cask-conditioned beers, in which sugar or yeast are added, continue to mature and even ferment up until the moment they are served. In addition, these beers are not pushed out of the cask by carbon dioxide, as is the case with most kegs, but instead are hand-pumped by the traditional vacuum method, which makes for a less carbonated but smoother and headier beer. Some brewers still use oak or other wood casks because they feel that the wood adds flavor, although metal or glass casks are used most often for cask-conditioned beer. In bottle-conditioned beers, additional yeast is added just before bottling to instill a final

> In 1935, the Kreuger Brewing Company of New Jersey offered the first beer in a can, Kreuger Cream Ale. Coors was the first to use aluminum cans in the early 1950s. The pull-top was introduced by the Pittsburgh Brewing Company in 1962.

fermentation or maturation in the bottle, which may continue for years. This procedure can increase the level of alcohol, sweetness or carbonation.

The first attempt at storing beer in hand-manufactured glass bottles was in the sixteenth or seventeenth century, though mass-production of glass bottles became possible with the steam-powered machinery developed during the Industrial Revolution. These early bottled beers were sealed with corks. (You will see the occasional corked beer even today, particularly in bottle-conditioned ales.) The metal crown cap was invented in the 1890s, and though not resealable, it was cheap and easy to manufacture. The improved bottling technology also led to a greater emphasis on producing brighter, more carbonated beers that would be shown off in the glass bottles.

Although canning technology had emerged by the nineteenth century, the high carbonation and pressurization of beer delayed attempts at packaging beer in cans. In the 1930s, an internal lining was introduced that strengthened the can's construction and also protected the contents from the can's tinny flavor. Still, most people agree that cans are not ideal for enhancing the flavor of beer, although the economic benefits are undeniable. (Interestingly, the equipment re-quired for canning is more expensive than bottling equipment, which is one reason why many of the smaller

Early automatic canned beer dispenser

Factory conveyor belt for canning

microbreweries do not package their beer in cans, in addition to the taste issues.) Some British brewers have introduced a device, the widget, that is supposed to simulate the draught-beer experience by releasing nitrogen into the beer when the can is opened.

Most beer not packaged in bottles or cans is kegged. Beer production in the United States is measured in 31-gallon barrels, and kegs come as half-and quarter-size barrels, holding 15.5 and 7.75 gallons, respectively. European beer usually is imported in 50-and 30-liter sizes.

MICROBREWERIES, BREWPUBS, AND A WORD ABOUT HOME-BREWING

Although the beer industry is still dominated by a few large brewing companies, the number of breweries producing high-quality, traditional beers has increased dramatically since the 1970s. Craft-brewing utilizes many of the same techniques as mass-market brewing, although the beers are generally produced in smaller batches and with greater attention to the finer points of the brewing process. Craft brews usually are all-malt beers without ad-juncts. Craftbrewers also tend to be more innovative in offering interesting specialty beers.

According to industry definitions, a microbrewery is a brewery that produces less than 15,000 barrels (17,600 hectoliters) of beer annually—though this number changes as the microbrew industry grows. A microbrewery can sell its beers to the public in three ways, depending on the laws and individual marketing preferences: 1) through wholesalers, which in turn distribute the beer to retail outlets such as supermarkets, liquor stores, bars or restaurants; 2) directly to retailers; or 3) directly to the consumer by offering packaged beer on premises. A restaurant-brewery that sells more than 50 percent of its beer on site is considered a brewpub, although brewpubs too can sell their beers "to go." Breweries that fall between a microbrewery and the large national and multinational companies are known as regional breweries. A contract brewery is a company that hires another brewery to brew and package its beer according to its recipes. Some of the largest and best-known craft breweries in the United States, such as Pete's Brewing Company and Samuel Adams, contract-brew their beer at other breweries.

Another component of the renewed interest in craft-brewed beers has been the growing popularity of home-brewing. A loosening of the laws in the United States and elsewhere opened the door for individuals who wanted to experiment with brewing beer on their own (although restrictions remain with regard to amounts and distribution). In many instances, the homebrewers of yesterday are the leading microbrewers of today. Recipes for home-brewing can be widely found in books and on the Internet, and homebrew supply stores and mail-order companies offer the basic equipment and ingredients for home-brewing needs. There are homebrew clubs all over the world. In addition, brew-on-premises establishments allow you to brew beer using the equipment provided by the facility; this is a useful avenue to pursue before investing money in your own equipment.

Ales are easier to brew than lagers and so are preferable for the beginning homebrewer. Most of the equipment needed can be purchased from homebrew suppliers as beer kits. At a minimum, all that is needed to brew beer is a large pot, in which to boil the wort; a long-handled metal or plastic spoon; two large plastic buckets, with lids, which serve as the primary and secondary fermentation vessels; an airlock to fit over the fermenter, which lets air out and prevents air from coming in; plastic tubing, to transfer the wort from bucket to bucket; a bottling tube and racking cane, for transferring the beer from the secondary fermenter to the bottles; bottles and bottle caps; a bottle capper; a bottle brush, to clean the inside of the bottles; and a hydrometer, which measures the gravity of the brew, thus allowing you to determine the alcohol content. The malt, yeast and hops can also be obtained as kits in easy-to-use forms, such as malt extracts and hop pellets. Water can be treated or purified to obtain the desired mineral content, or bottled water may be used. The entire process of making home-brewed ale can take as little as a week or ten days if using extracts. More information on home-brewing is widely available for anybody interested in pursuing this fascinating hobby.

BEER TASTING:
THE SIGHTS, THE SMELLS, THE TASTE

The history, ingredients and brewing of beer serve as only a preamble to its primary reason for existing: drinking. While consuming beer can simply mean chugging down a mugful as quickly as possible, the complete enjoyment of a fine brew comes only with proper storing and serving and the total sensory experience of seeing it, smelling it, and tasting it. And while a poorly brewed beer will not taste good even at the ideal temperature, in the perfect glass, and with the clearest senses, and conversely a good beer will still garner some enjoyment even under less-than-ideal circumstances, you can do a lot to maximize your enjoyment of a beer.

It all begins with proper storing. Few beers are meant to be stored for prolonged periods and most deteriorate over time. Some bottle-conditioned or especially strong beers can be aged for several years. Most beer should be stored upright, except in the case of corked beers, which should be stored on their side, like wine. Beer should be kept cool and away from bright light. Beer that has been spoiled by light is referred to as light-struck or skunky; darker bottles are more effective in keeping beer fresh. Standard refrigerators generally are kept at cooler temperatures than is optimal for beer drinking, and so it is a good idea to let a beer sit out for a few minutes before drinking it. Ales are best served at temperatures between 50° and 60°F (10° to 16°C), with the warmer end of the range best for such darker or stronger ales as porter, stout, strong ale, lambics, Trappist or abbey ales, and barley wine. Lagers should be served slightly colder, between 45° and 55°F (7° to 13°C); the lighter-bodied, lower-alcohol styles may be served at the cooler temperatures, including some wheat beers, kölsch, and American-style lagers. Although serving temperature is largely a matter of personal preference, colder temperatures tend to weaken the flavor and body of a beer. Bottle-conditioned or "live" beer in particular should not be exposed to temperatures that are too cold, as the active yeast will not function in that environment.

The proper treatment and selection of glassware also impacts the enjoyment of beer. Perhaps it goes without saying that your glass should be clean before you drink out of it, but beer can be affected by residues left on the glass, whether from grease or improperly rinsed soap. Hand-washed and air-dried glasses are best. Frosty mugs may look appealing, but serving beer in a chilled glass weakens the flavor and the ice that forms on the glass will water down the beverage. Rinsing a glass with water before pouring the beer can help ensure the proper head.

Drinking beer from a glass brings out more of the flavors than does drinking from a bottle or can since it allows for full access to the beer's many aromas. The proper drinking vessel allows you to bring together as one the various sensory pleasures of beer—sight, smell, and taste. Different types of glasses can bring out elements of specific beer styles.

The *stemmed beer flute* is ideal for fruit-flavored and heavily aromatic beers, since the glass's tall, curved shape directs the bouquet toward the nose and helps retain the carbonation. It is similar in appearance to a champagne glass.

A *flared tulip glass* is similar to a *brandy snifter*, though slightly taller and narrower. These glasses trap the beer's aromas near the rim and so are ideal for such aromatic beers as lambics and abbey beers as well as for the stronger ale styles like barley wine,

English old ale, and Belgian strong ale and red ale. The shape also helps preserve the beer's head.

Goblets are traditionally used for German wheat beers and some Belgian Trappist or abbey ales. The subtler aromas of those beer styles are more easily accessed with the wide bowl, and the shape also maintains proper head formation for well-carbonated beers.

The tall and narrow shape of the typical *pilsner glass* shows off that beer's golden color and high carbonation. The hop nose of pilsners and light German lagers are brought out by the shape as well, as the glass is slightly flared.

Pint glasses come in a variety of forms, the most familiar being the standard 16-ounce, tapering version. The *Imperial pint*, which has a slight bulge near the top, holds 20 ounces and captures the hop bouquet and fruity aromas of such styles as pale ales, India pale ales, brown ales, porters, and stouts.

The *dimpled pint mug* is the classic English pub glass. The large, open mouth allows for full enjoyment of the strong malt aromas and flavors of bitters and pale ales.

The clay or ceramic *stein* used to be the standard in Germany, often complete with the flip-top lid to keep out flying debris. They are efficient for maintaining the beer's temperature, although since they can be heavy, steins are not always practical. Similarly, the typically pewter *tankard* conceals the color of the beer and is good for temperature control.

The slim, straight-sided *tumbler* is a popular style of glass for altbier and kölsch. More-fluted tumblers may be best for certain aromatic lambics. The *weizenbier tumbler* is taller than a standard tumbler, often holding more than a pint, and is slightly flared near the mouth. It is designed to encourage the several inches of head typical for wheat beers.

Other interesting beer-drinking vessels include the *aleyard* or *yard-of-ale*, a long and skinny glass with a ball-shaped bottom that holds more than 2 pints of beer and comes complete with a stand; the *stiefel*, which is German for "boot" and is indeed shaped like one, with a capacity of several pints; and the much more modest *cordial*, good for sipping small servings of especially strong beers.

Proper pouring technique can also vary according to the kind of beer and the amount of head desired. Holding the glass at an angle and pouring down the side will minimize the formation of the head, while pouring straight down the middle will create a fuller head. The presence of a thick, creamy head is generally the sign of a good beer; little or no head can result from a flat beer or even a dirty glass. Head accentuates the beer's aroma, so the larger the head, the stronger and more clear the aromas. Generally speaking, one inch of head is appropriate for most beers, less for stouts and porters, more for pilsners, wheat beers and strong Belgian ales. Whatever the initial level, some head should remain for a minute or so, and as it subsides and the beer is consumed, consistent traces of foam should remain down the sides of the glass; this is known as Belgian or Brussels lace.

Because the foam brings out the aromas, which dissipate quickly, it is best to breathe in the aromas of the beer immediately after pouring. The smells of a beer can be described in terms of the aroma, bouquet, or nose, encompassing the underlying smells of the malt, hops and yeast. The fermentation of ale yeast produces esters that have a buttery or fruity aroma. Most lagers will not smell fruity but have more of a dry, herbal aroma. As described in the previous chapter, the degree of hop bouquet is directly affected by the timing of the addition of hops in the brewing process. The hop aroma or bouquet can be described as herbal, piney, floral, spicy, and perfumey. Nutty, roasty, buttery, chocolatey or grainy, among others, are the terms most often associated with malt aromas.

The olfactory sense (smell) is an important component of taste, and breathing out through your nose as you swallow can accentuate flavors. Obviously, sipping will allow for greater enjoyment than chugging the beer, and it is a good idea to let the beer sit in your mouth for a few seconds, making sure to swish it around the mouth, since the taste buds for sour, bitter, sweet and salty are located in different parts of the tongue. It may take several sips before certain subtleties emerge. Most beers, at least the better ones, should have a good balance yet maintain a complexity in the different layers of flavor: the sweetness of the malt, the bitterness of the hops, the fruitiness of the yeast, and any other flavors provided by additives. The fermentation can also contribute a slight alcohol taste or aroma, though this should be faint in all but the strongest of beers. Many of the same terms used for aroma are used to describe the various malt flavors as well. Caramel, chocolate, coffee, roasty, and toasty flavors indicate the use of kilned or deeply roasted malts; a smoky flavor results from malts that have been cooked over an open fire. The flavors imparted by hops can be bitter, citrus, sour or tart, as well as grassy, spicy, and an array of other expressions. Clove and other spices or fruits are common flavors found in beer. All in all, hundreds of different terms are used to describe the many flavors encountered in beer.

The International Bitterness Unit is a scientific method of measuring the amount of bitterness in a beer, determined by the level of alpha acids in the hops. Most wheat beers, for example, have an IBU rating between 10 and 20, whereas an Imperial stout can be as high as 70 IBUs or more.

The lingering flavors that emerge after swallowing are referred to as the aftertaste or finish. Like flavor, aftertaste is style specific, but it too should be balanced and clean and, most important, make you want to drink more. The dryness of the hops greatly influences the finish, but so can the body of the beer. Also known as mouthfeel, a beer's body can be thick or thin, though the most common designations are light-bodied, medium-bodied, or full-bodied. The body encompasses both the consistency of the liquid and the flavors contained within.

The appearance of a beer, though not directly related to taste, can reveal a lot about ingredients. However, beyond being consistent with the style of beer—be wary of a pale yellow stout, for example—color in itself should not be given too much weight in judging a beer. A light golden beer may very well be heavier and stronger than a dark brown one. A dark beer usually gets its color from the dark malts used in brewing, and the malt will certainly influence the flavor, but it is not always a direct correlation. Certain mass-market dark beers may actually be a standard lager with little more than food coloring added. The expressions of color most commonly used to describe beer are (in order of increasing darkness): pale, golden, amber, copper, red, brown and black, with many variations in between. The more technical measurement of beer color is known as the Standard Reference Method (SRM), which uses light to analyze the exact color; lighter beers have a lower SRM number.

Similarly, the degree of clarity or cloudiness does not in itself affect taste and thus should not be used to judge beer, though once again it should be consistent with the style. Expect sediment in certain unfiltered wheat beers and bottle-conditioned brews, but a lager that is very cloudy with sediment most likely is flawed in some way. Some excellent beers are cloudy or opaque, while others are crystal-clear. The sediment in bottle-conditioned beer should be a thin, densely packed layer at the bottom of the bottle; if it is loose and cloudy, allow it to settle before opening.

BEER STYLES

Beers can differ for a variety of reasons, whether it is the amount and types of malt and hops or the timing and temperatures employed in the brewing process. The two primary species of yeast used in brewing are top-fermenting vs. bottom-fermenting. As a general rule, lagers, which are bottom-fermenting, tend to be smoother and cleaner as a result of the more efficient yeast used and the colder temperatures of fermentation and aging. Ales, using top-fermenting yeast, might have more complex flavors and aromas, with the fruitier as well as more bitter beers generally falling under the ale category. What follows is a listing of some of the more common or traditional beer styles, each with a general description that broadly covers the beer produced within that style.

Alt or Altbier—*Alt* is the German word for "old," and in the case of altbier it refers to the old tradition of the brewing process. Predating the emergence of lager brewing, altbier is brewed at warmer temperatures using top-fermenting yeast, like ales, but conditioned at cooler temperatures, like lagers. It is a smooth, malty beer with a high bitterness.

Altbier is copper or amber to dark brown in color. This traditional beer style originated in northern Germany, particularly around Düsseldorf; today, alts are increasingly being brewed in Japan and North America.

Barley Wine—This very potent beverage is not a wine at all, of course, but the term was employed because of the high alcohol content, which can be as much as two to three times that of the average ale. Barley wine is often served in wine glasses, and certain bottle-conditioned varieties improve with age. It is full-bodied and has a generous dose of malt. Fruit aromas combine with a hop bouquet. Bittering hops are used at high levels to counteract the sweetness of the malt. The color is deep copper or gold ranging to deep brown. This heavy, powerful ale has a long and complex finish that warms the throat, making it appropriate as a winter beverage. It is also considered a good dessert beer.

Belgian Strong Ale—This rich, highly alcoholic beer from Belgium is similar to barley wine and English old ale. Also known as golden ale, strong ale is fermented with ale yeast but is cold-conditioned. It is malty sweet, and it ranges in color from pale golden to deep brown. The darker versions have a fuller body and are usually sweeter.

Bière de garde—Translated as "beer for keeping," this beer of northwestern France traditionally was brewed in winter and stored for drinking in summer. It can be made with either ale or lager yeast and has a spicy quality. The heavy maltiness often comes from using several different types of malt, which also offers a fruity aroma and finish. It is mildly hoppy. Dark amber in color, bière de garde is often sealed with wired corks like champagne.

Bitter—The term "bitter" was initially used in England to distinguish the newly introduced hopped beers, but beer that is labeled a bitter today may not be much more bitter than the average pale ale. As a rule, bitters are dry and heavily hopped, with a relatively low alcohol content. They are lightly carbonated and range from gold to reddish copper in color. Three sub-styles further divide bitters, increasing in complexity of flavor, depth of body, and alcohol content: ordinary bitter is the mildest form, followed by special or best, and finally extra special bitter (ESB). The maltiness and hoppiness come through most strongly in ESB.

Black Beer or Schwarzbier—A beer traditionally brewed in the Köstritz area of eastern Germany, black beer is now mostly brewed in Japan. It is, fittingly, very dark in color, though it has a medium body. With bitter-chocolate tones, this is a strong-tasting beer with a malty aroma. Black beers are now mostly lagers, although when the style first developed it most likely was made with top-fermenting yeast.

Bock—Bocks are strong but smooth all-malt lagers. The style is credited as having originated in the northern German city of Einbeck (pronounced *Ein-bock* in German), which likely provided the name. A long maturation period results in a cleaner and crisper flavor, usually with chocolatey overtones. Bock is lightly hopped to balance the malt, not to provide flavor. Some of the heavier, fuller-bodied bocks are consumed as dessert beers. American bocks, originating in Wisconsin, are less assertive than the German originals.

Bocks are divided into several sub-styles. Traditional bocks range from golden brown to dark brown in color, are malty sweet, and have a medium to full body. Doppelbock, or double bock, is stronger than bock—though not actually twice as strong—and has a more intense malt flavor and aroma. Eisbock (literally "ice bock") is richer and higher in alcohol than doppelbock, as it is made by freezing doppelbock and then removing the frozen water to leave behind more concentrated alcohol. The medium-bodied hellesbock and maibock are paler variations on bock beer, offering a less chocolatey maltiness and a little more bitterness from the hops.

Brown Ale—Similar to pale ales, but darker in color, brown ales are smooth and mild. There may be nutty or fruity overtones to the malt, and a slight taste of hop bitterness cuts the sweetness. Brown ale from northern England is drier and higher in alcohol than the version brewed in southern England, which is also darker in color. Traditionally a workers' drink in England, it is gaining in popularity among American microbreweries. The American brown ale, commonly called nut brown or honey brown ale, tends to have a more hoppy flavor and aroma, as is the case with most American interpretations of English ales. All varieties are medium-bodied.

The Flemish brown ale of Belgium is quite different from its British and American counterparts. Slightly redder in color, it has a complex mixture of malts and yeast, and a distinct sour flavor is provided by a long fermentation period. It is fruitier and less hoppy than English brown ale. It is known as *oud bruin* ("old brown") in Flemish.

Cream Ale—When American brewers attempted to reproduce the pilsner style of lager, they created a smooth beer using bottom-fermenting lager yeast (or lager and ale yeast mixed) but with a warm fermentation period, followed by cold conditioning. This beer came to be known as a cream ale and is very pale in color and light- to medium-bodied. It is fairly sweet, low in hop flavor and aroma, and highly carbonated.

Dortmunder or Dortmunder Export—The traditional beer of the western German city of Dortmund, this medium- to full-bodied lager is less hoppy and slightly sweeter than the typical pilsner, though it is dry. The malt's medium sweetness and the bitterness of hops are well-balanced. Its color is pale to golden.

Dunkel or Münchner Dunkel—The dark (*dunkel*) lager of Munich has a spicy maltiness and a slight chocolate or caramel sweetness. Hops provide some aroma and taste to counteract the malt, but dunkel is not bitter. It is copper to dark brown and has a medium body.

Helles or Münchner Helles—A lighter version of dunkel (*helles* is German for "light" or "clear"), this Munich-style pale or golden lager is well balanced, though slightly on the malty side. Helles is lighter than a Dortmunder but heavier and less hoppy compared to pilsner.

India Pale Ale—This style of pale ale was developed in England to withstand the long sea journey to the far reaches of the British Empire, such as India. Today's IPAs retain the high levels of hops and alcohol that were included to improve the preservative qualities, and the result is a bitter, medium-bodied ale. The hop flavor and aroma are balanced by medium maltiness. The oak flavor that resulted from the long voyage in oak casks on ships is still sought by some brewers through cask-conditioning. IPAs are golden to amber in color.

Irish or Irish Red Ale—This slightly sweet ale is malty and lightly hopped. The reddish hue is derived from roasted barley. A light- to medium-bodied beer, Irish ale is influenced by the brewing traditions of Scotland. Bottom-fermented lagers based on the style are also produced.

Kölsch—This pale blond, alt-style ale has a sour quality and medium bitterness. It is often cloudy from being unfiltered but has a clean taste. The body is light to medium, and it is popular as a refreshing summer beer. A beer designated as a kölsch must be brewed in the German city of Köln (Cologne) by a member of the city's brewers' union.

Lambic—The only style that retains the old method of spontaneous fermentation by wild airborne yeast, lambics cover a wide range, including many flavored with fruit. The name *lambic* most likely derived from the Belgian town of Lembeek, and a lambic must contain at least 30 percent unmalted wheat in order to be assigned that name. They are sour but clean, and hops are used only as a preservative, not for flavor or aroma. A medium-bodied brew, lambics have little carbonation and are cloudy in appearance. They are aged in large wooden casks for three months to a full year. Some are bottled "straight" while others contain a blend of different varieties. Lambics fall into several categories, including the following:

Faro: A weak lambic sweetened with sugar or rock candy, giving a complex, sweet-and-sour taste. It is cloudy and pale to golden in color.

Gueuze: A very sour blend of old and young lambics. The young lambic stimulates a secondary fermentation, and the beer is bottle-conditioned for an additional six months to a year or more.

Framboise or Frambozen: A raspberry-flavored lambic. It is amber in color with a slight purple tinge.

Kriek: A lambic flavored with cherries.

Märzen or Oktoberfest—A Munich derivation of the Vienna style, this amber-or copper-colored lager traditionally was brewed in March (*Märzen* in German) and aged until early autumn for consuming at Oktoberfest. Similar to a bock, it is very malty, though not as chocolatey since the toasty flavor is balanced by bittering hops. It is medium-bodied and smooth.

Mild Ale—As a traditional workers' drink, mild ale was until recently the dominant ale in England and Wales, though it is making a comeback. The mild classification refers to the hoppiness, and mild ales are not bitter; they are somewhat sweet and malty. Though some are pale or copper in color, most are dark brown. Mild ale is relatively low in alcohol.

Old Ale—Also known as strong ale or stock ale, English old ale is slightly lower in alcohol than barley wine. It is a rich, malty-sweet beer with a full body and a deep amber color. Old ale matures well and can be aged for several years. Popular as a winter warmer.

Pale Ale—The classic pale ale of England is, in actuality, not very pale, but this bronze- or amber-colored beer was named in contrast to the dark brown or black porters and stouts. A high level of hops gives pale ale a bitter flavor and a hoppy aroma, which tends to dominate any malt or fruit elements. The pale ale of the United States is lighter and less malty than the British equivalent, offering an acidy hop aroma.

Belgian pale ale has a spicy aroma and toasty malt and fruity flavors, which make this a sweeter ale than the American and British pale ales. Belgian pale ale also tends to be stronger and more carbonated.

Pilsner—The original pilsner lager was first produced in the Bohemian town of Plzen (Pilsen) in 1842, and today the pilsner style dominates the world beer market. Czech pilsners have a complex but well-balanced malty character, a flowery hop aroma, and a dry finish; the hops contribute a definite but not overwhelming bitterness. The German rendition of pilsner lager, often called simply pils, is lighter and crisper and lacks some of the complexity of the Czech original. Both have a light to medium body.

The style of pilsner lager common in the United States is a far cry from the Czech version. Commonly known simply as lager, in premium and standard designations, American pilsner is light-bodied, since it usually includes adjuncts like rice and corn, and is more carbonated. The malt flavor is mild and some slight hoppiness can be detected in the flavor and aroma. Dark malts added to standard lagers produce the dark lagers offered by the large American breweries. Lagers that are high in alcohol, but thin in body and taste, are known as malt liquor.

Porter—Another beer style that is seeing a resurgence in the craft-brew revolution, porter is a dry, dark brown to black, usually opaque ale that is a slightly lighter cousin of the heavier stout. Porter developed out of the practice in British pubs of mixing a lighter, less-expensive beer with a heavier and more matured dark beer, creating an "entire" beer. Mythology has it that it was given the name porter because it was a favorite drink of the porters at Victoria Station in London.

Robust porters have a medium to full body and the sharp, bitter taste of chocolate and black malt. A hoppy bitterness also contributes to the complex flavors. A slightly different, less bitter variety known as brown porter is lighter in both color and body. The bitterness of the hops and the sweetness of the malt are more moderate and better balanced than in a robust porter.

Rauchbier—This German smoked beer (*Rauch* = smoke) has a strong smoky aroma and flavor, which is obtained by drying the malt over beechwood fires. The smokiness can range from light to heavy, but it always will dominate any sweetness or bitterness underneath. It is dark amber to brown in color. Made famous in the Bavarian city of Bamberg, rauchbier can be made as either lager or ale.

Red Ale—The traditional red ale of West Flanders gets its reddish hue from Vienna malt. Tart in flavor, the sharp acidity comes from long aging in oak tuns. It is light to medium in body and not at all hoppy. It is common practice to add sweet syrup or younger, sweeter beer to a Belgian red ale to cut the tartness.

The so-called red beers that leapt onto the American scene in the mid-'90s mostly represented a marketing ploy and not any definite style, encompassing any reddish-toned, amber- or copper-colored beer.

Rye Beer—Rye is being used increasingly in specialty beers as a complement to barley malt, and the traditional roggen rye beer is still brewed in Germany and Austria. Rye was once the preferred brewing grain in the colder areas of northern Europe, though it is harder to work with than barley grain.

Saison or Sezuen—A tart but refreshing brew, saison is a highly hopped, spicy ale from Belgium that traditionally was brewed in winter for aging until summer. It is medium-bodied and usually well carbonated. Copper or orange in color, saison is bottle-conditioned, often aged in wine bottles and corked.

Scottish Ale—Ales from Scotland are generally maltier and less hoppy than their English counterparts, making them fuller in body. Scottish ales are divided into the categories of light, heavy and export, according to alcohol content, though these sub-styles are more commonly known in Scotland as 60-shilling, 70-shilling, and 80-shilling, based on the old price system. The strongest type is known as Scotch ale or Scottish strong ale and falls into the 90-to 120-shilling range. The fullest-bodied of the Scottish ales, Scotch ale can have a smoky character from the use of roasted barley or dark malt. It is roughly the Scottish equivalent of English barley wine or old ale and is traditionally known as "wee heavy."

Steam or California Common—This style developed in California during the gold rush in the mid-nineteenth century. A hybrid of ale and lager brewing, it uses lager yeast but is fermented in warm temperatures and in large, shallow fermenters. The result is a moderately hoppy flavor, aroma and bitterness and a light amber color. "Steam Beer" is now a trademark of the Anchor Brewing Company of San Francisco. The name is said to have been derived from the hissing sound when the casks are tapped.

Steinbier—Literally meaning "stone beer," this German specialty beer employs the ancient brewing technique of lowering very hot stones into the wort to bring it to a boil. Burnt sugars crystallize on the stones, which are returned to the green beer during aging to spark a second fermentation. It has a smoky but sweet flavor and a tawny color.

Stout—Originally developed as a full-bodied, "stouter" variety of porter, stout soon emerged as its own style. The dividing line between stouts and porters is still a little fuzzy, though stout is generally fuller-bodied and darker, most taking on an opaque black color. The stouts break down into several distinct classes:

Dry or Irish Stout: The traditional stout made famous by Guinness, dry stout lives up to its name and offers a roasted flavor, which comes from using unmalted roasted barley. Hops provide a medium to high degree of bitterness. Irish stout is medium-bodied and has the distinctive opaque black color of a stout.

Sweet Stout: Brewers in the London area tended to make sweeter stouts, and the sweet or London style today is still sweetened with sugar. It was formerly known as milk stout due to the use of milk sugar (lactose), until the term was eliminated so as not to suggest that actual milk was included in the beer. Sweet stout is brewed with chocolate malt, making it less roasty but more fruity than dry stout, and it has little hop bitterness. It has a medium to full body.

Oatmeal Stout: A kind of sweet stout in which oats are added to the barley malt. The oats give oatmeal stout a fuller body and also bring out some more of the burnt toffee or coffee overtones. Some brewers simply add oatmeal to the mash, while others use malted oats.

Russian Imperial Stout: Named as such because it was a favorite of Empress Catherine the Great of Russia, Russian Imperial stout was brewed extra-strong so that it could survive exporting. It has a certain fruitiness that goes along with the flavor of burnt malt. It is full-bodied and has a slight alcohol flavor. The color is dark copper to deep black.

Other Stouts: Though few brewers offer it these days, oyster stout was once fairly popular, particularly in port towns. It sometimes included oysters, but usually oyster extract. Espresso stouts are being offered by a number of microbreweries, and although most are called that simply because of a coffee-ish character, some brewers add actual crushed espresso beans.

Trappist or Abbey—In order to be designated a Trappist beer, it must be brewed by one of six Trappist monasteries, five of which are in Belgium and the sixth in the Netherlands; ales brewed or licensed by other religious orders, or styled after the Trappist ales, are known as abbey beers. The character of Trappist or abbey ales can vary, but they tend to be strong and rich and are bottle-conditioned. Some are sweet and some are dry, though most are malty. Trappist beers are subdivided into single, dubbel, and tripel, based on strength. Single is the weakest and is usually brewed to be consumed by the monks themselves. Trappist dubbel is slightly darker and fuller, offering a complex nutty and fruity aroma and a slight sweet taste. Tripel is the strongest category of Trappist ale, and it is also the palest in color.

Vienna—This amber-red lager was developed in the 1840s by the Austrian brewing pioneer Anton Dreher. It is medium-bodied and has a toasty, malty taste offset by mild hop bitterness. The style is now mostly reflected in the märzen-style beers.

Wheat Beer—German wheat beers are known as either weizen (meaning "wheat") or weisse (meaning "white"), though weizen generally is used to refer to the wheat beers of Bavaria and southern Germany while weisse is reserved for the wheat beer brewed in the north around Berlin, known as Berliner weisse. Whatever the name, wheat beer is made with 50 to 60 percent malted wheat, although it can be as little as 20 percent, and some brewers use unmalted wheat. It is top-fermented and so has the complex flavors of ale, often very fruity and a little spicy in aroma, particularly of clove and banana. A slight tang or sourness may be evident, although hops offer little bitterness. German wheat beer is highly carbonated, has a light to medium body, and is very refreshing, making it a popular summertime drink. The northern version, Berliner weisse, is more sharply acidic, and drinkers will sometimes sweeten it with woodruff or raspberry juice to cut the tartness. It is also slightly lower in alcohol.

Hefeweizen is unfiltered wheat beer that is conditioned with yeast in the bottle or keg, giving it a very cloudy appearance and a definite yeast sediment. By contrast, kristallweizen refers to a filtered wheat beer, which is smoother and cleaner tasting, without the yeast flavors and aromas of hefeweizen. The darker, deep copper-colored dunkelweizen combines the sourness of wheat beer with the roasty, chocolatey flavors of darker malts; it is fuller in body than other weizen beers. Weizenbock is a medium- to full-bodied bock made with wheat malt. The color can range from copper to dark brown, with the darker end of the spectrum offering some roasted flavor and aroma.

The American rendition of wheat beer, which is growing in popularity among craftbrewers, tends to be milder in flavor and aroma compared to the German weizenbier, though it is similarly highly carbonated and refreshing. It is popularly consumed with a slice of lemon.

Witbier or Bière Blanche—Belgium offers its own style of wheat beer that uses unmalted wheat and is usually flavored with orange peel and coriander or other spices. It is fruitier and less acidic than German wheat beer. Witbier, which means "white beer," is cloudy and very pale in appearance and has a light to medium body. The cloudiness as well as some sediment come from treating the beer with yeast during maturation.

Specialty Beers—In addition to the basic styles listed above, a variety of specialty beers include additives, providing a beverage distinct from typical beers. Some common flavor additives include honey, chocolate, maple syrup, smoke, or a variety of herbs and spices, such as allspice, chili pepper (sometimes even a whole pepper included in a bottle), cinnamon, clove, coriander, nutmeg or tarragon. Apricot, blueberry, cherry, lemon, orange and raspberry are just some of the fruits that may be added, either real fruit or extracts, to provide flavors to a standard ale or lager. Fruit beers have a long history in Belgium, particularly with lambics, though it is a time-honored tradition in the United States as well. The seasonal wassail, also known as holiday beer or yule ale, is a strong ale served around the winter holidays. Originating as an old English toasting beverage during the Middle Ages—*wassail* means "be in good health"—it is often served warm with various spices and fruit.

BEER AND FOOD

MATCHING BEER WITH FOOD

Although beer is often enjoyed as a session drink—consumed over the course of a long evening at the pub, perhaps with pretzels or peanuts—it also serves as a satisfying accompaniment to many foods. There are two approaches to choosing what beer to pair with a particular food: beer can be used to match the food's flavor, such as serving a kriek lambic with cherry pie or a smoky rauchbier with barbecued ribs, or to balance and counteract it, such as serving a sweet gueuze with salty, sour Stilton cheese. Given this precept, it would seem that one could not really go wrong when picking a beer to accompany a dish—and, happily, this is largely true. However, one must be careful not to overwhelm delicate food with a strong-tasting beer, or a weak beer with a rich meal. As a general rule, light beers go with light foods, and heavy beers with heavy foods.

One sure-fire way to match beer with food is to select a beer from the same region as the meal. You can't go wrong by serving an American pale ale with pizza, a pale lager like Singha with spicy pad thai, a märzen with zesty German sausages, or a Mexican Vienna-style lager with hot tamales. The following is a brief list of guidelines for pairing beer with a variety of cuisine.

Aperitif—The dry and bitter flavors of beer pique the appetite. Start a meal with a lighter beer to cleanse the palate and to ensure you are not weighed down before beginning your meal!

Cheese—When pairing beer and cheese, both should be acidic. Sweet or bitter beers counteract the salty flavor and sourness of many cheeses. Beers that have sherry- or port-like undertones, such as English old ale or barley wine, will go with similarly flavored cheese, and the smoky flavors of rauchbier and certain porters and stouts marry well with smoked cheeses. Pairing beer and cheese according to region is also effective.

Soup—With lighter soups, drink hoppy, dry, pale beers. Combine stews with thick, malty beers such as Scotch ales.

Cuisine	Suggested Beers	
Aperitif	Belgian ale	pale ale
	fruit lambic	Trappist ale
Cheese (soft)	gueuze	porter
	old ale	Trappist ale
Cheese (strong)	barley wine	gueuze
	bière de garde	old ale
	porter	stout
	rauchbier	Trappist ale
Soup	pilsner (for lighter soups, such as French onion)	
	Scotch ale (for stew)	
Salad	gueuze	pale ale
	wheat	
Asparagus	Trappist tripel	pale lager
Fish	pale ale	pale lager
	pilsner	wheat
	witbier	
Shellfish	pale ale	stout
	pale lager	wheat
	porter	
Chicken and Game	bock or doppelbock	Trappist ale
	brown ale	dark lager
	Vienna-style lager	fruit lambic
	winter or spiced ale	
Lamb	pale ale	brown ale
Pork	Vienna-style lager	maibock
	pale ale	wheat ale
	Trappist ale	

Vegetables—Any beer accompanying salad should be light. The spicy, herbal flavor of hoppy beers such as pale ales goes well with green salads. Acidic beers complement salads with vinegar-based dressings.

Fish—Pale, dry beers won't overwhelm the subtleties of fish and will sharpen its flavors.

Shellfish—Beer's tanginess is a fitting flavor match

Cuisine	Suggested Beers	
Sausages	German wheat	rauchbier
	Vienna-style lager	märzen
Hamburgers	pale ale	pale lager
Roast Beef	brown ale	pale ale
	old ale	porter
Barbecue	pale ale	rauchbier
	porter	stout
Steak	pale ale	porter
Roasted Meat	Vienna-style lager	dark lager
Smoked foods (fish, meat, cheese)	porter	rauchbier
Pizza	Belgian red ale	pilsner
	märzen	pale ale
	Vienna-style lager	
Spicy	bock	dark ale
Mexican food	Belgian red ale	chili beer
	Vienna-style lager	
Thai or Indian curry dishes	pale ale	
	pale lager	
Creamy desserts *(chocolate,*	barley wine	eisbock
	doppelbock	Imperial stout
pudding, ice cream)	porter	Trappist ale
Fruit desserts	fruit lambic	porter
	spiced or winter ale	stout
	wheat	witbier
Digestif	barley wine	doppelbock

for the saltiness of shellfish. A classic combination is savory oysters accompanied by a dry porter or stout. Oyster stout, with oyster extract or actual oysters as an ingredient, was historically offered by brewers, though it is less common today.

Chicken and Game—Bitter beer nicely contrasts with the richness of game, while sweet, malty beer complements it. When serving goose or turkey for the holidays, add a festive flavor by accompanying it with a spiced or fruity winter beer, particularly if the bird is prepared with cranberries or other fruit.

Red Meat—With heavy meals containing red meat, drink rich, heavy, dark beers that will not be overwhelmed by such foods as steak or roast beef.

Barbecue—Smoky beer is an obvious choice to serve with barbecue but may be too overwhelming. Dry beers such as pale ales and porters or stouts (ones that have a slight "burnt" taste in particular) couple well with barbecue. Bitter, hoppy and full-flavored beers will nicely balance a sweet barbecue sauce.

Pizza—To match the tomato sweetness of a pizza, quaff a malty, faintly sweet beer such as a märzen or Vienna-style lager. Belgian red ale can complement a pizza's spiciness.

Mexican, Thai and Indian dishes—Dry, hoppy beers assist in counteracting the heat of these ethnic dishes.

Desserts—When topping off a meal with chocolate, nothing beats a rich, sweet malty beer, most notably doppelbock, with its sherry-like overtones, or Imperial stout, often characterized as having a chocolatey or coffee flavor. Fruit desserts are aptly matched with fruit beer or balanced by a dry porter or stout.

Digestif—While light, dry beers should begin a meal, afterwards one should drink a rich, strong, sweet beer that encourages slow savoring.

COOKING WITH BEER

The history of cooking with beer, or cuisine à la bière, is rooted in Western Europe, where traditional dishes include Carbonade Flamande, a Flemish beef and onion stew with a beer base (see recipes later in this chapter), and Scottish gingerbread prepared with ale. The English typically marinate venison in ale, and the Irish poach salmon in porter. Other representative meals from this part of the world are steak-and-ale pie and beef-and-Guinness stew.

Today, cooking with beer is fast becoming a standard practice, and the types of meals incorporating beer include a varied repertoire, from heavy, meaty fare to light dishes such as soups and salad dressings. In an increasingly health-conscious world, beer is a welcome ingredient: because the caloric alcohol is steamed off when cooked, no fat or cholesterol is left behind. This makes beer a healthy and tasty alternative to bouillon or marinades.

The popularity of beer dinners, in which different beers are employed in the creation of each course as well as an accompanying beverage, is additional evidence of the growing trend of cooking with beer. With the rise of craft beers, and the coinciding emphasis on local and natural ingredients, brewpubs often incorporate their house beers into dishes.

Beer easily substitutes for wine or water in many recipes, bread and soup being primary examples. Lighter beer, such as pale ales and lagers, suitably thins batter, giving pancakes an added zing. Beer-steaming mussels, shrimp, or other shellfish lends a tanginess that counteracts the fish's saltiness. On the other end of the spectrum, cooking shellfish in a sweet beer such as gueuze creates a piquancy akin to steaming mussels in wine. The flavorful addition of beer marinade complements roasted chicken or grilled sausages.

Beer's ingredients have distinct flavors that can enhance conventional meals: yeast has tart, fruity, and acid flavors that awaken the taste buds and cut the richness of certain foods; malt lends sweetness and nuttiness to a dish; and hops give a spicy or herbal undertone. When cooking with beer, consider the primary flavors associated with the different styles and use them strategically. Also keep in mind that the bitterness of beer increases with reduction, so avoid cooking with extremely hoppy beers. Especially if your dish must cook for a long period, choose a maltier beer. Take into account the color of your meal—dark beer will darken your food, and the wrong combination could make a dish appear unappetizing.

Following are some simple recipes for common beer dishes. Experiment and enjoy!

FOOD RECIPES

BEER BATTER PANCAKES

2 to 3 servings

2 ¼ cups flour
3 tablespoons sugar
½ teaspoon salt
6 tablespoons melted butter (cooled to room temperature)
2 eggs, lightly beaten
1 teaspoon vanilla
2 teaspoons freshly grated orange rind
1 tablespoon orange juice
12 oz. pale ale

Combine flour, sugar, and salt. Add remaining ingredients and beat until smooth. Let batter sit until it cools to room temperature. Stir gently before pouring onto griddle.

FRENCH ONION SOUP

6 servings

¼ cup butter
4 medium onions, thinly sliced
¼ cup olive oil
2 tablespoons brown sugar
6 cups beef broth
22 oz. pilsner
1 oz. brandy, burgundy wine,
    cognac, sherry, or dry white wine
1 tablespoon fresh thyme (or ½ tablespoon dried)
salt and pepper to taste
1 tablespoon Worcestershire sauce
1 tablespoon Dijon mustard
sliced French bread
fresh grated parmesan or romano cheese

Melt butter in a large saucepan. Add olive oil and onions and sauté over medium heat until onions are

56

translucent (5–10 minutes). Add brown sugar and cook, stirring often, until onions turn brown. Add broth and continue to stir, scraping bottom of pan. Add pilsner, wine, thyme, salt and pepper, Worcestershire sauce and mustard. Bring to a boil. Reduce heat to simmer, then cover and cook for 1 hour. Skim off foam that rises to the top. Broil slices of French bread (one per serving) until toasted on both sides. To serve, pour soup into bowls, filling them three-quarters full. Add slice of toasted bread and top with cheese to taste. Place bowls on cookie sheet and broil until cheese is slightly browned.

Suggested beer accompaniment: porter, dry pilsner, Trappist ale

MIDWESTERN BEER CHEESE SOUP

6 servings

4 tablespoons butter
$1/4$ cup carrots, finely chopped
$1/4$ cup celery, finely chopped
$1/2$ cup onions, finely chopped
5 tablespoons flour
1 teaspoon paprika
1 teaspoon dry mustard
1 tablespoon Worcestershire sauce
12 oz. beer (try a porter or a bock for a deep-bodied flavor)
1 cup chicken broth
1 pound cheddar cheese, grated
1 cup whipped cream
Tabasco sauce
popcorn

Sauté carrots, celery and onions in butter until tender. Stir in flour. Cook on low heat for 3 minutes, taking care not to brown vegetables. Stir in paprika, mustard, Worcestershire sauce, beer and chicken broth. Whisk until smooth. Add grated cheese. Increase heat and bring to a boil. Reduce heat to medium-low and simmer 5–10 minutes, scraping the bottom of the pan periodically. Remove from heat and fold in whipped cream. Add Tabasco sauce to taste. For that authentic Wisconsin flare, serve with several kernels of popcorn floating in each bowl.

Suggested beer accompaniment: Trappist ale, old ale, porter, rauchbier

Chicken with Creamy Beer Sauce

4 servings

1 chicken, about 4 pounds, cut in 8 serving pieces or boned chicken breasts with skin, about 1 1/4 pounds, cut in 8 serving pieces
salt
fresh ground pepper
3 tablespoons butter
1 onion, chopped
1 garlic clove, chopped
2 bay leaves
2 cloves
1 teaspoon fresh sage, chopped
3 cups pale or amber-colored beer
1 tablespoon flour
¹/₂ teaspoon nutmeg
3 egg yolks, beaten
1 cup heavy cream

Rub salt and pepper on both sides of chicken. In large skillet, melt 2 tablespoons of the butter over medium heat. Sauté the chicken until golden-brown on all sides. Add onion, garlic, bay leaves, cloves, sage and beer. Bring to a boil and reduce heat. Simmer until chicken is tender to the fork—about 40 minutes. Remove chicken from skillet, set aside, and keep warm. Over medium heat, cook the remaining liquid, watching carefully, until is it reduced by a third. In a saucepan, melt 1 tablespoon of butter. Stir in flour and cook for 2 minutes. Gradually stir in sauce from the skillet and add nutmeg. Simmer for 10 more minutes. Place egg yolks and cream in a bowl. Whisking constantly, slowly add the bouillon. Return this mixture to the saucepan and slowly reheat it, whisking constantly. Do not boil. Extract the bay leaves and cloves, pour the sauce over the chicken, and serve over noodles.

Suggested beer accompaniment: brown ale

Three-Bean Chili for a Crowd

10 servings

4 tablespoons olive oil
2 large onions, chopped
12 large cloves garlic, minced

5 teaspoons ground cumin
4 heaping teaspoons dried oregano
²/₃ cup chili powder
2 teaspoons cayenne pepper
2 green peppers
1 red pepper
3 large tomatoes
2 ¹/₂ cups märzen lager, mixed with ¹/₃ cup cornmeal
2 cups canned beef or vegetable broth
2 16-oz. cans kidney beans, drained
2 16-oz. cans black beans, drained
2 16-oz. cans pinto beans, drained
salt and pepper to taste
sour cream, cheddar cheese, cilantro (optional)

Heat oil in a large pot over medium heat. Add onions and cook until clear. Lower heat and add garlic, cumin and oregano. Cook for 5 more minutes. Add chili powder and cayenne and cook for 1 minute. Add peppers and sauté for 3 minutes. Add beer, broth, beans and tomatoes. Simmer, stirring frequently, for 40 minutes. Add salt and pepper to taste. Serve with sour cream, cheddar cheese and cilantro as garnish.

Suggested beer accompaniment: bock

CARBONADE FLAMANDE

6 servings

1 ¹/₂ pounds beef boneless chuck or round steak
¹/₄ pound bacon
4 medium onions, sliced
1 minced clove garlic
3 tablespoons flour
1 cup water
16 oz. lambic, stout, or Flemish brown ale
1 bay leaf
1 tablespoon packed brown sugar
1 tablespoon Dijon mustard
2 teaspoons salt
¹/₂ teaspoon dried thyme leaves
1 teaspoon fresh ground pepper
1 tablespoon red wine vinegar
parsley, chopped
cooked pasta

Cut beef into 2-inch strips. Cut bacon into small pieces and fry until crisp. Remove bacon from pan. Pour off bacon fat and reserve. Sauté onions and garlic in 2 tablespoons of the reserved bacon fat until tender, about 10 minutes. Remove onions. Cook beef in remaining bacon fat until brown, about 15 minutes. Stir in flour to coat beef, and gradually stir in water. Add onions, beer, bay leaf, brown sugar, mustard, salt, thyme and pepper. Add just enough water to cover beef, if necessary. Heat to boiling, then reduce heat. Cover and simmer for 1–1 $^{1}/_{2}$ hours, until beef is tender. Remove bay leaf. Stir in vinegar, sprinkle with bacon and parsley. Serve over pasta.

Suggested beer accompaniment: brown ale, old ale, pale ale, porter

Tasty Sausages in Beer

Midwest version: bratwurst
                    beer
                    sliced onions
Suggested beer accompaniment: American pale ale

German version: German-style sausage
                    beer
                    sliced onions
Suggested beer accompaniment: German wheat beer, märzen

Italian version: Italian-style sausage
                    beer
                    sliced onions
Suggested beer accompaniment: Vienna-style lager

Sauté onions over medium-high heat in a small amount of beer. Add sausages and immerse in beer. Cook until half of beer is boiled off. Continue frying until sausage skin is crispy and tight, poking sausages periodically with a fork.

Quick 'n' Easy Sweet Beer Bread

---

3 cups flour
2 teaspoons baking soda
$^{1}/_{3}$ – $^{1}/_{2}$ cup sugar
1 cup grated cheddar cheese
12 oz. bock beer or dark lager

Preheat oven to 350°F. Mix all ingredients in a greased breadloaf pan. Bake for 30 minutes.

DRINK RECIPES

Recipes are for one serving unless noted

BEER BUSTER

12 oz. ice-cold beer
4 parts frozen 100-proof vodka
Tabasco sauce

Pour all ingredients into frosted beer mug and stir gently.

BLACK VELVET

1/2 pint chilled champagne
1/2 pint chilled stout (Guinness is recommended)

Slowly pour both ingredients at the same time into a chilled highball glass. Do not stir.

BLOODY BREW

2 oz. vodka
3 oz. beer
4 oz. tomato juice
salt to taste
dill pickle spear

Mix all ingredients, except pickle, in chilled highball glass with ice. Garnish with pickle.

BOILERMAKER

1/2 pint beer
1 1/2 oz. whiskey

Pour the whiskey into a shot glass. Drop shot glass into mug of beer.

BROWN VELVET

6 oz. port
6 oz. stout

Slowly pour both ingredients at the same time into a chilled highball glass.

DEPTH CHARGE

2 oz. schnapps (flavor of your choice)
16 oz. beer

Pour the schnapps, then the beer, into a frosted mug.

GINGER BEER

2 oz. ginger brandy
dark beer

Fill a frosted beer mug with dark beer and add ginger brandy. Do not stir.

GRANDMA'S SUMMERTIME "STRIP ME NAKED"

serves a crowd

750 ml vodka
12 bottles of beer
2 cans lemonade concentrate

Combine ingredients and stir vigorously.

LIME AND LAGER

1 teaspoon Rose's lime juice
1 teaspoon fresh lime juice
8 oz. cold lager

In a chilled mug, combine the two lime juices. Pour in beer. Garnish with lime slice.

SHANDY GAFF

6 oz. beer
6 oz. chilled ginger ale

Pour equal parts simultaneously into a chilled tumbler glass.

STOUT FLOAT

1 mug of stout
1 scoop of vanilla ice cream

Float the ice cream in the beer for an alcoholic twist on the traditional root beer float.

SUBMARINO

1 ¹/₂ oz. white tequila
¹/₂ pint beer

Fill chilled mug three-quarters full with beer. Pour tequila into a shot glass. Drop shot glass into beer.

WASSAIL BOWL

serves 10

6 12-oz. bottles of ale
1 cup cream sherry
¹/₂ cup bar sugar
¹/₂ teaspoon allspice
1 teaspoon ground cinnamon
2 teaspoons freshly ground nutmeg
¹/₄ teaspoon powdered ginger
lemon slices

In a large saucepan or stock pot, heat the sherry and one bottle of ale. Do not boil. Add sugar and spices and stir until dissolved. Add remaining ale and stir. Let stand at room temperature for about 3 hours. Pour into punch bowl and garnish with lemon slices.

YORSH

1 ¹/₂ oz. vodka
¹/₂ pint beer

Fill a mug three-quarters full with beer. Pour the vodka into the beer.

Table of Beer Style Definitions

The precise distinctions between beer styles are not always clear-cut. No single organization or internationally accepted guidelines oversee how breweries identify their beers. Of course, gaining the consumer's trust is a motivating factor in keeping breweries honest, but what one brewery calls a porter might be another brewery's stout. Three basic criteria are commonly used to distinguish the different style: the alcohol content, expressed in terms of alcohol by volume (*abv*); the amount of hop bitterness, based on the International Bitterness Unit (*ibu*); and the color of the beer, using the Standard Reference Method (*srm*). Other units are occasionally used in measuring these qualities—alcohol content, for example, may also be indicated by alcohol by weight or by original gravity, which measures the amount of fermentable sugars in beer before fermentation, often expressed as o.g. or degrees Plato.

The Association of Brewers, located in Boulder, Colorado, has developed a set of beer style descriptions as a reference for brewers and organizers of beer competitions. According to the AOB, the guidelines are compiled from information gathered from commercial brewers, beer industry experts, knowledgeable beer enthusiasts, and beer analyses. The styles that are described are based on historical significance or presence in the current beer market, which means that certain traditional styles rarely brewed today, as well as contemporary passing fads, are omitted. (The Belgian red ale, saison, and steam or California common styles are not presently described under the AOB guidelines; in the following table, the data presented for those styles, indicated with an asterisk(*), are compiled from other sources.)

Style	ABV	IBU	SRM
Alt or Altbier	4.3–5%	25–48	11–19
Barley Wine	8.4–12%	50–100	14–22
Belgian Strong Ale	7–11%	20–50	3.5–20
Bière de Garde	4.5–8%	25–30	8–12
Bitter, Ordinary	3–3.7%	20–35	8–12
Bitter, Best or Special	4.1–4.8%	28–46	8–14
Bitter, Extra Special or Strong	4.8–5.8%	30–55	8–14
Black Beer or Schwarzbier	3.8–5%	22–30	25–30
Bock	6–7.5%	20–30	20–30
Bock, Helles or Mai	6–8%	20–38	4–10
Bock, Doppel	6.5–8%	17–27	12–30
Bock, Eis	8.6–14.4%	26–33	18–50
Brown Ale, English	4–5.5%	15–25	15–22
Brown Ale, American	4–6.4%	25–45	15–22
Brown Ale, Flemish/Oud Bruin	4.8–5.2%	15–25	12–18
Cream Ale	4.2–5.6%	10–22	2–5
Dortmunder or Dortmunder Export	5–6%	23–29	3–5
Münchner Dunkel	4.5–5%	16–25	17–20
Münchner Helles	4.5–5.5%	18–25	4–5.5
India Pale Ale	5–7.5%	40–60	6–14
Irish or Irish Red Ale	4–4.5%	22–28	11–18
Kölsch	4.8–5.2%	20–32	3–5
Lambic	5–6%	11–23	6–13
Lambic, Gueuze	5–6%	11–23	6–13
Lambic, Fruit	5–7%	15–23	N/A
Märzen or Oktoberfest	5.3–5.9%	18–25	4–15
Mild Ale, Pale	3.2–4%	10–24	8–17
Mild Ale, Dark	3.2–4%	10–24	17–34
Old Ale or Strong Ale, English	5.3–11%	24–80	8–21
Pale Ale, English	4.5–5.5%	20–40	5–14
Pale Ale, American	4.5–5.5%	20–40	4–11
Pale Ale, Belgian	4–6%	20–30	3.5–12
Pilsner, Czech	4–5%	35–45	3–7
Pilsner, German	4–5%	30–40	3–4
Pilsner, American	5–6%	17–30	3–4
Porter, Robust	5–6.5%	25–40	30+
Porter, Brown	4.5–6%	20–30	20–35
Rauchbier	4.6–5%	20–30	10–20

Red Ale, Belgian *	6.2–6.5%	15–20	11–18
Rye Beer	3.8–5%	10–25	2–12
Saison or Sezuen *	5–6%	20–30	3.5–10
Scottish Ale, Light or 60/-	3–5%	9–20	8–17
Scottish Ale, Heavy or 70/-	3.5–4%	12–20	10–19
Scottish Ale, Export or 80/-	4–4.5%	15–25	10–19
Scottish Strong Ale, or Scotch Ale	6.2–8%	25–35	10–25
Steam or California Common	3.6–5%	35–45	8–17
Stout, Dry or Irish	3.8–5%	30–40	40+
Stout, Imperial	7–10%	5–80	20+
Stout, Sweet	3–6%	15–25	40+
Stout, Oatmeal	3.8–6%	20–40	20+
Stout, Foreign-Style	5.7–7.5%	30–60	40+
Trappist or Abbey, Dubbel	6–7.5%	18–25	14–18
Trappist or Abbey, Tripel	7–10%	20–25	3.5–5.5
Vienna	4.8–5.4%	22–28	8–12
Wheat, Berliner Weisse	2.8–3.4%	3–6	2–4
Wheat, Hefeweizen	4.9–5.5%	10–15	3–9
Wheat, Kristallweizen	4.9–5.5%	10–15	3–9
Wheat, Dunkelweizen	4.8–5.4%	10–15	16–23
Wheat, Weizenbock	6.9–9.3%	10–15	5–30
Wheat, American	3.8–5%	10–25	2–8
Witbier or Bière Blanche	4.8–5.2%	15–25	2–4

In addition to the classic styles listed above and discussed earlier in the chapter, several variations on these styles developed in the United States are defined by the guidelines of the Association of Brewers. While these are not traditional styles, they are commonly encountered in the U.S. and elsewhere and are a regular part of beer competitions.

American Lager	3.8–4.5%	5–17	2–4
American Amber Lager	4.5–5.4%	20–30	6–14
American Dark Lager	4–5.5%	14–20	14–25
American Dry Lager	4.3–5.5%	15–23	2–4
American Light Lager	3.5–4.4%	8–15	2–4
American Malt Liquor	6.25–7.5%	12–23	2–5
American Premium Lager	4.3–5%	13–23	2–6

THE
BEERS
OF THE
WORLD:
AN
INTRODUCTION

Beer is brewed in nearly every country of the world. Common styles, ingredients, and processes are employed from Portland to Rio de Janeiro, from London to Budapest, and from Nairobi to Beijing, yet the results take on a wide range of characteristics. In earlier eras, limited transportation, communication, and other technology meant that brewing practices often remained isolated, evolving with the unique traditions and available materials of the particular country, city, or even neighborhood. Over the centuries, prompted in particular by the era of European colonization and the Industrial Revolution, beer styles and brewing methods flowed freely across borders. Sometimes the newly introduced foreign principles usurped local ones, but oftentimes the myriad influences intermingled to create further innovation, as seen in the variation on the Irish stout style that emerged in such tropical areas as the Caribbean and Southeast Asia. The golden pilsner-style lager remains the most widely produced style of beer across the globe, but as beer-makers and beer-drinkers crave more creative options, a range of old styles are re-emerging alongside a varied selection of new types.

This section explores the variety and characteristics of beers being brewed today in specific regions of the world, offered in the context of local brewing history as

well as the current state of the beer industry. An exhaustive presentation of all breweries and beers is obviously beyond the scope of this book, but some of the more notable examples are featured, including a selection of the best, most innovative, or most influential. The individual beers offered by a brewery will change over time and geography—the name of a beer may even differ in the local and exported versions—though the basic philosophy will be established. The focus here, too, is on beers that are available over a relatively broad area, and so brewpubs or beer cafés that offer their beer only on-premises are largely omitted. Of course, beer served directly from the keg or cask will generally taste better, or at least fresher, than beer packaged in bottles or cans. So hopefully this book will encourage you to seek out the range of beers offered by microbreweries and brewpubs of a specific region. Local production does not guarantee quality, but exploring the offerings can be an exciting and tasty adventure.

A NOTE ON THE BEER RATINGS: Many brews listed in the following survey have been rated by Michael Jackson for quality on a scale of one to three mugs:

one mug	🍺
two mugs	🍺🍺
three mugs	🍺🍺🍺

A "no mug" rating indicates a beer which has yet to be scored, and is not indicative of quality. These ratings are based on prior tastings and have appeared in previously published material.

ENGLAND, SCOTLAND AND WALES

The British Isles have long been the world's leading proponent of traditional ales—porter, stout, bitter, mild, pale ale, brown ale and old ale are all classic styles of top-fermented beer that were developed or at least perfected here and subsequently spread to other areas of the globe. Mild ale was the preferred "everyman's" brew in the first half of the twentieth century, but in recent decades bitters have assumed that role. Whatever the style, ales are consumed at a greater level in the United Kingdom than in any other nation of the world.

Although the British have always stuck by their ales, a veritable beer crisis hit the nation in the 1960s and early 1970s, as the large national breweries began acquiring or closing down many smaller, regional breweries. In an effort to maximize cost efficiency, these breweries abandoned the traditional method of serving ales from casks in favor of the cheaper and less-labor-intensive keg system, which meant filtered, pasteurized and blander beers. In response, a small group of consumers launched the Campaign for Real Ale (CAMRA) in the early 1970s to preserve the tradition of the cask- or bottle-conditioned ale—"real ale"—and to protect the smaller breweries against domination by the major breweries. In the quarter century since CAMRA's founding, the number of breweries in England has more than doubled, and even the major national breweries returned to producing cask- or bottle-conditioned ales. Classic styles that had all but faded from pub taps, such as porter, were again being produced. The real ale campaign in England inspired an international beer revival.

While CAMRA did succeed in saving many smaller breweries from buyouts and closures, the brewery industry in the United Kingdom consists of several conglomerates. The Bass brewing group—which already included Worthington, Mitchells and Butlers, Tennents, and Hancock—merged with Carlsberg-Tetley in 1997, making it the nation's largest brewing group. Scottish Courage is another national giant, encompassing McEwan's, Younger's, Newcastle, Theakston and others. Based outside of London, The Whitbread Beer Company brews its own line of beers in addition to those of Boddington's, Castle Eden, Flowers and Mackeson.

England's tradition of quality ales is due in part to the quality of its beer-related natural resources. Although England was a long holdout against using hops in beer, it is home to some of the world's finest hop varieties. Goldings and Fuggles hops from Kent are very highly regarded, and farms in Suffolk and East Anglia produce premier barley for malting. Several cities in England developed reputations for great beer based on their natural water sources, as in such historic beer capitals as Burton-on-Trent, Dublin and parts of London.

LONDON AREA AND SOUTHEAST ENGLAND

The London area was once home to many great breweries, and though a number of them have moved away (with the notable exception of Fuller's and Young's), new brewpubs and micros have begun to emerge. Not far to the southeast of London is the hop-growing capital of England—county Kent, land of the renowned Goldings and Fuggles varieties—and the influence of Kent's hop gardens can be tasted in the ales of the region.

YOUNG & COMPANY'S BREWERY

LONDON   FOUNDED 1675

The Young family has owned this long-established south London brewery since acquiring Ram Brewery in 1831, and the traditionalist Young's stuck by the casked "real ales" when most English breweries were turning to kegs in the 1970s. In a combination of traditional and

modern equipment, Young's ales  are brewed primarily from English malt and hops. The **Ordinary Bitter** and **Special Bitter** are representative of the brewery's dry style, with the latter having stronger hop and malt flavors. The full-bodied **Ram Rod** is a well-balanced extra special bitter. **Special London Ale** (known as Strong Export Ale within the U.K.) is an excellent example of an India pale ale. Young's also brews a barley wine, **Old Nick** and a roasty **Oatmeal Stout**. The recently introduced line of seasonal ales includes the rich **Winter Warmer**; the Belgian-style **Wheat Beer**; and the spring-season **Best Mild Ale**.

W. H. BRAKSPEAR & SONS
HENLEY-ON-THAMES, OXFORDSHIRE   FOUNDED 1799

From a traditional two-story, gravity-based brewery, Brakspear produces the amber-colored and hoppy **Bitter**; a maltier **Special**, **Mild**; and **OBJ**, a rich winter ale. Traditional English barley malt and hops, often dry-hopped, are used.

FULLER, SMITH & TURNER
LONDON   FOUNDED 1845

Fuller's has garnered many awards at CAMRA's Great British Beer Festival over the years. The three main brews are **Chiswick Bitter**, a classic "ordinary" bitter, low in alcohol but high in hops; **London Pride**, a fuller and fruitier special bitter; and **ESB**, which is a premier example of the style. The bottle-conditioned old ale **Fuller's 1845** was released in celebration of the brewery's 150th anniversary. Seasonal or limited-edition brews include **Honey Dew Spring Ale**, **Summer Ale**, **Old Winter Ale**, **Golden Pride Strong Ale** and **London Porter**.

HARVEY & SON
LEWES, EAST SUSSEX   FOUNDED 1790

This classic family brewery uses traditional brewing equipment and methods. Harvey's **Elizabethan** barley wine was first brewed in honor of Queen Elizabeth's coronation in 1953. Standard offerings are **Armada Ale**, **Sussex Best Bitter**, **Sussex Mild** and **Sussex Pale Ale** and the seasonal **1859 Porter**, **Knots Of May Light Mild**, **Sussex XXXX Old Ale**, **Christmas Ale**, and **Tom Paine**, a strong and hoppy summer pale ale.

MAULDONS BREWERY
SUDBURY, SUSSEX   FOUNDED 1982

This relatively new microbrewery was founded by a family whose brewing traditions go back to the late eighteenth century. Mauldons produces a wide range of beers, such as **Black Adder** dry stout and **Mauldon Special Bitter**.

MORRELLS BREWERY
OXFORD   FOUNDED 1782

Still family-run, Morrells is the oldest brewery in the town of

Oxford, and its ales are appropriately named **College**, **Varsity** , and **Graduate** . Morrells also brews a **Mild** and a **Bitter** .

Shepherd Neame

Faversham, Kent   Founded 1698

The oldest brewery in England, Shepherd Neame is located in the heart of English hop country in Kent. The brewery's steam engines and teakwood mash tuns date from the early twentieth century. The strong **Bishops Finger** , has fruity-malt tones, while **Spitfire** is a hoppy, bottle-conditioned mild. Real licorice root is used in the **Original Porter** . Shepard Neame also produces **Master Brew Bitter** , and **Best Bitter**.

OTHER BREWERIES

Hogs Back Brewery, Tongham, Surrey: Hop Garden Gold, A Pint-a Bitter, Traditional English Ale, A Over T (Aromas Over Tongham), Brewster's Bundle

Hook Norton Brewery, Banbury, Oxfordshire: Best Bitter , Best Mild , Old Hooky Strong Ale

King & Barnes, Horsham, West Sussex: Broadwood, Festive Ale , Harvest Ale , Rye Beer

McMullen & Sons, Hertford, Hertfordshire: AK Mild , Country Best Bitter, Gladstone, Stronghart

Morland, Abingdon, Oxfordshire: Old Speckled Hen , Old Masters, Original Bitter

Pilgrim Ales, Reigate, Surrey: Saracen, Saracen Stout, Progress, Surrey Bitter, Springbock

---

SOUTHWEST ENGLAND

A small handful of national breweries are located in Southwest England, but the region has cultivated a thriving microbrewery industry. The microbrew pioneer Peter Austin—who has consulted and helped establish microbreweries across North America and in Asia—set up his own shop in Hampshire County, Ringwood Brewery, in the late 1970s. The new microbreweries are introducing more flavorful beers to the region, in the true spirit of the real ale renaissance.

Eldridge Pope & Company

Dorchester, Dorset   Founded 1837

Eldridge Pope's best-known beer honors the famous Dorchester novelist, Thomas Hardy. A classic English old ale, **Thomas Hardy's Ale** (12% ABV) is one of the strongest beers in the world. This bottle-conditioned ale matures well in the bottle, for as long as twenty-five years. Each bottle is dated and numbered. **Royal Oak Pale Ale** is a reddish-amber ale. Eldridge Pope also brews the dry **Thomas Hardy Country Bitter** , **Blackdown Porter** and **Dorchester Bitter** .

GEORGE GALE & COMPANY
HORNDEAN, HAMPSHIRE   FOUNDED 1847

This family-run brewery is housed in a late-nineteenth-century Victorian tower brewery. Gale's beers tend to be fruity, most notably the rich **Prize Old Ale** 🍺🍺🍺. Matured for up to a full year in the tanks, it is hand-bottled and corked and ages well for many years. **HSB** (Horndean Special Bitter) is hoppier than most of Gale's brews, though just as flavorful. **Butser Bitter**, **Festival Best Mild** and **GB Best Bitter** are other regular offerings, in addition to the seasonal **Anniversary Ale**, **Hampshire Glory**, **Christmas Ale** and **Trafalger Ale**.

GIBBS MEW
SALISBURY, WILTSHIRE   FOUNDED 1858

This independent was one of the first British breweries to keg beer. It is best known for **The Bishops Tipple** 🍺🍺 strong old ale, which has a rich maltiness, and also brews the bitters **Wiltshire Traditional Bitter**, **Salisbury Best Bitter** and **Deacon**.

HOP BACK BREWERY
SALISBURY, WILTSHIRE   FOUNDED 1987

Opened as a brewpub, Hop Back quickly expanded to include a separate brewery. **Summer Lightening** 🍺🍺 is a pale bitter, and the brewery also produces **GFB** bitter, **Entire Stout** 🍺, **Thunderstorm** wheat ale 🍺🍺, and others.

WADWORTH & COMPANY
DEVIZES, WILTSHIRE   FOUNDED 1885

From a traditional tower brewery, Wadworth 🍺🍺 brews its full-bodied flagship bitter, **6X**, as well as **Henry's Original IPA**, **Farmer's Glory** bitter and seasonals such as **Malt and Hops**, **Summersault** and **Old Timer**.

OTHER BREWERIES

BUTCOMBE BREWERY, Bristol, Avon: Butcombe Bitter 🍺

COTLEIGH BREWERY 🍺, Wiveliscombe, Somerset: Harrier SPA, Tawny Bitter, Barn Owl Bitter, Old Buzzard

COTTAGE BREWING COMPANY, West Lyford, Somerest

DONNINGTON BREWERY, Stow-on-the-World, Gloucestershire: XXX, SBA

EXMOOR ALES 🍺, Wiveliscombe, Somerset: Exmoor Gold, Stag, Exmoor Beast

RINGWOOD BREWERY, Ringwood, Hampshire: Fortyniner 🍺, Ringwood's Best Bitter 🍺, Old Thumper 🍺🍺

SMILES BREWING COMPANY 🍺, Bristol, Avon

USHERS 🍺🍺, Trowbridge, Wiltshire: Founder's Ale, Autumn Frenzy, 1824 Particular

---

MIDLANDS

The Midlands area of England was made famous in the nineteenth century with the emergence of Burton-on-

Trent as a leading brewing center. Known for the high quality of its natural water source, Burton spawned several successful breweries and the development of the pale ale style, Bass being the most important practitioner. Ind Coope's Double Diamond and Worthington's White Shield are the other classic examples. The Burton Unions method of fermentation produced cleaner, drier and more bitter beers, ideal for the pale ale variant. In this method, the fermenting beer flowed from the barrels and circulated through a series of long, open troughs. Today, few breweries employ the Burton Unions, as it is more costly and labor-intensive.

The area around Birmingham in the industrial West Midlands remains partial to the traditional workers' brew: the sweeter, darker mild ales. The classic mild is also still produced by some breweries in the region, most notably Highgate and Banks's ales.

BASS BREWERS

BURTON-ON-TRENT, STAFFORDSHIRE   FOUNDED 1777

Located in the famous brewing center of Burton, Bass is one of England's best-known breweries. The flagship **Draught Bass** is the top-selling cask-conditioned ale in England, though many claim that it has lost something since the brewery abandoned the Burton Union System; **Bass Ale** is the export version. **Worthington White Shield** is a bottle-conditioned pale ale.

HIGHGATE BREWERY

WALSALL, WEST MIDLANDS   FOUNDED 1895

Highgate is one of the few remaining British breweries to specialize in mild ales. **Highgate Dark Mild** has a dark brown color and malty flavor, and **Highgate Old Ale** is a rich winter ale. In 1995, management bought the company from Bass.

IND COOPE BURTON BREWERY

BURTON-ON-TRENT, STAFFORDSHIRE   FOUNDED 1845

Ind Coope joined with fellow Burton brewer Allsopp in 1934 and is now part of Carlsberg-Tetley. It still produces its famous Burton pale ale **Double Diamond**, which is available both bottled and on cask, as well as **Ansells Mild** and **Ind Coope's Burton Ale**, among others.

MARSTON, THOMPSON & EVERSHED

BURTON-ON-TRENT, STAFFORDSHIRE   FOUNDED 1834

The only remaining brewery to use the Burton Unions fermentation system, Marston's brews with English malt and hops, the latter featuring prominently in many of its beers. **Pedigree** is a classic example of a Burton pale ale. Marston's produces the very hoppy, amber-colored **Bitter**, the rich and fruity **Owd Roger** old ale, and a creamy **Oyster Stout**. It offers a range of limited-edition specialties under the Head Brewer's Choice label.

WOLVERHAMPTON & DUDLEY BREWERIES

WOLVERHAMPTON, WEST MIDLANDS   FOUNDED 1890

This brewery is known for its Banks's line of beers, including the reddish-amber mild **Banks's Ale** 🍺🍺 and **Banks's Bitter**. It is a large regional brewery.

OTHER BREWERIES

BATHAM, Delph Brewery, Brierley Hill, West Midlands: Batham Mild 🍺, Batham's Best Bitter 🍺

BURTON BRIDGE BREWERY, Burton-on-Trent, Staffordshire: Bridge Bitter, Summer Ale 🍺, Top Dog Stout, Burton Porter 🍺🍺

HANBY ALES 🍺, Wem, Shropshire: Drawwell Bitter, Nutcracker Bitter, Black Magic Mild, Shropshire Stout

HARDYS & HANSONS 🍺, Nottingham, Nottinghamshire: Kimberley Mild, Kimberley Bitter, Kimberley Classic

HOLDEN'S BREWERY COMPANY, Dudley, West Midlands, Black Country Mild 🍺🍺, Black Country Bitter 🍺

MANSFIELD BREWERY 🍺, Mansfield, Nottinghamshire: Riding Bitter, Riding Mild, Mansfield Bitter

THE WOOD BREWERY, Craven Arms, Shropshire: Shropshire Lad, Wood's Special Bitter, Wood's Wonderful 🍺

EAST ANGLIA

In addition to several established independent breweries, a good number of microbreweries have opened in East Anglia since the 1970s. Although the region is the barley and malting center of England, the beers produced in eastern England exhibit more of a tart fruitiness rather than a straight malty character.

ADNAMS & COMPANY
SOUTHWOLD, SUFFOLK   FOUNDED 1890

Adnams 🍺🍺🍺 has been in the same location for more than one hundred years and is still family-run. In addition to the standard **Mild and Bitter**, this traditional brewery produces the pale **Broadside Ale** and **Suffolk Extra** (also known as Suffolk Strong). Seasonal brews are also offered, such as **May Day, Barley Mow, Old Ale** and **Tally Ho** barley wine.

GEORGE BATEMAN & SONS
WAINFLEET, LINCOLNSHIRE   FOUNDED 1874

Rejuvenated by CAMRA's "real ale revolution" in the 1970s, Bateman's brews a smooth **Dark Mild** 🍺🍺, the full-flavored pale ale **Victory Ale**, **Salem Porter** 🍺🍺, the fruity **Valiant** bitter, **XB Best Bitter** and the strong and complex **XXXB** 🍺🍺 premium bitter. The Zodiac Mystic line consists of twelve limited-edition ales for each of the signs of the zodiac. More typical seasonal ales are also produced.

GREENE KING
BURY ST. EDMUNDS, SUFFOLK   FOUNDED 1799

Greene King is a large regional independent brewery with a long history. **Abbot Ale** 🍺🍺 is a popular, strong bitter, and **Strong**

Suffolk is a blend of a well-aged old ale with a dark ale. **Winter Ale** is one of the brewery's several seasonals.

TOLLEMACHE & COBBOLD BREWERY
IPSWICH, SUFFOLK   FOUNDED 1723

The Cobbold Brewery dates back to 1723, and it merged with Tollemache Brewery in 1957. Familiarly known as Tolly Cobbold, this traditional brewery produces the hoppy **Cobbold's IPA** and **Tolly's Strong Ale** as well as a range of bitters and milds.

CHARLES WELLS
BEDFORD   FOUNDED 1876

Still family-run, Wells brews with recipes that date back to its nineteenth century origins. Its best-known ales are the malty **Bombadier Premium Bitter** and **Fargo Strong Ale**.

OTHER BREWERIES

CROUCH VALE BREWERY, Chelmsford, Essex: Millennium Gold, Strong Anglian Special (SAS), Essex Porter, Willie Warmer

ELGOOD & SONS, Wisbech, Cambridgeshire: Black Dog Mild, Cambridge Bitter, North Brink Porter, Barleymead

NETHERGATE BREWERY COMPANY, Clare, Suffolk: Old Growler, Umbel Ale, Umbel Magna, Nethergate Bitter

T.D. RIDLEYS & SONS, Chelmsford, Essex: ESX Best Bitter, Old Bob, Bishops Ale, Mild, IPA

WOODFORDE'S, Norwich, Norfolk: Mardler's Mild, Wherry Best Bitter, Norfolk Nog, Emerald Ale, Headcracker

---

NORTHEAST ENGLAND & YORKSHIRE

Yorkshire is one of the largest counties in England, and it is a leader in beer production as well. Such brewing giants as Samuel Smith, Newcastle and Tetley are located here, alongside dozens of microbreweries. The creamy and nutty character particular to the region's beers can be found in such classics as Newcastle Brown, Theakston's Old Peculier and a range of Samuel Smith's offerings. A unique method of fermentation also developed in and around Yorkshire. A system of massive, open-slate fermenters, called Yorkshire Squares, circulates the fermenting ale between the two levels, giving the yeast a very distinctive character. Only a few traditional breweries still use the Yorkshire Square method. The popular bitter ale of northern England tends to be stronger and maltier than that of southern England, which is more carbonated and hopped.

SAMUEL SMITH OLD BREWERY
TADCASTER, NORTH YORKSHIRE   FOUNDED 1758

The Old Brewery in Tadcaster has been owned by the Smith family

since the 1840s, and the sense of tradition is clear from the continuing use of slate fermentation squares and wooden casks. Samuel Smith brews a wide range of ales that are classics in their style. **Samuel Smith's Old Brewery Pale Ale** 🍺🍺 is mahogany-orange in color, with a slight hoppiness coming through the malt flavors. Nutty in both color and flavor, **Samuel Smith's Nut Brown Ale** 🍺🍺 is somewhat sweet and full-bodied. The flavorful **Taddy Porter** 🍺 is a premier example of a porter-style ale. Samuel Smith also produces two excellent stouts: the smooth **Oatmeal Stout** 🍺🍺🍺, with chocolate, coffee and roasty notes, and the dark and rich **Imperial Stout** 🍺🍺🍺. **Samuel Smith's Winter Welcome** 🍺🍺 is relatively low in alcohol for a barley wine (6% abv) but offers strong fruity flavors and a dry finish. The Old Brewery even brews a lager: **Pure Brewed Lager Beer**.

Black Sheep Brewery

Masham, North Yorkshire   Founded 1992

After the family lost control of the T&R Theakston Brewery, Paul Theakston established his own brewery in the same small town. Using the traditional Yorkshire Square system, it produces **Black Sheep Best Bitter**, **Special Strong Bitter** 🍺🍺 and the roasty dark ale **Riggwelter**.

Castle Eden Brewery

Hartlepool, Cleveland   Founded 1826

Originally know as Nimmo's Brewery and now owned by Whitbread, Castle Eden is an innovative brewer of specialty ales, employing flavors such as ginger, licor-ice and others in many of its beers. Regular offerings include **Castle Eden Ale**, **Fuggles Imperial IPA** 🍺🍺 and **Whitbread Porter** 🍺🍺.

John Smith's Brewery

Tadcaster, North Yorkshire   Founded 1883

John Smith built his own brewery next to the family's Old Brewery. The classic **Imperial Russian Stout** 🍺🍺🍺, a rich and strong bottle-conditioned stout, uses a variety of malts and ages well. John Smith's also brews **Magnet Mild** 🍺 and **Webster's Yorkshire Bitter**. The brewery is now owned by Scottish Courage.

TETLEY & SON

LEEDS, WEST YORKSHIRE   FOUNDED 1822

Part of the massive Carlsberg-Tetley group, the Tetley brewery produces a range of beers using the Yorkshire Square fermentation method. **Tetley Mild** and **Tetley Bitter** are brewed at the Leeds brewery, along with several seasonals.

T & R THEAKSTON

MASHAM, NORTH YORKSHIRE   FOUNDED 1827

Theakston's has been at its present site since 1875, though the Theakston family lost control in the 1970s and the brewery is now owned by Scottish Courage. Its renowned **Old Peculier**—the spelling comes from the Peculier of Masham parish—is a classic English old ale with deep flavors of fruit and roasted malt. Other Theakston beers include **Theakston Best Bitter**, **Mild** and **XB**.

OTHER BREWERIES

BIG LAMP BREWERS, Newcastle-on-Tyne, Tyne and Wear: Big Lamp Bitter, Prince Bishop Ale

CAMERONS BREWERY COMPANY, Hartlepool, Cleveland: Camerons Bitter, Strongarm

MALTON BREWING COMPANY, Malton, North Yorkshire: Pale Ale, Crown Bitter Double Chance Bitter, Pickwick Porter, Owd Bob

TIMOTHY TAYLOR & COMPANY, Keighley, West Yorkshire: Landlord, Best Bitter, Golden Best, Ram Tam, Porter

VAUX BREWERIES, Sunderland, Tyne and Wear: Double Maxim, Samson, Vaux Bitter

---

NORTHWEST ENGLAND

The industrial cities of Northwest England, such as Manchester and Liverpool, are home to both storied family breweries and modern-day micros. The beers of the region tend to be dry, and dark and pale milds are still popular among the locals.

BODDINGTONS

MANCHESTER   FOUNDED 1778

Boddingtons has brewed its classic dry ales at Strangeways Brewery since the late eighteenth century, though in 1989 it was acquired by Whitbread. The dryness of **Boddingtons Draught** bitter has decreased over the years. Boddingtons also offers a Mild and the bitter ale **Manchester Gold**.

JOSEPH HOLT

MANCHESTER   FOUNDED 1849

Holt is known for its dry beers and low prices, and it still delivers its beers to local pubs in giant hogsheads (54-gallon casks). Two well-hopped beers are Holt's only regular offering: **Mild** and **Bitter**. Seasonal ales are brewed on occasion.

JENNINGS BROTHERS

COCKERMOUTH, CUMBRIA   FOUNDED 1828

One of the oldest standing breweries in the region, Jennings🍺 brews dry, flavorful bitters such as **Jennings Bitter**, **Cocker Hoop**, **Cumberland Ale** and the rich and malty **Sneck Lifter**.

J.W. LEES & COMPANY

MANCHESTER   FOUNDED 1828

This independent brewery is still owned by the Lees family, producing malty but dry ales. The winter-seasonal **Harvest Ale**🍺🍺🍺 is a very strong (12% abv) vintage ale that can be laid down to age. **Moonraker**, **GB Mild** and **Lees Bitter** are additional Lees products.

DANIEL THWAITES

BLACKBURN, LANCASHIRE   FOUNDED 1807

This old regional brewery still delivers its beers by horse cart in the local area. They include **Thwaites Bitter**🍺, the dark **Thwaites Best Mild**🍺🍺 and **Craftsman**🍺🍺 golden ale.

OTHER BREWERIES

BURTONWOOD BREWERY, Warrington, Cheshire: Burtonwood Bitter, James Forshaw's Bitter🍺, Top Hat, Buccaneer

ROBERT CAIN & COMPANY, Liverpool, Merseyside: Dark Mild, Cains Bitter, Traditional Bitter🍺🍺, Formidable Ale🍺

COACH HOUSE BREWING COMPANY, Warrington, Cheshire: Blunderbus Porter🍺, Coachman's Best Bitter, Posthorn Premium Ale🍺, Gunpowder Strong Mild, Innkeeper's Special Reserve

HYDES' ANVIL BREWERY, Manchester: Anvil Bitter, Anvil Mild, Anvil Light🍺, 4X

MITCHELL'S OF LANCASTER, Lancaster, Lancashire: Lancaster Bomber🍺🍺, William Mitchell's Original Bitter🍺, Single Malt

MOORHOUSE'S BREWERY, Burnley, Lancashire: Black Cat Mild, Pendle Witches' Brew🍺, Owd Ale

OAK BREWING COMPANY, Heywood, Greater Manchester: Best Bitter🍺, Old Oak Ale, Wobbly Bob🍺🍺

FREDERIC ROBINSON, Stockport, Cheshire: Frederic's Golden Ale, Robinson's Best Bitter, Dark Best Mild, Old Tom🍺🍺, Hatters Mild🍺🍺

WALES

The Welsh brewing tradition extends far back to the Celts of the early Middle Ages, when cloves, honey and various sweetish spices were used to flavor beer. Today, Welsh beers are not quite so unconventional, but they do tend to be sweeter and maltier than their English equivalents. The three major breweries—Brain's, Crown Buckley and Felinfoel—are concentrated along Wales's southern coast, although the northern regions are home to many microbreweries, such as Dyffryn Clwyd and Plassey.

S. A. BRAIN & COMPANY
CARDIFF   FOUNDED 1882
This family-owned brewery continued to brew traditional ales even through the lull of the 1960s and 1970s. Using Kent hops and a variety of malts, Brains brews only three regular beers: **Brains Bitter**, **Brains Dark** 🍺🍺 mild and **SA Best Bitter** 🍺🍺, affectionately known as "Skull Attack." **Brains Smooth** and **Brains Dark Smooth** are available on draught.

CROWN BUCKLEY BREWERY
LLANELLI, DYFED   FOUNDED 1767
The Jenkins Brewery became the Crown Brewery in the 1910s and then merged with Buckley in 1989. In addition to a quality line of milds and bitters—**Buckley's Best Bitter**, **Buckley's Dark Mild** and **Crown Pale Ale**—Crown Buckley brews the powerful and spicy **Reverand James Original Ale** 🍺.

DYFFRYN CLWYD BREWERY
DENBIGH, CLWYD   FOUNDED 1993
This new-wave microbrewery produces a range of flavorful ales, such as **Archdruid**, **Cwrw Castell** (Castle Bitter), **Pedwar Bawd** (Four Thumbs), **Jolly Jack Tar Porter** and **Dr Johnson's Draught**.

FELINFOEL BREWING COMPANY
LLANELLI, DYFED   FOUNDED 1878
Aside from holding the distinction of being the first European brewery to can its beers (the brewery had connections to a tinplate factory), Felinfoel produces traditionally malty ales. The premium bitter **Double Dragon Ale** 🍺 (exported as Welsh Ale) is its most popular, but Felinfoel also brews **Dragon Bitter**, **Dragon Dark** and **Cambrian Best Bitter**.

HANCOCK BREWERY
CARDIFF   FOUNDED 1884
Hancock was long Wales's largest brewery before being taken over by Bass Brewers in the late 1960s, along with several other Welsh breweries. **Hancock's HB**, a malty "ordinary" bitter, is the only Hancock original still regularly produced.

OTHER WELSH BREWERIES

BULLMASTIFF BREWERY, Cardiff: Bullmastiff Best Bitter, Brindle, Ebony Dark, Gold Brew, Son of a Bitch

CAMBRIAN BREWERY COMPANY, Dolgellau, Gwnyedd: Best Bitter, Original, Premium

PEMBROKE BREWERY COMPANY, Pembroke, Dyfed: Main Street Bitter, Off the Rails

Plassey Brewery, Wrexham, Clwyd: Plassey Bitter, Dragon's Breath, Tudno

Tomos Watkin & Sons, Llandeilo, Carmarthenshire: Watkin's Bitter, Watkin's Old Style Bitter

---

Scotland

Farther north in Scotland, the beers tend to be sweeter, maltier and darker compared to the English varieties. Many breweries still use the old currency-based system of identifying the range of strengths in Scottish ales as 60-shilling (60/-), 70-shilling (70/-), 80-shilling (80/-) and 90-shilling (90/-), the latter also commonly referred to as Scotch ale or "wee heavy." Innovation in the Scottish brewing industry was hampered somewhat by a series of mergers and takeovers that consolidated much of the market starting in the 1960s and 1970s—most notably Scottish Courage, though Bass and Carlsberg-Tetley have gotten their hands on several of Scotland's breweries. The city of Edinburgh, once a thriving brewing center, is only now starting to see a resurgence in a number of new microbreweries.

Caledonian Brewing Company
Edinburgh, Founded 1869

The sole remaining survivor of Edinburgh's once-vibrant brewery industry—having narrowly escaped impending closure in the late 1980s—Caledonian is Scotland's leading brewery and one of the world's largest. From a red-brick Victorian brewhouse that dates back to the nineteenth century, Caledonian brews in traditional open copper kettles heated over open fires. The brewery pays tribute to several former Edinburgh breweries in the names of its beers: **Deuchar's IPA**; **Murray's Heavy**; and **Campbell, Hope & King's Double Amber Ale**. Caledonian's **Edinburgh Strong Ale**, which is exported to the United States as **MacAndrew's Stock Ale**, is a strong, copper-colored ale that has a complex balance of tartness, hop bitterness and rich maltiness. Caledonian Golden Promise was one of the first organic beers; **Caledonian Golden Pale**, also organic, is hoppier and slightly lower in alcohol. Other Caledonian brews include the reddish-bronze **Merman XXX** pale ale and the traditional range of Scottish ales: **60/-**, **70/**, and **80/- Export Ale**.

BELHAVEN BREWERY COMPANY

DUNBAR   FOUNDED 1719

Belhaven, built on ancient monastic lands, is Scotland's oldest brewery, and its beers were reputed to have been a favorite of the Austrian emperor in the early 1800s. Today Belhaven brews the malty **Sandy Hunter's Ale**🍺🍺, **St. Andrew's Ale**🍺🍺 and the full range of Scottish ales 🍺🍺.

BROUGHTON BREWERY

BIGGAR   FOUNDED 1980

Founded by a descendant of the Younger brewing family, the Broughton microbrewery produces several distinctive ales: **Greenmantle Ale**, **Merlin's Ale**, **Old Jock**🍺🍺, **Special Bitter**, **The Ghillie** and the draught **Scottish Oatmeal Stout**🍺🍺.

MACLAY & COMPANY

ALLOA   FOUNDED 1830

Maclay's traditional tower brewery dates back to the 1860s, and this rare independent is still family-run. Its ales tend to be drier and less malty than those of other Scottish breweries. Standard offerings are **60/- Ale**🍺, **70/- Ale**🍺, **80/- Export**🍺, and **Scotch Ale**🍺, plus Broadsword golden pale ale, **Wallace IPA**, **Oat Malt Stout**🍺🍺 and **Kane's Amber Ale**. **Leann Fraoch**🍺🍺 is a spicy traditional Scottish ale flavored with heather.

ORKNEY BREWERY

QUOYLOO   FOUNDED 1988

Located on the main Orkney island off Scotland's north coast, this is the northernmost brewery in the British Isles. Orkney Brewery makes the rich **Dark Island**🍺🍺 ale, the reddish **Raven Ale**🍺, **Red MacGregor**, **Dragonhead Stout** and **Skull Splitter**🍺🍺 barley wine.

SCOTTISH COURAGE

EDINBURGH   FOUNDED 1749

The oldest piece of the brewing giant Scottish Courage was established in 1749 with the William Younger Brewery. McEwan's, founded in 1856, joined with Younger's in 1931 to form Scottish Brewers, which subsequently merged with Newcastle Breweries. In 1995, Scottish and Newcastle merged with Courage, the roots of which date back to 1787. The Younger's and McEwan's lines are brewed at McEwan's Old Fountain Brewery in Edinburgh, including **McEwan's Export**; **McEwan 70/-**, also known as **Younger Scotch Bitter**; **McEwan's 80/-**, or **Younger IPA**🍺; **McEwan 90/-**; and **Younger No. 3**. **McEwan's Scotch Ale**🍺🍺 is the expert version. Other beers in the Scottish Courage stable include **Courage Best Bitter**, **Webster's Yorkshire Bitter**, **Matthew Brown Dark Mild** and **Home Bitter**, which are produced in Scottish Courage breweries around England. The renowned **Newcastle Brown Ale**🍺🍺, which has been brewed since the 1920s, is made at the Tyneside Brewery in northern England.

TRAQUAIR HOUSE BREWERY

INNERLEITHEN   FOUNDED 1965

The Traquair manor house dates back to the early twelfth century, and in 1965 a long-abandoned brewhouse was discovered and revived. Traquair brews a rich Scotch ale, known as **Traquair House Ale**🍺🍺🍺, fermented in oak casks. **Bear Ale**🍺🍺 and **Jacobite Ale**, also fermented in oak, are the brewery's other regular offerings, in addition to such seasonals as **Fair Ale** and **Festival Ale**.

OTHER SCOTTISH BREWERIES

ALLOA BREWERY COMPANY, Alloa: Arrol's 80/-, Archibald Arrol's 80/- 🍺

BORVE BREW HOUSE, Ruthven

HARVIESTOUN BREWERY 🍺, Dollar: Waverley 70/-, Original 80/-, Montrose, Nouveau

TOMINTOUL BREWERY, Tomintoul: Culloden, Stag, Highland Hammer, Laird's Ale, Wild Cat

IRELAND

Workers pose in front of a ten ton stainless steel fermenting tun.

For many, Irish beer begins and ends with stout—Guinness stout to be precise. However, not only are quality stouts other than Guinness brewed in Ireland, namely the Cork-based Murphy's and Beamish, but the nation's beer comes in other distinctive styles as well, including Irish red ales. Still, stouts dominate the Irish market, accounting for more than half of all beer sales. Pubs remain the favored venue for beer consumption, and new brewpubs and microbreweries are slowly beginning to emerge.

Arthur Guinness & Sons

Dublin   Founded 1759

After signing a nine-thousand-year lease on an abandoned brewery in Dublin in the late eighteenth century, Arthur Guinness turned his attention to the dark porters being brewed around London. Guinness's son, also named Arthur, introduced the practice of using unmalted roasted barley in the mash, giving the dark, extra-stout porter its distinctive roasty "bite." Guinness was the largest brewery in the world by the end of the nineteenth century, and over the next century it built additional breweries in Ireland as well as in exotic locations around the globe, from the Caribbean to Africa to Southeast Asia. Today Guinness stout is brewed in more than fifty nations and available in at least one hundred more. It comes in many variations of strength and character, depending on the market. **Draught Guinness** is creamy and smooth due to the injection of nitrogen and carbon dioxide; the canned version contains a nitrogen-releasing plastic "widget." The bottled **Guinness Extra Stout** is a more bitter and complex version, close to Arthur's original brew. **Foreign Extra Stout** is strong, made with a portion of concentrated, well-matured stout. Arthur Guinness & Sons also makes Harp Lager, brewed at its Dundalk brewery, and the slightly stronger **Harp Export**.

Beamish & Crawford

Cork   Founded 1792

After an early period of rapid growth, Beamish & Crawford hit upon hard times in the 1960s and is now owned by Scottish Courage. **Beamish Stout** is a chocolatey stout and the brewery also produces **Beamish Red Irish Ale**.

Biddy Early Brewery

Inagh   Founded 1995

Ireland's first modern-day brewpub, Biddy Early produces **Red Biddy Irish Ale**, **Blonde Biddy** lager, **Black Biddy** stout, and the cask-conditioned **Real Biddy**, in addition to seasonals.

Hilden Brewery

Lisburn, Northern Ireland   Founded 1981

Hilden is one of the few independent microbreweries in Northern Ireland. Its cask-conditioned ales include the bitter **Hilden Ale** and **Hilden Special Reserve**.

Murphy Brewery

Cork   Founded 1854

Owned by Heineken since the 1980s, Murphy's Lady's Well Brewery in Cork still brews the classic **Murphy's Irish Stout**, a smooth dry stout. Bottled or canned versions come with the nitrogen-injecting widget to give it a creamier feel. The brewery also makes **Murphy's Irish Red Beer**.

E. Smithwick & Sons

Kilkenny   Founded 1710

Smithwick's is the oldest brewery in Ireland. **Smithwick's Ale** is a classic example of the Irish red ale style; **Kilkenny's Irish Beer**, originally produced as the export version of Smithwick's Ale, is now available on draught in the United Kingdom as well. **Smithwick's Barley Wine** is produced by Macardle in Dundalk.

MACARDLE BREWERY 🍺, Dundalk: Macardle's Ale, Phoenix
PORTER HOUSE, Dublin (brewpub): Plain Porter, Oyster Stout, Red Ale
THOMAS CAFFREY, Belfast, Northern Ireland: Caffrey's Irish Ale

FRANCE

rance is of course better known as a wine-making and -consuming nation, but it has a long tradition of beer drinking as well. Two world wars and economic difficulties caused most of the one thousand-plus turn-of-the-century breweries to close by the 1950s, but starting in the 1970s, as in many other countries, small specialty breweries began to emerge through the dominance of the few large-scale, lager-producing breweries. The most significant resurgence was seen in the traditional bière de garde style of northeastern France, exemplified by breweries such as Castelain and Duyck, among others. Golden lagers remain the dominant beer in France today—those of Alsace-Lorraine, in particular, reflect a German influence, though they are often sweeter and less hoppy than the equivalents across the border. The brewing giants Kronenbourg and Kanterbräu, both owned by the conglomerate Danone, are the leading lager producers of Alsace. Aside from the Kronenbourg-Kanterbräu group, a large portion of the market is controlled by the Dutch company Heineken, which owns Pelforth, Mützig and most recently, Fischer. Nevertheless, brewpubs and beer cafés are becoming more common around Paris and in such rural areas as Brittany. Wheat beers are even starting to find their way in craft breweries in the north.

BRASSERIE ST. SYLVESTRE
ST. SYLVESTRE-CAPPEL   FOUNDED 1918

Located in the heart of the hop-growing region of French Flanders, St. Sylvestre is a classic farmhouse brewery specializing broadly in the bière de garde style. Influence from neighboring Belgium is evident in its line of top-fermented beers. **Trois Monts** 🍺 🍺 🍺, named for the three hills that surround the town, is a premier example of a bière de garde. Subtitled a "Flanders Golden Ale," Trois Monts has a gold color but retains a slight yeasty haze from partial filtering. It is dry and hoppy. Slightly more complex in aroma and flavor is **Trois Monts Grand Reserve**, a bottle-conditioned and cork-sealed variation that is suitable for aging. St. Sylvestre also produces the distinctive **Bière de Noël**, or **Flanders Winter Ale**, a full and malty seasonal ale. **Bière de Mars** is occasionally offered in late winter or early spring.

BRASSERIE CASTELAIN
BÉNIFONTAINE   FOUNDED 1966

Castelain's line of bières de garde are fruitier and less spicy than others of the style. They are bottom-fermented and packaged in corked

bottles. **Ch'ti Blonde** 🍺 is a deep gold color, **Ch'ti Ambrée** 🍺 is a slightly maltier, amber-colored version, and **Ch'ti Brune** 🍺🍺 is the darkest (Ch'ti is slang for someone from northern France). Castelain also brews the pale-gold **Jade** 🍺, the only certified organic beer in France. The abbey-style **St. Arnoldus** 🍺 is filtered and then given additional yeast for bottle-conditioning.

BRASSERIE LA CHOULETTE
HORDAIN   FOUNDED **1885**
La Choulette 🍺🍺🍺 is an old farmhouse brewery of northern France that returned to brewing specialty beers in the 1980s, including a range of top-fermented bières de garde: **Blonde**, **Ambrée**, **Robespierre** and **Bière des Sans Culottes** 🍺🍺🍺. They are bottle-conditioned and only partially fermented, leaving some yeast sediment behind. A raspberry-flavored Framboise is also offered.

BRASSERIE DUYCK
JENLAIN   FOUNDED **1922**
The family-owned Duyck has been producing traditional beers since its origins as a farmhouse brewery. **Jenlain** 🍺🍺 is a classic bière de garde. It is top-fermented, reddish amber in color and has complex flavors of malt spice and fruitiness. Duyck also brews the blond bière de garde **Sebourg** and such seasonals as **Bière de Noël** and **Printemps**.

BRASSERIE ENFANTS DE GAYANT
DOUAI   FOUNDED **1919**
Enfants de Gayant is known for brewing the strongest golden lager, **Bière du Démon** 🍺🍺 (12% abv), but it also produces traditional, if strong, lagers in the bière de garde style, including **Lutèce** 🍺 and **Goudale**. Several abbey-style beers under the **Saint Landelin** brand are brewed for Crespin Abbey.

BRASSERIE FISCHER/PÊCHEUR
SCHILTIGHEIM   FOUNDED **1821**
This Alsatian brewery focuses on lager beers, such as the hoppy **Fischer Bitter** 🍺 and **Fischer Gold**. La Bière Amoureuse, the so-called

aphrodisiac, is flavored with ginseng and other herbs. The Adelshoffen Brewery, owned by Fischer, produces the smoky-flavored **Adelscott** and **Adelscott Noir** 🍺🍺.

GRANDE BRASSERIE MODERNE
ROUBAIX   FOUNDED **1896**

Grande Brasserie Moderne brews various brews under the Terken label, such as **Terken Blonde** and **Terken Brune**. The bière de garde **Septante Cinq** 🍺🍺 is a strong, complex lager, and the toasty **Brune Spéciale** is another bottom-fermented offering.

BRASSERIES KRONENBOURG
STRASBOURG   FOUNDED **1664**

France's best-known beer is **Kronenbourg** pale lager, which accounts for more than one-quarter of the French beer market. In addition, the brewery produces **Kronenbourg 1664** and **1664 Brune**, which are lagers fuller in flavor and body, and the seasonal **Bière de Noël** and **Bière de Mars**.

BRASSERIE SCHUTZENBERGER
SCHILTIGHEIM   FOUNDED **1740**

The rare Alsatian independent, Schutzenberger produces two German-influenced bocks, **Jubilator** 🍺 and **Patriator**, the strong, copper-colored **La Cuivrée** 🍺🍺 and several other specialty and seasonal offerings.

OTHER FRENCH BREWERIES

BRASSERIE AMOS, Metz

BRASSERIE ANNOEULLIN, Annoeullin: Pastor Ale 🍺🍺, L'Angelus 🍺🍺

BRASSERIE ARTISANALE ST. MARTIAL, Limoges

LES BRASSEURS, Lille

BRASSERIE DE GRANGES-SUR-BAUME, Granges-sur-Baume: Nébuleuse
    Ambrée, Nébuleuse Blonde

BRASSERIE JEANNE D'ARC, Ronchin

BRASSERIE METEOR, Hochfelden: Mortimer 🍺, Pils, Ackerland

BRASSERIE PELFORTH, LILLE: Pelforth Brune 🍺, George Killian's Bière
    Rousse 🍺🍺, Pelican Export

BRASSERIE DE SAVERNE, Saverne

BELGIUM

Belgium produces some of the most distinctive beers in the world, with traditional styles that have been brewed for centuries. Most Belgian beers are provided with additional yeast or sugar in the bottle to impart a second, or in some cases third, fermentation; this bottle-conditioning is referred to as méthod champenoise. Several varieties are sealed with wired corks—some bottles are even wrapped in tissue paper—and are meant to be laid down for years to age. Certain styles or individual brands even have their own distinct glass in which they are to be drunk—Orval has its wide-mouthed goblet, Duvel is usually served in a flared tulip glass, and Kwak in a bulbous-ended aleyard, to name a few.

Traditionally, beer-making in Belgium was primarily done by two segments of the community: artisan or farm-house breweries and monastery breweries. Many of the breweries that exist today had their origins as family-run, rural operations that ultimately put agricultural pursuits behind them to focus exclusively on brewing. Some remain independent and family-owned, while others have gone public or have been bought out by large conglomerates. Interbrew is the main brewing group in Belgium and the second largest in all of Europe, encompassing Artois, Jupiler, Belle-Vue, De Kluis and St. Guibert's Leffe abbey ales, among others. Riva controls such breweries as Liefmans, Straffe Hendrik and Het Anker. Most of Belgium's one hundred-plus breweries remain independent, however, and new microbreweries and brewpubs are entering the scene.

The Belgian monastery breweries are some of the most storied breweries in the world, most notably the five Trappist monasteries: Chimay, Westmalle, Orval, Rochefort and Westvleteren. Monks may serve as head brewers, based on brewing traditions extending back many centuries. In addition to the Trappists, other monastic sects brew beer, either on the abbey premises or by license at secular breweries. Secular breweries produce "abbey-style" beers bearing the names of saints, shrines or churches.

Lambics are probably the most distinctive of Belgian beers in that they are made by the old technique of spontaneous fermentation. Most of the lambic breweries are concentrated in the area to the south and west of Brussels, along the Senne River Valley. Lambic was the most popular style around Brussels from the mid-1700s until the First World War, and it has recently seen a resurgence in Belgium and elsewhere.

Other Belgian beer styles developed around specific geographic regions, although improved distribution and marketing has extended their appeal. The Belgian wheat beer known as witbier was once widely brewed in the town of Hoegaarden to the east of Brussels, though the style had all but disappeared until Pierre Celis reintroduced it in the 1960s at De Kluis brewery. Celis has since brought witbiers to a wider international market with Celis White, from his brewery in Austin, Texas. The sweet-and-sour brown ale, or *oud bruin*, is the brew of the East Flanders town of Oudenaarde. West Flanders has its own sour-tasting style of beer known as red ale—most clearly represented by Rodenbach—which is redder in color and tarter in flavor than the East Flanders brown. In areas to the north of Brussels and around Antwerp, several notable breweries produce the copper-colored, fruity Belgian ale, while the classic example of the golden strong ale by Moortgat, Duvel, is also brewed in the north, though imitators have popped up in other areas of the country, particularly Flanders. In the French-speaking provinces to the south along the border with France, saison beer has developed from its origins as a farmhouse ale to being exported worldwide. Fruit-flavored beers are produced by most of the lambic brewers in western Belgium, although not all fruit beers are lambics. The

excellent fruit beers from Liefmans are based on the brown ale of East Flanders, for example.

Despite this exciting array, it is actually a "foreign" style that dominates the Belgian beer market: pilsner-style lagers. Interbrew and Alken-Maes, in particular, offer several brands of light lagers. Nevertheless, Belgium's specialty and traditional ales are finding greater markets internationally, spurred by the "real ale" or craft-brew revolution of the last few decades.

ABBAYE DE NOTRE DAME DE SCOURMONT—CHIMAY

FORGES   **FOUNDED 1862**

Chimay is the largest and best-known of Belgium's five Trappist breweries. The monastery was established in 1850 and began brewing on a commercial scale in 1862. The abbey's well-water and house yeast give Chimay ales their distinctive spicy character. The brewery offers three bottle-conditioned ales, identified by the color of the label and crown cap in the smaller 33-cl bottle. **Première**, or **Chimay Rouge** 🍺 🍺, is the original Chimay beer and the lowest of the three in alcohol (7% abv). It is a reddish-brown dubbel ale with a mix of fruity and spicy malt flavors. The next strongest is **Cinq Cents**, or **Chimay Blanche** 🍺 🍺 (8% abv), a golden-amber tripel that is hoppier than the other Chimay brews. The richest and most complex is **Grand Réserve**, or **Chimay Bleu** 🍺 🍺 🍺. At 9% abv, it is a strong beer exhibiting a port-like sweetness. When packaged in the larger-size corked bottles, all are suitable for aging—three to six months for the Première and Cinq Cents and several years for the Grand Réserve.

Brouwerij Liefmans
Oudenaard
Founded 1679

Liefmans has been the premier brewer of the tart brown ale (oud bruin) of East Flanders for more than three centuries. Containing a mixture of several malts and roasted barley, the beer is fermented in open copper vessels and then aged for about three months. This straight, young brown is sold as **Oud Bruin**. Liefmans' most renowned ale, **Goudenband** , is made by blending the young beer with a stronger, more aged one, which is then bottled with fresh yeast and sugar and conditioned further at the brewery. Goudenband is a rich, sweet-and-sour brew and can be laid down in the bottle for several years. Liefmans also adds raspberries or cherries to its **Oud Bruin** to produce **Framboz-enbier** and **Kriekbier**, respectively. In 1990 Liefmans was acquired by Riva of Dentergem, and its beers are currently brewed in Dentergem until Liefmans' brewery is renovated, though the ales are still fermented, conditioned and bottled in Oudenaarde.

Brouwerij Moortgat
Breendonk-Puurs
Founded 1871

The independent, family-run brewery of Moortgat produces one of Belgium's best-known specialty beers. Originally based on a dark Scottish ale, **Duvel** transformed to a lighter golden color in the late 1960s in response to the trend toward golden lagers. The name means "devil"—apparently inspired by the exclamation that it was "a devil of a beer" when first sampled in the 1920s. This Belgian strong ale undergoes a complex triple-fermentation process using two yeast strains. First is a warm fermentation, followed by a cold secondary fermentation and several weeks of cold maturation. The beer is then bottled with another dose of yeast to undergo a third conditioning. Two strains of hops give it hoppy bitterness and aroma, and Duvel develops a large, frothy white head when poured. Moortgat also brews a pale and hoppy-dry pilsner lager, Bel Pils, as well as a range of bottle-conditioned abbey ales under license: the dubbel **Maredsous 6**, a darker **Maredsous 8** and **Maredsous 10** tripel.

Abbaye de Notre Dame de Saint-Remy
Rochefort
Founded 1899

Brewing at the Trappist abbey in Rochefort dates back to the late 1500s. Rochefort's three ales are identified by the old brewing degree system and the color of the bottle caps. **Rochefort 6**, or **Red Cap**, is the weakest of the three—"only" 7.5% abv. **Rochefort 8**, **Green**

Cap, is darker brown and fruitier. The strongest, **Rochefort 10**, or **Black Cap**, is very rich and complex.

ABBAYE DE NOTRE DAME D'ORVAL
VILLERS-DEVANT-ORVAL   FOUNDED 1931

Although the abbey was established in the twelfth century, Ovral's beer was not offered commercially until the 1930s. The orangish-colored **Orval Trappist Ale** is brewed from a special blend of malts, hops, several yeast strains and candy sugar. It undergoes three fermentations—twice in the brewery and then in the bottle—and it may be laid down for up to five years. Dry-hopping gives Orval a stronger hop presence compared to other Trappist ales.

ABDIJ ST. SIXTUS
WESTVLETEREN   FOUNDED 1839

The abbey at Westvleteren is the smallest of the Trappist breweries, and its sweet, flavorful ales are the hardest to come by outside of West Flanders. **Special 6** (red cap) is dark in color and malty in flavor. Next strongest is **Extra 8** (blue cap), followed by the powerful **Abt 12** (yellow cap).

ABDIJ DER TRAPPISTEN VAN WESTMALLE
MALLE   FOUNDED 1836

The Trappist abbey of Westmalle brewed the first **Tripel**, which is pale in color, although the dark **Westmalle Dubbel** is also a classic. They are given additional yeast and sugar before bottling to induce a secondary fermentation. Both display a fruity malt taste along with hop flavor and a dry finish.

BRASSERIE D'ACHOUFFE
ACHOUFFE   FOUNDED 1982

This farmhouse microbrewery produces two strong ales. **La Chouffe** is spicy and well-balanced, and the darker **McChouffe** is based loosely on Scottish ales.

ALKEN-MAES BREWERY
ALKEN AND WAARLOOS   FOUNDED 1988

Alken and Maes, two breweries dating from the 1880s, merged in 1988 to form the second-largest brewing group in Belgium, which is now owned by the French Kronenbourg. **Cristal Alken Pils** and **Maes Pils** are the leading products, but Alken-Maes breweries produce a variety of beers, including Du Keersmaeker's **Mort Subite** lambic line and the **Grimbergen** abbey ales from Brasserie de l'Union.

BELLE-VUE
BRUSSELS   FOUNDED 1913

Owned by Interbrew, Belle-Vue is Belgium's largest brewer of lambics. The blended Gueuze and the fruit-flavored **Kriek** and **Framboise** are aged in oak barrels. The unfiltered gueuze **Séléction Lambic** is also offered on a limited scale.

BROUWERIJ BOSTEELS
BUGGENHOUT   FOUNDED 1791

This family brewery's best-known beer is named for the eighteenth-century innkeeper, **Pauwel Kwak**, who served his ale to passing horseriders in a glass that could fit in the stirrup. The spicy and strong **Kwak** is still served in the distinctive, bulbous-ended glass with a wooden stand to keep it upright. Bosteels also offers Prosit Pils.

BRASSERIE CANTILLON
BRUSSELS   FOUNDED 1900

This traditional brewery produces its lambics only during the cool months of the year, when wild yeast is most active. Cantillon's distinctively sour brews include **Kriek**, **Framboise**, **Gueuze** and **Faro**, but it also offers Rosé de Gambrinus, flavored with cherries and vanilla in addition to the dominant raspberries, and the unblended **Grand Cru**, which matures for three to four years before bottling.

DE DOLLE BROUWERS
ESEN   FOUNDED 1980

De Dolle Brouwers, or "The Mad Brewers," is a small brewery with a range of strong ales bearing very colorful labels. **Oerbier** was the first creation, followed by the Christmas seasonal **Stille Nacht**, the summer **Arabier**, and **Boskeun**, which translates as "Wood Rabbit" and is brewed for Easter.

BROUWERIJ DE KLUIS
HOEGAARDEN   FOUNDED 1966

Former milkman Pierre Celis reintroduced the witbier style in the town that first made it famous. **Hoegaarden Witbier** offers the orange and coriander spice characteristic of this cloudy, white wheat beer. De Kluis also brews the amber-colored Das, **Julius**, and the strong **Grand Cru** and **Verboden Vrucht** ("Forbidden Fruit"). The brewery was destroyed by a fire in 1985 and was subsequently taken over by Interbrew.

BROUWERIJ DE KONINCK
ANTWERP   FOUNDED 1833

This brewery resisted the pilsner trend that swept over most of its local rivals; **De Koninck** is a classic Belgian ale, with fruity malt flavors balanced with hop spice. **Cuvée de Koninck** is the stronger version.

BROUWERIJ DE SMEDT
OPWIJK   FOUNDED 1790

The family-owned De Smedt brewery has been producing abbey beers for Affligem since that abbey's brewery was destroyed during World War II. In addition to **Affligem Dobbel**, **Affligem Tripel** and **Affligem Noël**, De Smedt brews the amber **Op Ale**.

BRASSERIE DUBUISSON FRERES
PIPAI   FOUNDED 1769

This family-run brewery produces the Belgian strong ale **Bush**, which is sold in the United States as **Scaldis Belgian Special Ale** (in the unlikely event of confusion with Busch beer). A similar but hoppier **Bush Noël (Scaldis Noël)** is brewed for Christmas. Both are 12 percent alcohol by volume.

BRASSERIE DUPONT
TOURPE   FOUNDED 1850

Dupont is a small farmhouse brewery that produces traditional beers. Packaged in corked bottles, **Saison Dupont** is bottle-conditioned and thick with yeast. It is the classic saison-style beer. Dupont's other variations on the saison style include **Moinette Blonde**, **Moinette Brune** and the organic **Foret**.

Brouwerij Frank Boon
Lembeek   Founded 1976
Frank Boon was a pioneer in reintroducing the ancient lambic style to the world. Boon brews a range of classic lambics, including **Gueuze**, **Kriek**, **Framboise** and **Pertotale Faro**, as well as blended varieties under the **Mariage Parfait** label.

Brasserie Lefebvre
Quenast   Founded 1876
Lefebvre produces ales in a variety of styles, from the ginger-spiced **Saison 1900** to the fruit-spiced witbier **Student** and the honey-flavored **Barbar**. Abbey beers are brewed under the Floreffe label: **Floreffe La Meilleure**, **Floreffe Dobbel** and **Floreffe Tripel**.

Brouwerij Lindemans
Vlezenbeek   Founded 1869
The Lindemans family began brewing in the 1810s and opened a commercial brewery on their farm half a century later. Lindemans specializes in sweet fruit lambics, such as **Framboise**, **Kriek** and the less-conventional **Peche** (peach-flavored). It blends its own **Gueuze Cuvée René** for export, and also sells its lambics to other gueuze producers.

Martens Brewery
Bocholt   Founded 1758
Martens is a large independent that brews a variation on the saison style. **Sezoens** is a hoppy, golden-colored ale, and the amber **Sezoens Quattro** is higher in alcohol. Martens also has a range of pilsners, including **Premium Pilsner**.

Brasserie Palm
Steenhuffel   Founded 1747
This large independent brewery produces the popular **Palm Spéciale**, an amber-colored malty ale, and a darker version brewed for winter, **Dobbel Palm**. Palm also brews the powerful **Aerts 1900** and **Steendonk Witbier**.

Brouwerij Rodenbach
Roeselare   Founded 1836
Rodenbach produces the quintessential red ale of West Flanders, and the magnificent brewery houses hundreds of massive wood tuns in which the ales are aged for up to two years. The wood and the yeast living in it give the beers their sour quality. The reddish-brown ale known simply as **Rodenbach Belgian Red Ale** is the well-aged ale mixed with freshly fermented ale, while **Rodenbach Grand Cru** is unblended ale bottled directly from the vats. A third variety, **Alexander**, is Grand Cru laced with cherry essence.

Brasserie de Silly
Silly   Founded 1850
This farmhouse brewery is best known for its saison—the blended **Saison de Silly**—but its varied offerings also include **La Divine**, a strong abbey-style ale; **Titje**, a spicy wheat beer; and **Double Enghien Blond** and **Double Enghien Brune**, both sweet and strong ales.

TIMMERMANS
ITTERBEEK   FOUNDED **1888**

Timmermans is a traditional lambic brewer. Its selection of pure and blended lambics includes **Kriek**🍺🍺, **Pêche**, **Framboise**🍺🍺, **Gueuze Caveau** 🍺 🍺 and the wheat lambic **Blanche Wit**🍺. **Bourgogne de Flanders**🍺 is a blend of lambic and Belgian red ale.

BROUWERIJ VAN HONSEBROUCK
INGELMUNSTER   FOUNDED **1900**

This specialty brewery offers a range of beers, including the strong and rich **Kasteelbier** 🍺 🍺, which is laid down in the bottle to mature in the cellar of the family "castle." **Brigand** 🍺 🍺 is another strong ale from Van Honsebrouck, along with the red ale **Bacchus**🍺 and several lambics.

OTHER BELGIAN BREWERIES

BROUWERIJ ARTOIS, Leuven: Stella Artois🍺, Loburg

BAVIK-DE BRABANDERE, Bavikove: Petrus Oud Bruin🍺🍺, Bavik Premium Pils, Bavik Witbier

BRASSERIE LA BINCHOISE, Binche: Bière des Ours, Fakir, Spéciale Noël

BREWERY DE BLOCK, Peizegem: Satan Ale

BROUWERIJ BOCKOR, Bellegem: Bellegems Bruin, Bockor Ouden Tripel🍺🍺, Jacobins Lambic

BROUWERIJ CORSENDONK, Oud Turnhout: Agnus Dei (Monk's Pale Ale), Pater Noster (Monk's Brown Ale)🍺🍺

BRASSERIE FRIART, Le Roeulx: St. Feuillien Cuvée de Noël, St. Feuillien Blonde🍺🍺, St. Feuillien Brune🍺🍺

BROUWERIJ DE GOUDEN BOOM🍺, Bruges: Blanche de Bruges, Brugse Tripel, Steenbrugge Dubbel, Steenbrugge Tripel

BROUWERIJ HAACHT, Boortmeerbeek: Coq Hardi Pils, Gildenbier🍺🍺, Haecht Witbier🍺, Primus Pilsner,

BROUWERIJ HET ANKER, Mechelen: Gouden Carolus🍺🍺, Mechelsen Bruynen🍺🍺, Toison d'Or Tripel

BROUWERIJ HUYGHE, Melle: Delerium Tremens

BROUWERIJ RIVA, Dentergem: Lucifer🍺, Vondel, Dentergems Wit🍺

ROMAN, OUDENAARDE: Oudenaards🍺, Dobbelen Bruinen🍺🍺, Sloeber🍺, Ename Dubbel Abbey🍺, Romy Pils

BROUWERIJ ST. BERNARDUS🍺, Watou: Pater 6, Prior 8, Abt 12, St. Bernardus Tripel

BROUWERIJ ST. JOZEF, Opitter: Pax Pils🍺, Limburgse Witte🍺🍺, Bosbier, Bokkereye🍺

BROUWERIJ SLAGHMUYLDER, Ninove: Witkap-Pater Abbey Singel Ale, Witkap-Pater Abbey dubbel🍺🍺, Witkap-Pater Abbey Tripel🍺🍺

STRAFFE HENDRIK, Bruges: Bruges Straffe Hendrik🍺

STRUBBE BREWERY, Ichtegem: Ichtegem Oud Bruin🍺

BRASSERIE DE TROCH, Wambeck: Gueuze Lambic🍺 🍺, Kriek Lambic, Peche Lambic, Exotic Lambic, Tropical Lambic

VANDER LINDEN, Halle: Duivelsbier🍺, Frambozenbier, Vieux Foudre Gueuze🍺

LUXEMBOURG

The tiny Grand Duchy of Luxembourg on Belgium's southern border is home to a handful of breweries, producing mostly light lagers and the occasional dark lager or seasonal. A large portion of Luxembourg beer is exported. Among Luxembourg's breweries, Brasserie de Diekirch brews Diekirch Premium, Diekirch Exclusive and Diekirch Grande Reserve; Brasserie Mousel et Clausen offers Altmunster, Mansfield Pilsner and Mousel Pilsner; Brasserie Nationale, of Bascharge, brews Bofferding Lager Pils, Bofferding Hausbeier and Bofferding Christmas; and Brasserie de Wiltz produces Simon Pils and Simon Noël.

THE NETHERLANDS

The beers of neighboring Germany and Belgium are increasingly influencing the Dutch beer industry. Although the Netherlands is best known for its golden lagers, such as those brewed by Heineken and Grolsch, even the mass-market companies offer dark lagers, bocks (or boks, as they are known), or abbey-style ales. Dutch breweries also produce beers in the oud bruin style of Belgium and, increasingly, wheat beers, spiced ales and even stouts and porters. The focus of beer culture and consumption in the Netherlands is located in the south. Beer cafés are established in most cities, and new microbreweries are opening up.

GROLSCH BIERBROUWERIJ
ENSCHEDE FOUNDED 1615

Peter Cuyper established a brewery in the town of Groenlo, then called Grolle. The swing-top bottles first used by Grolsch around the end of the nineteenth century remain a distinctive character of this independent brewery, as the brewery stuck by the crafted bottles when others were abandoning them for cheaper containers. **Grolsch Premium Lager** is a golden pilsner with hop flavors balanced by a slight maltiness. The top-fermented **Grolsch Amber Ale** is a reddish-amber color and uses a small amount of wheat malt in addition to two types of barley malt. Seasonal brews include the light **Grolsch Summerblond** (Zomergoud) and two bock beers, **Meibok** and **Bokbier**. All Grolsch products are unpasteurized, even the exported versions.

ALFA BROUWERIJ
SHINNEN   FOUNDED 1870
This small independent adheres to the German beer purity law, offering only all-malt beers with hop character. **Super Dortmunder** is a strong, sweet beer based on that German style. Alfa's hoppy pilsner beer is **Alfa Edel Pils**, and **Lente Bok** is a classic Dutch-style bok beer.

ARCEN BIERBROUWERIJ
ARCEN   FOUNDED 1981
Though a buyout by the Belgian-based Interbrew has shifted the focus slightly more to lagers, Arcen produces several specialty ales, including the dark barley wine **Grand Prestige** (10% abv), the strongest beer brewed in the Netherlands.

BAVARIA BREWERIES
LIESHOUT   FOUNDED 1719
Still run by the founding family, Bavaria Breweries is one of the Netherlands's oldest breweries. It switched to lagers early in the twentieth century, which prompted the adoption of the name Bavaria. Its lagers—**Bavaria Lager**, **Swinkel's Export Beer** and others—tend to be lighter than those of the Bavarian region of Germany.

BRAND BIERBROUWERIJ
WIJLRE   FOUNDED 1871
Although it has been called Brand only since the 1870s, this brewery was established in the fourteenth century. Now controlled by Heineken, Brand continues to brew distinctive beers, including two rich bocks, the single **Imperator** and **Brand Dubbelbock**; **Sylvestor** strong winter ale; and flavorful pilsners, **Brand Urtyp Pilsner** (UP) and **Brand Pils**.

BUDELS BROUWERIJ
BUDEL   FOUNDED 1870
Budels brews several specialty beers along with the standard **Budels Pilsner**. **Budels Alt** and **Parel** are interpretations of the traditional beers of Düsseldorf and Cologne, respectively, while Capucijn is a spicy and smoky abbey-style beer.

DE DRIE RINGEN BROUWERIJ
AMERSFOORT   FOUNDED 1989
One of the more successful new microbreweries, De Drie Ringen ("The Three Rings") brews mostly top-fermented ales, including the pale ale **Hopfenbier**; the spicy wheat beer known as **Amersfoort Wit**; the abbey-style **Tripel**; and a spring bock, **Meibok**, among other seasonal and specialty brews.

GULPENER BIERBROUWERIJ
GULPEN   FOUNDED 1825
Among this brewery's interesting beers is **Sjoes**, which is

Gulpener's standard, all-malt pilsner mixed with a shot of sweet, dark oud bruin lager; the pilsner is sold separately as **X-Pert** . **Mestreechs Aajt** is a blend of oud bruin and a wild-fermented, lambic-like beer, although other beers have also been used. **Korenwolf** is a wheat beer that includes oats and rye in addition to barley and wheat. Gulpener also offers **Dort** and **Meibock**, among others.

HEINEKEN

AMSTERDAM   FOUNDED 1863

Heineken is the second largest and probably most international brewing company in the world, with breweries or licensing agreements in more than one hundred countries. The lager known simply as **Heineken** is the flagship brand. More flavorful, all-malt offerings are **Tarwebok** , **Van Vollenhoven Stout** and the Irish-style **Kylian** . Heineken brews the export **Amstel Light** and others of the now-defunct Amstel brewery, which Heineken purchased in the 1960s.

ABDIJ VAN KONINGSHOEVEN—TRAPPISTEN BIERBROUWERIJ "DE SCHAAPSKOOI"

EINDHOVENSWEG   FOUNDED 1884

At its Schaapskooi brewhouse, the Trappist abbey at Koningshoeven brews traditional, bottle-conditioned ales using a house yeast and the abbey's well-water. **Dubbel** is ruby-brown in color and has a spicy or bitter element. The next-strongest are the dark gold **Tripel**, which is hoppier than the others, and the vintage-dated **Quadrupel**. The most recent introduction is the single **Enkel**, an amber-colored pale ale. The beers are sold under both the La Trappe and Koningshoeven labels.

ORANJEBOOM BIERBROUWERIJ

BREDA   FOUNDED 1670

Oranjeboom was purchased by Allied Breweries of England and moved from its Rotterdam home to the Three Horseshoes (Drie Hoefijzers) brewery. The products include **Oranjeboom Pils** and **Oranjeboom Oud Bruin**.

BROUWERIJ DE RIDDER

MAASTRICHT   FOUNDED 1852

This small brewery is owned by Heineken. It brews a spicy, unfiltered wheat beer, **Wieckse Witte** , and a strong, malty Dortmunder-style lager, **Maltezer** .

BIERBROUWERIJ ST. CHRISTOFFEL

ROERMOND   FOUNDED 1986

Leo Brand, of the Brand brewing family of Wijlre, opened this microbrewery focusing on lagers. Named for the patron saint of Roermond, St. Christoffel brews the hoppy, all-malt **Christoffel Blond** , a highly regarded example of the pilsner style. **Christoffel Robertus** is a Munich-style dark lager.

BROUWERIJ 'T IJ

AMSTERDAM   FOUNDED 1984

Built under a windmill, this microbrewery produces a range of ales. **Natte** is a dark abbey-style dubbel; **Zatte** is a spicier tripel; **Columbus** is strong pale ale; and **Struis** is a strong but dark ale.

DOMMELSCHE BIERBROUWERIJ, Dommelen: Dominator💀, Pilsner

DE KROON BIERBROUWERIJ, Oirschot: Briljant, Meibok💀

DE LEEUW BIERBROUWERIJ, Valkenburg: Jubileeuw Pils💀,
    Superleeuw💀, Valkenburgs Wit, Venloosch Alt💀

DE LINDEBOOM BIERBROUWERIJ, Neer: Pilsner💀, Gouverneur💀💀

MAASLAND BROUWERIJ, Oss

RAAF BROUWERIJ, Heumen: Witte Raaf💀

GERMANY

G ermany consistently ranks near the top in beer production and consumption, and there are well over
one thousand breweries currently producing beer
in Germany. Munich's huge beer halls and the annual
beer festivals are highly regarded traditions in German
culture. Though the sixteenth-century Reinheitsgebot no
longer dictates what ingredients can be used in beer,
German brewers stand proudly behind the purity and
high quality of their beers. Germany has a wide range of
styles and specialty beers, much of it locally based. As a
result, few truly national brands have emerged, as people
remain loyal to the beers of their region. Nevertheless,
large brewing conglomerates control a number of formerly independent breweries. The largest brewing group,
Bräu und Brunnen, owns such breweries as Bavaria St.
Pauli, Dortmunder Union (DUB), Einbecker, Jever,
Küppers and Schultheiss. The Henninger and Binding
brewing groups each consist of several smaller breweries,
and the Munich-based Spaten-Franziskaner and
Löwenbräu breweries merged in 1997.

In general, the beers of northern Germany are dry
and hoppy while those of the south tend toward the sweet
and malty. Breweries in and around Hamburg and
Bremen, most notably Holsten, Beck's and Jever, brew
dry, pilsner-style lagers. Several cities developed their
own individual beer styles over the centuries, and in the
northwest, Cologne (Köln) has its kölsch, Dortmund has
its Dortmunder export, and Düsseldorf has its altbier.
Berlin is known for its tart wheat beer, Berliner weisse. In
Bavaria, Munich is an obvious contender for the title of
world's leading brewing center, offering a wide variety of
beers ranging from Münchner dunkel (dark) to Münchner
helles (light) lagers, and from rich doppelbocks to cloudy
weizenbiers. There is much brewing throughout Bavaria,
and other areas, such as Franconia in northern Bavaria,

also produce distinct styles: the rauchbier of Bamberg, the unfiltered kellerbier and the schwarzbier style of Köstritz and Kulmbach are all classic German beers.

Brauerei Ayinger

Aying   Founded 1878

Located in a picturesque countryside outside of Munich, the Ayinger brewery has been owned by the Inselkammer family since its

inception. It is a relatively small brewery, but Ayinger produces a broad range of award-winning beers that are now widely exported. The hops and malt used in the brewery's traditional Bavarian-style beers come from this region of southern Germany. Ayinger's excellent doppelbock, **Celebrator** 🍺🍺🍺, is rich in malty aromas and flavors and dark reddish-brown in color. The dark lager **Altbairisch Dunkel** 🍺🍺 also exhibits strong maltiness. **Jahrhundert-Bier** 🍺, brewed originally to celebrate the brewery's centenary, is in the style of a Dortmunder export lager. Ayinger's pale **Maibock** 🍺 has mostly hop but also some fruit flavors, and the fall-season **Oktober Fest-Märzen** 🍺 is another pale and malty offering. Two wheat beers are brewed by Ayinger: **Ur-Weisse** 🍺🍺, a reddish unfiltered wheat beer, and **Bräu-**

Weisse, a tart and pale variation.

Paulaner Salvator Thomas Bräu

Munich   Founded 1634

The monks of the Order of St. Francis of Paula began selling beers commercially in 1780, and the brewery was taken over by secular own-

ers in the early 1800s. Acquiring Thomas Brothers Brewery in the 1920s and, more recently, Hacker-Pschorr, Paulaner is now the largest brewery in Munich. It has been a pioneering brewery throughout its history in such areas as lager brewing and refrigeration, but perhaps its greatest innovation was the development of the doppelbock style. A rich, strong beer had been brewed by the monks to consume during Lent, and the secular brewers continued the style, naming it Salvator, meaning "savior." (Many other breweries give their doppelbocks names ending in "-ator" in tribute.) The **Salvator** 🍺🍺🍺 brewed today remains rich and strong and is ruby-brown in color. Paulaner's beers are drier than those of other Munich breweries.

Dray horses pulling a beer carriage at a German Oktoberfest.

The dark **Münchner Dunkel** lager and the classic German-style **Premium Pils** display some of that dry but malty character. In addition, Paulaner brews **Original Münchner Hell**, **Oktoberfest** and a good Bavarian style **Hefe-Weizen**.

SPATEN-FRANZISKANER-BRÄU
MUNICH FOUNDED 1397

Spaten, the oldest of the Munich breweries, has been making beer since the late 1300s, and the Franziskaner (Franciscan) brewery (which has been owned by Spaten since the 1920s) can trace its origins

to even earlier in the fourteenth century. Spaten was taken over by Gabriel Sedlmayr, brewmaster of the Bavarian Royal Court, in 1807, and he expanded the brewery and its reputation significantly. His sons Gabriel II and Joseph continued that legacy of innovation, doing pioneering work in the areas of refrigeration and steam power as well as in brewing techniques. Spaten was an early promoter of lagers and is credited with originating the märzen style. Spaten's **Premium Lager** and **Pils** are hoppy, bottom-fermented beers, while **Dunkel Export** has more of a malty quality. **Optimator** is Spaten's rich, fairly spicy doppelbock. The original **Oktoberfest Ur-Märzen** is amber-red in color and has strong malty aromas. The wheat beers brewed by Spaten-Franziskaner include **Franziskaner Hefe-Weissbier**, **Franziskaner Hefe-Weissbier Dunkel** and the filtered **Franziskaner Club-Weissbier**.

AUGUSTINER BRAUEREI
MUNICH   FOUNDED 1803

Though less well-known internationally than the major Munich breweries, Augustiner is a favorite within that Bavarian city.

Raucos crowd at an Oltoberfest celebration in Munich

Augustiner Hell and **Augustiner Dunkel**, both of which are available in export versions, are true to the malty character of Munich's lagers. Augustiner also brews a **Weissbier**.

BRAUEREI BECK & COMPANY
BREMEN   FOUNDED 1873

A giant in the international beer market, Beck's is Germany's largest beer exporter. Its lagers are produced at the Bremen brewery. These include **Beck's Beer**, **Beck's Dark**, **Haake Beck Non-Alcoholic** and the seasonal **Beck's Oktoberfest**.

BERLINER KINDL BRAUEREI
BERLIN   FOUNDED 1872

The Kindl brewery produces one of the few remaining examples of the classic Berlin-style wheat beer. The refreshing **Berliner Kindl Weisse** is a sour, somewhat fruity wheat ale that is brewed with milk sugar, or lactose. Kindl also brews other German standards, such as **Kindl Pils** and **Kindl Schwarzbier**.

Binding Brauerei
Frankfurt   Founded 1870

Binding is the second-largest brewing group in Germany, consisting of Berliner Kindl, DAB, and others. It makes traditional beers such as **Romer Pils**, **Carolus Doppelbock**, and **Kutscher Alt**, but it is best known for its pioneering non-alcoholic **Clausthaler**.

Bitburger Brauerei Th. Simon
Bitburg   Founded 1817

Shortly after Theobald Simon took over the brewery founded by his grandfather, Bitburger turned to brewing the new pilsner-style lagers in the 1880s. The company is still run by Simon descendants, producing **Bitburger Premium Pils** 🍺🍺, the leading draught pilsner in Germany, as well as **Bitburger Light** and the alcohol-free **Bitburger Drive**.

Privatbrauerei Diebels
Issum   Founded 1878

This large family-run brewery makes **Diebels Alt** (also known as Diebels German Premium Beer), a premier example of the altbier style. Diebels offers low-calorie and low-alcohol versions of its alt.

Dortmunder Actien Brauerei (DAB)

Dortmund   Founded 1868

DAB's interpretation of the Dortmunder-style lager, **DAB Export** , is malty dry, though the brewery is focusing more on its **DAB Meister Pils**. It also produces **Dortmunder Actien Alt** and beers of its subsidiary Dortmunder Hansa, such as **Dortmunder Hansa Export**.

Dortmunder Kronen Brauerei

Dortmund   Founded 1430

The oldest of Dortmund's three main breweries, the family-owned Kronen is also the smallest. The slightly malty **Export**, the pale **Classic** and **Kronen Pils** are its main beers.

Dortmunder Union Brauerei (DUB)

Dortmund   Founded 1873

Dortmunder Union formed when a dozen or so breweries in Dortmund merged in the late nineteenth century. **DUB Export** is a mild Dortmunder beer. DUB's pilsner-style lagers include **Siegel Pilsner** and **Brinkhoff's No. 1**. Dortmunder Ritter, which brews **Ritter First Pils**, is now a part of DUB.

Einbecker Bräuhaus

Einbeck   Founded 1967

Located in the town that is credited with inventing bock beer, Einbecker has links to breweries from centuries ago. Today it brews three varieties of the ur-bock ("original bock") style: **Ur-Bock Hell**, **Ur-Bock Dunkel** and **Miabock**. A dry pilsner, **Brauherren Pils**, is also produced.

Erdinger Weissbräu

Erding   Founded 1886

Erdinger, the leading producer of wheat beers in Germany, brews exclusively wheat beers, including **Hefe Weissbier**, **Dunkel Weissbier**, **Kristall Weissbier** and **Erdinger Pinkantus**, a weizenbock. It uses mostly locally grown wheat.

Hacker-Pschorr Bräu

Munich   Founded 1417

This major Munich-based brewery has been part of Paulaner since the 1970s. Hacker-Pschorr brews traditional German-style beers such as **Braumeister** pilsner, **Edelhell** and **Oktoberfest Märzen**, as well as the wheat beers **Pschorr Weisse** and **Pschorr Weisse Dunkel**.

Brauerei Heller-Trum, Schlenkerla

Bamberg   Founded 1678

Aecht Schlenkerla Rauchbier is the classic smoked beer of Bamberg. It has been brewed at the Schlenkerla tavern, first by the Heller family and then by the Trums, since the seventeenth century. This märzen-style lager has definite smoky flavors and aromas, which is achieved by kilning the malt over open beechwood fires.

Holsten Brauerei

Hamburg   Founded 1879

This large Hamburg brewery is known for its hoppy pilsners, among them **Holsten Pils** and **Holsten Premium Beer**, although it also brews **Urbock**, which is really a maibock, and **Holsten Export**.

Irseer Klosterbräu

Irseer   Founded 1390

Klosterbräu means "cloister brewery," and although the monks were expelled from Irseer centuries ago, the brewery still brews from those monastic recipes. **Kloster Urtunk** is an unfiltered märzen lager, and the Irseer brewery also produces a wheat beer and the rich and strong **Abts Trunk**.

Brauerei Gebrüder Maisel

Bayreuth   Founded 1887

Maisel's has benefited from the recent resurgence of German wheat beers, producing **Maisel's Weiss**, **Kristall Weizen** and **Weizen Bock** 🍺🍺, among others. The brewery also offers **Maisel's Pilsner** and the unusual **Dampfbier** ("steam beer") 🍺🍺, a top-fermented ale similar to an English bitter.

Reichelbräu Aktien-Gesellschaft

Kulmbach   Founded 1846

Kulmbacher Reichelbräu brews the quintessential eisbock. Known as **Reichelbräu Eisbock Bayrisch G'frorns** ("Bavarian Frozen") 🍺🍺🍺, this very strong lager (10% abv) is made with several different malts and three hop varieties.

Küppers Kölsch   Cologne

Küppers is the largest producer of the kölsch beers of Cologne, but in addition to its fairly sweet **Küppers Kölsch** 🍺, the brewery offers an unfiltered version, **Küppers Wiess** 🍺🍺 (*not* "Weiss").

Brauerei Löwenbräu

Munich   Founded 1383

Probably the most widely known Munich brewery internationally, Löwenbräu brews typical Munich-style beers—**Münchner Dunkel**, **Münchner Helles**, **Münchner Oktoberfest**, **Premium Pilsner** and others—that tend to have a malty character. In 1997 Löwenbräu was acquired by Spaten.

Brauerei Pinkus Müller

Münster   Founded 1816

Pinkus Müller is a family-run brewery and pub that brews only organic beers. The golden **Pinkus Pils**, **Pinkus Weizen** 🍺 and **Pinkus Alt** 🍺🍺, which is made partly with wheat, are the standard offerings.

Schlossbrauerei Kaltenberg

Kaltenberg and Furstenfeldbruck   Founded 1872

Located in an old Bavarian castle, Schlossbrauerei Kaltenberg is best known for its **König Ludwig Dunkel** 🍺🍺 lager and **Prinzregent Luitpold Weissbier** 🍺🍺, which is available in both hefe and dunkel varieties. This castle brewery also brews **Kaltenberg Pils**.

Privatbrauerei G. Schneider & Sohn

Kelheim   Founded 1856

Wheat beer has been brewed on the site of the Schneider brewery since the 1600s, and in the mid-1850s, Georg Schneider purchased the exclusive right to produce wheat beer. The original **Schneider Weisse** 🍺🍺 is a relatively dark hefeweizen made with 60 percent wheat that offers complex aromas and a tart, spicy flavor. **Aventinus** is a bottle-conditioned wheat doppelbock that has richer fruit tones than the hefeweizen.

BAYERISCHE STAATSBRAUEREI WEIHENSTEPHAN

FREISING   FOUNDED 1040

Weihenstephan claims to be the oldest brewery in the world, tracing its origins to an eleventh century monastery brewery. Now state-owned, the brewery makes several wheat beers, including **Hefeweissbier** and **Kristallweissbier**, as well as **Edelpils**, the dark **Export Dunkel** and **Korbinian Dunkels Starkbier**, a doppelbock. Weihenstephan also houses the renowned Faculty of Brewing.

WEISSBRAUEREI HANS HOPF

MIESBACH   FOUNDED 1910

The Hopf family brewery in Bavaria makes wheat beers exclusively, including **Weisse Export**, **Dunkel Weissbier** and **Weisser Bock**.

OTHER GERMAN BREWERIES

BRAUEREI BAVARIA ST. PAULI, Hamburg: Astra Pilsner, Astra Exclusive, Astra Urbock

EICHBAUM BRAUEREI, Mannheim: Ureich Pilsner, Export Altgold, Apostulator

BRAUEREI FELSENKELLER, Herford: Herforder Pils, Herforder Export

FORSCHUNGS BRAUEREI, Munich: St. Jakobus, Pilsissimus

FRIESISCHES BRÄUHAUS ZU JEVER, Jever: Jever Pilsener

FÜRSTENBERG BRAUEREI, Donauchingen: Fürstenberg Pilsner

FÜRSTLICHE BRAUEREI THURN UND TAXIS, Regensburg: Thurn und Taxis Pilsner, Thurn und Taxis Hell, Schierlinger Roggenbier

PRIVATBRAUEREI GAFFEL, Cologne: Gaffel Kölsch

HANNEN BRAUEREI, Mönchen-Gladbach: Hannen Alt

HENNINGER BRAUEREI, Frankfurt: Kaiser Pilsner, Henninger Dunkel

KLOSTERBRAUEREI WELTENBURG, Kelheim: Kloster Pils, Kloster Barock Hell, Kloster Barock Dunkel, Kloster Hefe-Weissbier, Kloster Asam Bock

KÖNIG BRAUEREI, Duisberg: König Pilsner

KÖNIGSBACHER BRAUEREI, Koblenz: Königsbacher Alt, Königsbacher Pils, Königsbacher Urbock

KÖSTRITZER SCHWARZBIERBRAUEREI, Bad Köstritz: Köstritzer Schwarzbier

PRIVATBRAUEREI KROMBACHER, Krombach: Krombacher Pils

PRIVATBRAUEREI MODSCHIEDLER, Buttenheim: St. Georgen Kellerbier, St. Georgen Märzen

SCHULTHEISS BRAUEREI, Berlin: Schultheiss Berliner Weiss

ST. PAULI BRAUEREI, Bremen: St. Pauli Girl, St. Pauli Girl Dark

BRAUEREI SPEZIAL, Bamberg: Lagerbier, Märzenbier

STAATLICHES HOFBRÄUHAUS, Munich: Münchner Kindl Weissbier, Dunkel, Maibock

Unertl Weissbier, Haag: Hefeweissbier, Weisser Bock, Leichtes
    Weisse

Warsteiner Brauerei, Warstein: Warsteiner Premium Verum ,
    Warsteiner Light

Zum Uerige, Düsseldorf: Alt

SWITZERLAND

St. Gallen in Switzerland contains remnants of one of the oldest commercial breweries in Europe, dating from the ninth century. The German-speaking areas of Switzerland began producing lagers around the middle of the nineteenth century, but since then the number of breweries has steadily declined. Despite a minor resurgence in microbreweries and brewpubs, the industry is dominated by the Feldschlösschen-Hürlimann conglomerate. Feldschlöss-chen and Cardinal merged in 1992 and then joined up with fellow giant Hürlimann in 1996. The Zurich-based Löwenbräu (no relation to the Munich brewery of the same name) is a subsidiary of Hürlimann. Switzerland's beers are characterized by light, clean lagers known as blonds—they do not use the term pilsner, which is reserved for lagers from the Czech Republic. A few wheat beers and dark lagers constitute a small percentage of the remaining market.

BRAUEREI HÜRLIMANN
ZURICH   FOUNDED 1836

The Hürlimann family brewery moved to its present site in the 1860s to allow easier access to the ice and cool caves of the nearby Alps for lagering. Active in yeast research (it supplies hundreds of breweries with different yeast strains), Hürlimann discovered a strain of yeast that could withstand high alcohol levels, which led to the introduction of one of the strongest beers around. **Samichlaus**, which is the German-Swiss name for Santa Claus, is a strong, brownish-amber lager (14.7% abv). It is brewed on one day each year, St. Nicholas's Day (December 6), and is released on the following St. Nicholas's Day after a full year of lagering. The result is a rich, almost creamy beer with a complex range of flavors, from roasted malt to slightly spicy tones and an alcohol taste. By contrast, Hürlimann also brews a low-alcohol lager, **Birell**, using a specific yeast strain, rather than distillation, to remove the alcohol. The brewery's malty, dunkel lager is called **Hexen Bräu**, which means witches' brew and is produced only during periods of a full moon. **Dreikönigs** is a strong pale lager.

Unfortunately, in late 1998 Hürlimann decided to discontinue production of Samichlaus. Those lucky few who caught the last bottling and decided to lay down their supply for aging can revel in enjoying a last taste of this fine brew, once the strongest in all the world.

BRASSERIE DU CARDINAL
FRIBOURG   FOUNDED 1789

Now part of the Feldschlösschen-Hürlimann group, Cardinal brews a range of light lagers, including the golden **Cardinal Lager**, as well as **Anker** altbier and the non-alcoholic **Moussy**.

BRAUEREI FELDSCHLÖSSCHEN
RHEINFELDEN   FOUNDED 1874

Feldschlösschen 🍺 has long been a leading brewery in Switzerland. It brews **Hopfenperle**, a very hoppy lager; the dark **Dunkle Perle**; **Schlossgold**, a non-alcoholic beer; and **Ice Beer**.

BRAUEREI FISCHERSTUBE
BASEL   FOUNDED 1974

In the mid-1970s, the Fischerstube café in Basel began brewing beers with the name Ueli, which means jester. The small brewery offers **Ueli Lager** and **Ueli Weizenbier**.

OTHER SWISS BREWERIES

BACK UND BRÄU, several locations (brewpub)

CALANDA HALDENGUT BRAUEREI, Chur

EICHHOF, Lucerne: Eichhof Lager

LOCHER, Appenzell: Vollmond

BRAUEREI LÖWENBRÄU, Zurich: Löwenbräu Lager, Celtic Whiskey
    Brew

RUGENBRÄU, Matten-Interlaken

STADTBÜHL, Gossau

WARTEK BREWERY, Basel: Wartek Alt 🍺, Wartek Brune 🍺

AUSTRIA

Located on the border of two beer giants—Germany and the Czech Republic—Austria does have a brewing tradition of its own. Brewing in Austria dates back to the thirteenth century, but the most important development came in the 1840s, when renowned Viennese brewer Anton Dreher pioneered the Vienna-style lager. This reddish, malty lager was distinct from the dunkel lagers of Germany and the lighter Czech pilsner lagers. In recent years, the style has been carried on most faithfully in Mexico, although similar lagers continue to dominate the Austrian beer scene. In addition, a small percentage of the market consists of wheat ales, pilsners, and bocks, while more experimental styles, such as rye beer and "whiskey malt" beer, are becoming more common. Though brewpubs and microbreweries are finding some success, in January 1998, nearly two-thirds of Austria's beer production was combined under a single conglomerate, Brau Union Österreich AG. It formed from the union of the nation's two largest brewing groups, Brau AG and Steirerbrau AG. Among the brands consolidated under this group are Edelweiss, Falkenstein, Gösser, Innsbruck, Kaiser, Kaltenhausen, Puntigam, Reininghaus, Schwechat, Wieselburg and Zipf.

SCHLOSSBRAUEREI EGGENBERG
VORCHDORF   FOUNDED 1681

Eggenberg produces a range of specialty beers, most notably the strong and creamy **Urbock 23**. With strong malt flavors and aro-

mas, this deep golden lager is a classic bock. Aged for several months at the brewery, it is also one of the strongest Austrian beers, just short of 10% abv. In addition, Eggenberg brews an interesting "whiskey-malt" beer, **MacQueen's Nessie**, that uses smoked malt imported from Scotland and has a bronzy-gold color and smoky flavor. **Hopfen König** is a hoppy lager similar to a pilsner, while other offerings include **Eggenberg Märzen** and **Eggenberg Spezial Dunke**l.

GÖSSER BRAUEREI
LEOBEN-GÖSS
FOUNDED 1913

This brewery produces Austria's most widely-known lagers, including the light **Gösser Gold**, **Gösser Spezial**, **Gösser Märzen** and the fuller and darker **Gösser Export**.

PRIVATBRAUEREI JOSEF SIGL
OBERTRUM   FOUNDED 1601

The independent Sigl brewery makes the dry, hoppy **Trumer Pils** and a range of wheat beers under the Weizen Gold brand, such as **Weizen Gold Dunkel Hefeweizen** and the spritzy **Weizen Gold Champagner**. Sigl bottles display pop-art characters on the labels.

OTTAKRINGER BRAUEREI
VIENNA   FOUNDED 1837

A traditional family brewery, Ottakringer brews classic Vienna-style lagers with distinctive malty flavors. Among its offerings are the pale **Gold Fassl Pils**; **Gold Fassl Spezial**, which is a deeper gold color; **Ottakringer Helles Bier**; and **Ottakringer Bock**.

Brauerei Schwechat

Vienna · Founded 1632

With roots tracing back to the seventeenth century, Schwechat came to prominence as the brewery of Anton Dreher, beginning in the 1830s. The innovative brewer expanded the company throughout Austria, and in the early 1900s it merged with several other independents. The brewery's light lagers include **Steffl Export**, **Schwechater Lager Beer** and the hoppy **Hopfenperle**.

Stiftsbrauerei Schlägl

Schlägl · Founded 1580

The only monastery brewery in Austria brews by traditional methods to create flavorful, malty beers. **Gold Roggen** is a golden rye ale, and the brewery also produces **Schlägel Pils**, **Schlägel Kristall**, **Schlägel Märzen**, and **Schlägel Doppelbock**.

Brauerei Wieselburg

Wieselburg · Founded 1770

One of Austria's oldest-running breweries, Wieselburg produces traditional Austrian lagers, such as **Wieselburger Gold** and **Wieselburger Stammbräu**. The Kaiser line—**Kaiser Premium**, **Kaiser Märzen**, **Kaiser Bock**, **Doppelmalz**—are also brewed at Wieselburg.

OTHER AUSTRIAN BREWERIES

Adambräu, Innsbruck: Adambräu Lager

Brauerei Fohrenburg, Budenz

Privatbrauerei Fritz Egger, Unterradlberg

Brauerei Hirter, Hirt: Hirter Private Pils

Bräuhaus Nussdorf, Vienna: Doppelhopfen-Hell, Old Whiskey Bier, St. Thomas Brau, Sir Henry's Stout, Zwickel Bier

Brauerei Stiegl, Salzburg: Stiegl Goldbräu, Steigl Weihnachtsbock

CZECH REPUBLIC

The Czech Republic is probably best-known for the pilsner style of lager, which was developed in the town of Plzen (Pilsen) in the mid-nineteenth century. This pale, clear lager remains the nation's leading brew, although within the country the term pilsner is used only for beers produced in the town of Plzen. Aside from the original Pilsner Urquell, Staropramen and Budweiser Budvar are other classic examples, though slightly sweeter than the Plzen variety. But there is much more to this county's beer traditions than the one style of lager. The hops that are grown around the Bohemian town of Saaz (Zatec) are among the most highly regarded in the world, and Czech brewers were early advocates of using hops in beer. The barley from Moravia is also prized for its fine malting qualities. The Czech Republic ranks highest in per capita consumption of beer, and for centuries each town or village had its own brewery, providing one light and one dark beer to the local community. Today, many breweries identify their various products according to the old degree method of measuring alcohol levels—8 degrees, 10 degrees, or 12 degrees, in increasing order of strength.

Although the overthrow of the Communist regime in the "Velvet Revolution" of 1989 paved the way to a free-market system and opened the market to smaller breweries and brewpubs, it has also led to consolidation and a rush toward modernization. In addition, many foreign companies are buying out or entering into joint ventures with Czech breweries. Bass of England owns several Czech breweries, including Branik, Mestan, Ostravar and Staropramen. Pilsner Urquell is the largest brewing group in the Czech Republic, encompassing neighboring rival Gambrinus as well as the Domazlice and Karlovy Vary breweries. The South Bohemia brewery group includes Platan, Regent and Samson.

PILSNER URQUELL—PLZENSKY PRAZDROJ
PLZEN   FOUNDED 1842

Beer had been brewed in the Bohemian town of Plzen (Pilsen is the German spelling) since the thirteenth century, but the name of the town

first became famous in the mid-1800s when a local brewery abandoned the unreliable top-fermented ales in favor of the newly emerging bottom-fermented lager style. Hiring a young brewmaster from Bavaria, the brewery produced the first pale, clear lager in 1842, using pale Bohemian malt, the renowned local Saaz hops, and the town's quality water. **Pilsner Urquell** 🍺🍺🍺, which means "original source pilsner," remains a classic example of the style: pale golden in color, crystal clear, thick white head, hoppy aromas, hoppiness balanced by a slightly sweet malt character and dry finish. The Pilsner Urquell brewery has modernized its facilities in recent years, foregoing the traditional oak open fermenting vessels and aging casks in favor of the closed conical fermenters.

BUDWEISER BUDVARCESKE
BUDEJOVICE   FOUNDED 1895

Despite being excluded from the American market due to trademark disputes with Anheuser-Busch, Budweiser Budvar is a fast-growing brewery. The name Budweiser was originally used to define any beer from the city of Budweis (the German spelling). Using traditional equipment, the brewery's flagship **Budweiser Budvar** 🍺🍺🍺 is a premier example of the Czech lager style, slightly malty and golden-copper in color. The beer is now exported to the United States under the name **Crystal Lager**.

GAMBRINUS BREWERY
PLZEN   FOUNDED 1869

Though in the shadow of the larger and more widely known Pilsner Urquell, Gambrinus brews quality lagers in the brewery located next door. **Gambrinus 12** is a golden, somewhat hoppy lager true to the town's tradition.

PIVOVAR HEROLD
BREZNICE   FOUNDED 1720

The Communist government closed the old Herold brewery in 1988, but it was reopened in 1990 after the Velvet Revolution. Herold brews two pale lagers, **Pale 10** and **Pale 12**, and the black **Dark 13**. **Herold Wheat** is a tart wheat beer.

PIVOVAR OLOMOUC
OLOMOUC   FOUNDED 1896

Using its own maltings and well-water, Olomouc makes both traditional, unfiltered lagers and beers brewed under license for American companies. **Granat 12** is a rich, deep red lager, while **Holan 10** and **Vaclav 12** are standard pale lagers, the latter particularly hoppy.

PIVOVAR RADEGAST
NOSOVICE   FOUNDED 1970

Radegast has grown rapidly since privatization in the early 1990s to become one of the three leading breweries in the Czech Republic. Its lagers include the golden **Radegast Premium Light** and **Radegast Premium Dark**.

PIVOVAR REGENT
TREBON   FOUNDED 1379

This traditional brewery is one of the oldest in the Czech Republic. **Regent Black** is a full-bodied dark lager with roasty licorice and coffee notes. The popular **Bohemia Regent** is a copper-colored lager.

STAROPRAMEN BREWERY
PRAGUE   FOUNDED 1869

This large Prague brewery still uses open fermenting vessels and traditional lagering tanks to produce its beers. **Staropramen** is a flavorful golden lager, and there is also a darker version, **Staropramen Dark**.

U FLEKU
PRAGUE   FOUNDED 1499

Claiming to be the oldest brewpub in the world, U Fleku brews classic Czech beers in its historic brewery, including the rich and dark **Flekovsky Lezek**.

PIVOVAR VELKE POPOVICE
VELKE POPOVICE   FOUNDED 1874

Velke Popovice has roots extending to the sixteenth century and has grown fast since privatization in the early 1990s. It brews beers under the Kozel label: **Kozel Pale**, **Kozel Dark**, **Kozel Premium Lager**, and **Kozel Special Dark Beer**, with the latter two being maltier and slightly higher in alcohol.

OTHER CZECH BREWERIES

PIVOVARY BRANIK, Prague

PIVOVAR DOMAZLICE, Domazlice

PIVOVAR KARLOVY VARY, Karlovy Vary: Karel IV,
    Karel Svelte

PIVOVARY KRUSOVICE, Krusovice

LOBKOWICZ PIVOVAR, Chlumec

PIVOVAR NACHOD, Nachod: Primator

PIVOVAR OSTRAVAR, Ostrava: Ondras 12, Konik Pilsner, Vranik Porter

PIVOVAR PLATAN, Protivin: Platan Premium 12, Platan Dark 10

PIVOVAR SAMSON, Ceske Budejovice: Crystal Pale 12, Zamec Pale 11
    (Diplomat Dark)

PIVOVARY STAROBRNO, Brno

PIVOVAR ZATEC, Zatec: Chmelar, Lucan

OTHER SLOVAKIAN BREWERIES

PIVOVARE KOSICE, Kosice: Cassovar 🍺🍺

PIVOVARE MARTIN, Martin: Martinksy, Martin Porter

EASTERN EUROPE AND THE BALTIC REGION

The tradition of brewing beer is not as firmly entrenched in Eastern Europe as it is in the West, as hard alcohol and spirits have long been the preferred libation. However, past German influences in such nations as Poland and Hungary have had some residual effects, and Czech-and German-style lagers characterize the majority of the region's beers. English influences are stronger in the Baltic nations, as demonstrated by the porters commonly brewed there. Due to economic limitations, beer often includes rye, corn, or other locally grown grains as adjuncts.

During the Communist era, breweries in the Eastern Bloc were government-owned. Since the breakup of the Soviet Union, many Eastern European breweries have been acquired in foreign joint-venture operations. The Belgian Interbrew owns breweries in Hungary, Bulgaria, Romania and Poland; the Dutch Heineken has a large share in one of Poland's largest breweries; and the large Scandinavian joint company known as Baltic Beverages Holding has partnerships with major breweries in Latvia, Estonia, Lithuania and Russia. In Poland, which has many breweries, Elbrewery was created by the merging of Elblag and Hevelius, with Australian investment and in association with Grolsch. There has also been a certain amount of microbrew activity, particularly in Hungary.

SAKU OLLETEHAS BREWERY
TALLINN, ESTONIA   FOUNDED 1820

Now largely controlled by the Baltic Beverages Holding group, Saku brews dark beers in addition to the standard light lagers. **Saku Pilsner** and **Saku Original** are of the lighter variety, while **Saku Porter** and **Tume** are quality beers in the darker, richer category.

KOBANYAI SORGYAR
BUDAPEST, HUNGARY   FOUNDED 1854

Established in the hills around Budapest in order to take advantage of the cool mountain caves for lagering, Kobanyai was purchased by Viennese brewer Anton Dreher in 1862. The Dreher family expanded the Kobanyai brewery, merging with several local rivals in the pre-World War II era. After the war, any ties to the Germanic Dreher name were eliminated, though the Hungarian government continued producing beer in the facility. With a return to privatization in the 1990s, Dreher's legacy—including his recipes—was re-embraced, and the brewery offers several brands bearing the Dreher name. **Dreher Pils** is dry and hoppy, like a typical pilsner-style lager, while **Dreher Export** is fuller in body and darker in color. **Dreher Bak** is a dark bock with toasty flavors. South African Breweries purchased the company in 1993. Kobanyai remains Hungary's largest brewery.

ALDARIS BREWERY
RIGA, LATVIA   FOUNDED 1937

A Bavarian brewmaster established the Waldschlosschen brewery in the outskirts of Riga in 1865. By the turn of the century it was exporting its five brands across the Baltic region and Russia. In 1937, the government formed the Aldaris joint stock company out of the Waldschlosschen brewery. During the Soviet era, Aldaris was a leading brewery in the vast country. After the breakup of the Soviet Union, Aldaris became part of the joint-venture Baltic Beverages Holding. Today Aldaris produces six brands of beer. **Aldara Pilzenes** is a light, hoppy lager, and **Aldara Zelta** is a stronger but smooth beer. Aldaris also brews the dark **Aldara Porter**, as well as the amber-colored **Aldara Luksusa**, **Aldara Baltijas** and **Aldara Latvijas**.

ELBLAGU BROWAR
ELBLAG, POLAND
FOUNDED 1872

Elblag is part of Elbrewery (EB), the largest brewing group in Poland. Its flagship, **EB Special Pils**, is a pale yellow lager.

OKOCIM BROWAR
OKOCIM, POLAND
FOUNDED 1845

Founded by an Austrian, located near the Czech border, and now owned by the German brewing giant Bräu and Brunnen, the old Okocim brewery has connections with classic European brewing traditions. In addition to the light and hoppy Czech-style **Okocim Premium Pils**, the brewery produces the strong, dark brown **Okocim Porter**.

TYSKIE BROWAR
TYCHY, POLAND   FOUNDED 1629
Brewing in the town of Tychy dates back to the seventeenth century. The third-largest brewery in Poland, Tyskie brews Gronie, which accounts for more than three-quarters of production, **Karmen la Bella**, and **Mocne**.

ZYWIEC BROWAR
ZYWIEC, POLAND   FOUNDED 1856
Located near the town of Krakow, Zywiec produces Poland's most widely exported beer. Owned initially by the Hapsburg Royal Court, the brewery expanded into broader markets under state control during the Communist era. Since the fall of the Iron Curtain, Zywiec has modernized its facilities and is now partially owned by the Dutch Heineken. It controls the second-largest segment of the domestic beer market. The main beers are light, pilsner-style lagers, such as the dry **Zywiec Full Light**, but it also brews fuller-bodied beers. **Zywiec Porter** is a smooth, dark red porter with hints of coffee flavors, while a strong golden lager is produced as Eurospecjal.

BALTIKA BREWERY
ST. PETERSBURG, RUSSIA   FOUNDED 1978
Since joining Baltic Beverages Holding, Baltika has grown to become the largest brewery in St. Petersburg. Baltika's **Classic** and **Original** are standard, hoppy lagers, with Original being slightly darker. Baltika also brews a **Porter**.

OTHER BALTIC BREWERIES

KALNAPILIS, Panavezys, Lithuania

RAGUTUS, Kaunas, Lithuania

OTHER BULGARIAN BREWERIES

BULGARSKA PIVO, Sofia

ZAGORKA BREWERY, Stara Zagora

OTHER HUNGARIAN BREWERIES

BORSODI SORGYAR, Bocs: Borsod Premium

KANIZSAI SORGYAR, Nagykanizsa

KOMAROMI SORGYAR, Komaron: Talleros

SOPRONI SORGYAR, Sopron

OTHER POLISH BREWERIES

BIALYSTOKU BROWAR, Bialystok: Dojlidy

BYDGOSZCZKI BROWAR, Bydgoszcz

Hevelius Browar, Gdansk

Poznani Browar, Poznan: Lech Premium, Lech Porter

Warszawski Browar, Warsaw: Warszawski Porter

OTHER RUSSIAN & UKRAINIAN BREWERIES

Moscovskoye Brewery, Moscow

Obolon Brewery, Kiev

Zhigulevskoye Brewery, Moscow: Zhigulevskoye Lager

SCANDINAVIA

With the exception of Denmark, Scandinavia has a history of anti-alcohol sentiments that has somewhat restricted the growth of the brewing industry around the region. In Sweden, Norway and Finland, the domestic industry is dominated by a very small number of large breweries. Three of the biggest breweries in the region—Pripps of Sweden, Ringnes of Norway, and Hartwall of Finland—joined to form the massive Baltic Beverages Holding group. In addition to holding a significant share of the Scandinavian market, BBH is a major partner in ventures throughout the Baltic nations, Russia and the Ukraine.

The beers of Scandinavia are mostly golden lagers based on German or Czech traditions. Dark lagers, either of the bock or Münchner dunkel variety, also have a long local history. A British influence is evident in some beers of the region, though for the most part these are bottom-fermented adaptations.

DENMARK

Denmark, perhaps due to its close proximity to Germany, is among the highest consumers of beer per capita in Europe. In addition, the crucial role that the Carlsberg Brewery played in yeast research and developing the lager style in the 1880s gives the country historic significance. Carlsberg and Tuborg have long been the dominant beer producers, and since 1970 they have been a single entity, United Breweries, accounting for more than three-quarters of the Danish beer market. Carlsberg has also been an important force on the international market, and was further solidified by its union with the British-based Tetley group. The Carlsberg and Tuborg breweries focus on pilsner-style lagers, although a few darker styles are being brewed, including dunkel lagers and even porters and stouts. Denmark's second-largest brewing group formed with the union of the Ceres, Faxe and Thor breweries.

CARLSBERG BREWERY
COPENHAGEN
FOUNDED 1847

Carlsberg is among the largest breweries in the world, and its place in brewing lore is secure due to its being the first to isolate a pure culture of lager yeast, which allowed for large-scale and more consistent lager brewing—the yeast strain was originally called Saccharomyces carlsbergensis. Carlsberg was also an early exporter of beer and quickly gained an international market for its light, mild lagers. Today nearly 85 percent of Carlsberg's sales are outside of Denmark, and its beers are brewed under license in dozens of countries. **Carlsberg Pilsner** (also sold as Hof) is the standard offering. The darker and stronger **Elephant Beer** is similar to a bock, with an element of sweet malt flavors. Other dark beers produced by Carlsberg are **Special Dark Lager** and **Porter Imperial Stout**. **Carlsberg Let** is a light-beer offering.

BRYGGERI ALBANI
ODENSE   FOUNDED 1859

The best-known beer of this large independent brewery is **Giraf**, a strong golden lager, but Albani also brews the dark and malty **Albani Porter** and the traditional **Albani Pilsner**. It produces seasonal beers for Christmas and Easter.

CERES BRYGGERIERNE
AARHUS   FOUNDED 1865

Ceres specializes in strong beers with a British influence. These include **Ceres Porter** and **Ceres Stowt**, while **Ceres Royal Export** and Dansk Dortmunder are based on more Germanic traditions. **Bering** is a blend of lager and stout.

TUBORG BREWERY
COPENHAGEN   FOUNDED 1873

Tuborg has a distinguished brewing history going back more than a century. Its beers are similar but hoppier and drier than those of its parent, Carlsberg. **Tuborg Beer**—known as **Tuborg Grøn** because of the green label—is its main pilsner, but Tuborg also brews **Tuborg Porter** and **Tuborg Gold**.

OTHER DANISH BREWERIES

FAXE BRYGGERI, Fakse: Faxe Premium, Faxe Pils

THOR BRYGGERIERNE, Aarhus: Buur Beer

HARBOES BRYGGERI, Skaelskor: Bear Beer, Gold Export

WILBROE BRYGGERI, Elsinore

Government regulation and taxation, spurred in part by temperance movements, limited brewing in Finland over the centuries, but the country does produce flavorful lagers and even some ales in addition to the common golden lagers. Sinebrychoff and Hartwall control most of the industry, with the latter being the Finnish member of the Scandinavian triumverate that makes up Baltic Beverages Holding. Nevertheless, the number of micro-breweries has been on the rise.

The traditional farmhouse beer known as sahti—which is brewed with rye and oats and often flavored with juniper or other spices—remains a popular drink. Sahti is offered by several commercial breweries, including Lammin Sahti.

SINEBRYCHOFF BREWERY
KERAVA
FOUNDED 1819

Founded by a Russian merchant, Sinebrychoff is Finland's oldest and largest brewery. It recently moved from the original brewery in Helsinki, but the company continues to brew an innovative range of beers under the Koff name. **Koff Export Beer** is a pilsner-style lager, which also comes in a stronger version as **Koff Extra Strong**. Sinebrychoff brewed a top-fermented porter in its earliest days, and **Koff Porter** 🍺 🍺 🍺 remains a classic, though it might be considered more of a stout than a porter. Almost black in color and full-bodied, it has rich roasty and malt flavors. In addition to the porter, **Jouloulot** 🍺 🍺 and **Brewmaster's Brown** are other dark and rich offerings. The brewery's Russian roots are reflected in the lager called **Leningrad Cowboy**.

HARTWALL BREWERY
HELSINKI   FOUNDED 1873

From several breweries around Finland, Hartwall brews a pale lager, **Lapin Kulta** 🍺, which means "gold of Lapland" after a local gold mine, and a German-style wheat beer, **Weizenfest**.

OTHER FINNISH BREWERIES

OLVI BREWERY, Iisalmi

MALLASJUOMA, Lahti

With tight government control and high taxes, Norway does not have a major brewing industry, and what exists is largely regionally based. Taxes are based on alcohol levels, but the stronger beers, including seasonal brews, bocks, and other dark lagers (known as bayer), are among the more popular.

AASS BRYGGERI
DRAMMEN
FOUNDED 1834

Aass is Norway's oldest brewery. Located in the port city of Drammen south of Oslo, Aass hosts a beer guild with hundreds of members. It produces nearly a dozen different varieties of beer, including a premier example of a Scandinavian bock. **Aass Bock** is a creamy, dark reddish-brown beer offering rich malt flavors. **Jule Øl**, or "yule ale," is a Vienna-style reddish lager that is traditionally brewed around Christmas; the year-round **Aass Amber** is similar. A Bavarian-style dunkel lager known as **Bayer** is also a regular offering. Aass brewery's **Pilsner** uses Czech hops and reflects those influences in the taste and bouquet.

HANSA BRYGGERI
BERGEN   FOUNDED 1890

This large independent brews a juniper beer in addition to a range of standard lagers: **Hansa Premium Pilsner**, **Hansa Bayer** and **Hansa Export Øl**.

MACKS OLBRYGGERI
TROMSO   FOUNDED 1977

Norway's northernmost brewery brews traditional lagers with a Bavarian influence. These include the golden **Mack Arctic Pils**, the dark **Mack Bayer** and **Mack Polar Beer**, an amber lager.

RINGNES BRYGGERI
OSLO   FOUNDED 1877

Comprising several breweries around Norway, Ringnes is the country's largest brewing group. It produces dryish beers, most notably the pale **Ringnes Pilsner Beer**. Ringnes also brews **Special Bock**, the strong **Ringnes Export** and the seasonal **Christmas Ale** (or **Jule Øl**). **Frydenlund Pilsener** and **Dahl's Pils**, as well as beers under the Lysholmer and Schous brands, are now brewed by Ringnes.

OTHER NORWEGIAN BREWERIES

AKERSHUS BRYGGERI, Oslo
MIKROBRYGGERI, Oslo

SWEDEN

The Swedish beer industry has been similarly hampered by government restrictions, although the number of breweries is slowly beginning to increase again, largely in response to Sweden's joining the European Union. In addition, a greater variety of flavorful and strong beers are being brewed, though golden lager is the leading style.

PRIPPS BRYGGERI

STOCKHOLM   FOUNDED 1828

The largest brewing entity in Sweden, Pripps began in Göteborg and then merged with its chief rival, Stockholm Breweries, in the 1960s. Since then Pripps has extended throughout Scandinavia and northern Europe, largely through the formation of Baltic Beverages Holding with the prominent breweries of Norway and Finland. Pripps' association with a nineteenth century Scottish-owned Carnegie brewery in Göteborg is demonstrated by one of its premier beers: **Carnegie Porter** is a full and roasty top-fermented porter. The brewery's main brew is the **Pripps Bla** (meaning blue) lager, which is the best-selling beer in Sweden. It is available in various strengths, with **Extra Strong** being in the strongest class. The seasonal, märzen-style **Julöl** is available in limited quantities.

SPENDRUPS BRYGGERI

STOCKHOLM   FOUNDED 1859

One of the few remaining independent breweries in Sweden, Spendrups brews all-malt lagers in the pilsner style. These include **Old Gold**, which is dry and hoppy, **Spendrups Original** and **Norrlands Gold**.

OTHER SWEDISH BREWERIES

ABRO BRYGGERI, Vimmerby: Abro Guld
FALKEN BRYGGERI, Falkenberg: Bayerskt, Export, Julöl

ICELAND

All but the weakest of beers were outlawed in Iceland for more than seven decades before the ban was lifted in the late 1980s. The lagers of this small island nation are still very light and weak, and only a few breweries are in operation. Among them are Egill Skallagrimsson of Reykjavik and Viking Brugg of Akureyri.

SOUTHERN EUROPE

The countries of southern Europe are better known for their wine-making than for their beer, though Spain in particular is home to a number of traditional breweries. Light, thirst-quenching lagers loosely in the German tradition predominate in these warm-climate nations, although some Italian and Portuguese breweries are also expanding into the darker märzen and bock styles. A quality brewery on the island of Malta brews English-style ales. The Mediterranean region has also been characterized by market domination by a small number of breweries: Central de Cervejas and Unicer of Portugal control nearly 100 percent of the market between them; in Italy, Moretti and Peroni account for about three-quarters of the beer produced; and the Spanish market is dominated by four or five independents. Furthermore, international companies like Interbrew, Heineken and Carlsberg are buying into many local breweries throughout the region. Greece and Turkey have minimal beer industries, and most of it is foreign-owned.

BIRRA MORETTI
UDINE, ITALY   FOUNDED 1859

Although Birra Moretti is no longer the small, family-run brewery it once was—and in fact is owned by international brewing giant Heineken—it still offers a range of quality German-style beers. The mustachioed man gracing the label of Moretti bottles is also a classic and enduring image. This northeastern Italian brewery offers the refreshing, lightly hopped, yellow lager known simply as **Birra Moretti**. The Dortmunder-style **Sans Souci** is a flavorful lager, very malty but well-balanced with hops, while **Bruna** is an all-malt, dunkel-style brew. Another Moretti beer based on a Bavarian style is **La Rossa**, a deep copper-red, all-malt lager that is similar to a märzen, though with an alcohol content more in the range of a doppelbock (7.5% abv). **Baffo d'Oro**, which means "golden mustache" in honor of the brewery's famous trademark image, is another all-malt, golden lager from Moretti.

CENTRAL DE CERVEJAS
LISBON, PORTUGAL
FOUNDED 1934

Though its roots extend back to the 1880s, Portugal's largest brewing group resulted from a union of several Lisbon-area breweries in the 1930s. German influences characterize the brewery's lagers. Two versions of the main Sagres brand are brewed: the pale yellow, hoppy-dry **Sagres Golden** and the dark brown, richly malty **Sagres Dark**, which is in the style of a Münchner dunkel. Centralcer (as the company is commonly known) also brews **Europa Beer**, a gold-amber beer that is similar to a malty pilsner; the golden **Topazio**; **Onix**; and **Imperial**.

El Aguila
Madrid, Spain　　　　　　　FOUNDED 1902
Long one of Spain's largest breweries, Aguila produces mostly light-bodied, golden lagers, such as **Aguila Pilsner** and **Aguila Reserve**. It is now owned by Heineken.

Damm
Barcelona, Spain　　　　　　FOUNDED 1876
Established by an Alsatian brewer named Damm, this brewery reflects those origins in its German-style lagers, such as the golden, märzen-style **Voll Damm** and the dark **Bock Damm**. **Estrella Damm** is reminiscent of a pilsner but slightly stronger.

Birra Peroni
Milan, Italy
FOUNDED 1846

Peroni is a leading, long-established Italian brewery that produces several quality, if light, golden lagers. **Nastro Azzurro** is on the more flavorful end, while **Birra Peroni** is its basic dry and hoppy pilsner-style offering. Peroni also brews the bitter **Raffo** pilsner and an occasional specialty beer.

Birra Poretti
Varese, Italy
FOUNDED 1877
Now part of the Carlsberg brewing group, this brewery near Milan produces the golden lager **Poretti Oro** and a specialty line that includes **Splügen Bock** and **Splügen Dry**.

San Miguel
Lerida, Spain　　　　　　　FOUNDED 1954
Founded by the Filipino company of the same name, the Spanish San Miguel is now owned by France's Kronenbourg. It brews such lagers as **San Miguel Pale Pilsner**.

Simonds-Farsons-Cisk Brewery
Mriehel, Malta　　　　　　　FOUNDED 1889
Dating from its historic role as a stopover for British sailors, the tiny island nation of Malta is home to a brewer of classic English-style ales using malt, hops and yeast imported from England. Farsons, as the brewery is best known, brews the dark **Lacto Milk Stout**, which is made with milk sugar (lactose) and offers a rich mixture of sweet, chocolatey, and roasted flavors. **Blue Label** is a mild ale, while **Hop Leaf** and **Brewer's Choice** are pale ales. A lager is also produced under the **Cisk** label.

La Zaragozana
Zaragoza, Spain　　　　　　FOUNDED 1900
This traditional, independent brewery produces flavorful bottom-fermented beers. **Ambar** and the strong **Export** are its leading brews.

GREEK BREWERY

Athenian Brewery, Athens

OTHER ITALIAN BREWERIES

Birra Dreher, Milan: Dreher Export, Dreher Pilsner
Birra Forst, Lagundo
Birra Wührer, Brescia
Wunster, Bergamo

OTHER PORTUGUESE BREWERIES

Empresa de Cerveja de Madeira, Madeira: Coral
Unicer-Uniao Cervejeira, S. Mamede de Infesta: Cristal, Super Bock

OTHER SPANISH BREWERS

Cervezas Alhambra, Granada
La Cruz del Campo, Seville
Mahou, Madrid

TURKISH BREWERY

Efes Pilsen Breweries, Istanbul

ASIA

The first barley-based brewed beverage was introduced to Asia in the mid-nineteenth century, brought, as in most non-European regions of the world, by European traders and colonizers. Of course, Asian peoples had been producing and consuming a brewed grain drink for thousands of years before the first ales and lagers were brought to the Far East—sake, brewed with rice grain, is technically a kind of beer. Other traditional fermented drinks indigenous to such regions as Southeast Asia are made from coconut sap, sweet potatoes and certain vegetables. The Islamic nations of southwestern Asia do not produce beer for domestic consumption since alcohol is not allowed under the Muslim faith, although some breweries have been established in the region for exporting beer.

Beginning in the 1850s, Western travelers, primarily from Germany, England and the United States, brought with them the technology and equipment necessary to provide their merchants, troops and colonial settlers with suitable brews in the traditional styles of their homelands. Some of the best-known Asian breweries, such as Kirin in Japan and Tsingtao (Qingdao) in China, were established by Westerners, only later to be bought out by the national governments. This European influence is evident in the beers brewed in Asia more than a century later. Pilsner lagers are the most common style, although many breweries produce stouts as well. In addition, the Japanese have been active brewers of specialized German-style beers, such as altbier and black beer (schwarzbier), and Japan has seen greater innovation in recent years with the opening up of the market to microbreweries and brewpubs.

JAPAN

The first brewery in Japan was founded by an American in 1870 and was the origin of the Kirin Brewery. Around the same time, the Japanese government began construction of a brewery in Sapporo, on Hokkaido, based on the techniques of the German brewing industry—this Bavarian-style brewery eventually became known as Sapporo Breweries. By the late 1880s, two more major breweries were established: the Osaka Beer Company, which produced Asahi Beer, and the Japan Beer Company, brewers of Yebisu Beer. In 1906 Sapporo, Osaka and the Japan Beer Company merged to form the Dainippon Brewery Company. Dainippon controlled more than two-thirds of the market until the government broke it up in 1949 into Asahi Brewery and Nippon Brewery, with the latter eventually retaking the name Sapporo. From that point on, Kirin has been the nation's dominant brewery.

Beer consumption increased dramatically in the period following World War II, although the industry was limited to Kirin, Sapporo and Asahi, until a fourth enterprise, the Suntory distillery company, began making beer in 1960s. Until the mid 1990s, legislation prohibited breweries that produced less than 17,000 barrels (about 450,000 gallons) of beer annually, and so the monopoly by the so-called Big Four went unchallenged. In 1994, however, the law was changed, and although some restrictive regulations remain (such as high taxes), the microbrewery revolution has begun to take hold in Japan.

The Japanese beer industry is characterized by high-tech processes, resulting in very light, clean beers. The American-style pilsner is the predominant style, although all the major breweries produce a version of the German black beer and some have experimented with wheat beers, altbiers and other dark lagers. Japanese lagers often include a portion of rice in addition to barley malt, and they tend to be drier tasting and higher in alcohol than the American equivalent. An extremely dry, nearly flavorless style developed first by Asahi Brewing, known simply as "Dry Beer," is quite popular in Japan. The opening up of the beer industry has spurred further innovation into new beer styles.

KIRIN BREWERY COMPANY

TOKYO   FOUNDED 1870

Norwegian-American William Copeland established a brewery in the outskirts of Tokyo in 1870; in 1888 it introduced Kirin Lager Beer—

named for the half-horse, half-dragon creature from Chinese mythology that appears on the beer's label. By the mid-1960s, the Kirin Brewery controlled more than 50 percent of the Japanese beer market, and today it operates at least a dozen breweries throughout the country. Kirin is the fourth-largest brewery in the world. The flagship **Kirin Beer** is aged for one to two months, making it fuller in body than many other Japanese pilsners. Kirin's second–best selling brand, **Kirin Ichiban**, uses only the first runnings of the wort from the mash tun to give it a maltier flavor. The brewery also produces **Kirin Light**, as well as the limited-release **Kirin Alt** 🍺🍺, **Kirin Stout** 🍺🍺 and **Kirin Black** 🍺🍺, a smoky version of the popular black beer.

ASAHI BREWERIES

TOKYO   FOUNDED 1889

Asahi's rise to competitiveness with the larger Kirin and Sapporo was accomplished with the release of the first dry beer, in 1987. Currently one of Japan's top-selling beers, **Asahi Super Dry** is a practically flavorless lager; the top-fermented Z is another very light creation. Asahi also makes the much richer **Black Draft Beer** (or Kuronama, in Japan) 🍺🍺 and **Asahi Stout** 🍺🍺🍺, a traditional English-style stout. **First Lady** is Asahi's light-beer offering.

SAPPORO BREWERIES

TOKYO   FOUNDED 1876

Japan's longest continuously operating brewery, Sapporo was also the country's first Japanese-owned. Sapporo Cold Beer was the first beer produced by Pioneers Brewery, founded by Seibei Nakagawa, who had recently returned from researching breweries in Germany. Sapporo brewed Japan's first German-style dark lager in 1892, and the nearly opaque **Sapporo Black Beer** 🍺🍺 remains a premier example of the style. The flagship light lager, called **Original Draft Black Label** 🍺🍺 in Japan and sold as **Sapporo Draft** abroad, is available in the popular 22-ounce silver can as well as the 2-liter "Mini Keg." The Dortmunder-style

Yebisu Premium🍺🍺 is an all-malt beer and therefore more flavorful than other Japanese lagers. Sapporo also produces **Black Stout Draft**, in addition to several regional beers.

SUNTORY
OSAKA   FOUNDED **1899**
The smallest and most recent addition to Japan's Big Four began as a whiskey distillery and wine producer before entering the beer-brewing arena in 1963. Suntory's flagship beer is **Malt's**, a pale amber-colored all-malt lager. It also brews the light **Super Hop's** and such specialty offerings as **Suntory Black Beer**, **Suntory Weizen** and **Suntory Alt**.

OTHER JAPANESE BREWERIES

CHOJUGURA, Itami

DOPPO, Okayama (part of the Miyashita sake brewery)

GOTENBA KOHGEN BREWERY, Gotenba

KIRISHIMA HIGHLAND BREWERY, Kagoshima-Ken

MOKU MOKU, Nishiyubune

ORION BREWERIES, Okinawa: Orion Lager, Orion Draft

OTARU, Otaru: Otaru Dunkel, Otaru Helles

UEHARA SHUZO COMPANY/ECHIGO, Nishikanbara-Gun

CHINA

B rewing was introduced to China in the German-occupied port city of Tsingtao (now Qingdao) in the 1890s. Today China is the second largest beer producer in the world, surpassing Germany; it is predicted that it will be the largest producer by the beginning of the new millennium. In per capita consumption, however, China ranks in the high twenties among beer-drinking nations.

A handful of foreign-and Chinese-owned breweries were established in the first half of the twentieth century, and when the Communist government took control, all breweries were nationalized and hop farming encouraged. The majority of the current eight hundred–plus breweries in China have been built since 1980. Nearly every town has its own brewery, and beer production is very localized due to limited transportation systems as well as strong regional loyalties. In fact, protectionist laws often prohibit beers or ingredients from other regions. As

China moves closer to an open-market economy, an increasing number of foreigners are undertaking joint ventures with regional breweries. Anheuser-Busch bought a stake in Tsingtao, and Beck's, Fosters and other well-known foreign companies are investing in China's breweries—but the Chinese-owned regional breweries continue to have the greatest success.

Almost all beers produced in China are in the pale lager style, although dark beers and even the occasional stout or porter make periodic appearances. Chinese lagers tend to be thin and relatively low in alcohol. Aside from Tsingtao (Qingdao), other notable brands include Snowflake Beer, by Shenyang Brewery, Five-Star Beer and Guangzhou Brewery's Double Happiness Guangzhou Beer and Hua Nan Beer. Most are rare to find outside of China.

TSINGTAO (QINGDAO) BREWERY

QINGDAO   FOUNDED 1903

Tsingtao is China's leading beer and its most widely exported one. The brewery was established around the turn of the century to supply

Germany's merchants and troops living in China with German-style beers. The flagship **Tsingtao Beer** is a pale, hoppy pilsner-style lager, typical of Chinese beers. The company has also produced **Tsingtao Dark Beer**. With Anheuser-Busch's purchase of shares in Tsingtao, the brewery has broadened its distribution, increasing the emphasis on exporting as well.

KHAN BRÄU
ULAN BATUR, MONGOLIA
FOUNDED 1996

This Mongolian brewery was established as a joint venture with a German company, and its **Khan Bräu** pilsner-style lager is brewed according to the 1516 Bavarian beer purity law and uses German technology and equipment.

OTHER CHINESE BREWERIES

BEIJING BREWERY, Beijing: Tientan Beer

BEIJING SHUANGHESHENG BREWERY, Beijing: Five-Star Beer, Nine-Star Premium

CHU JIANG BREWERY, Guangzhou: Chu Sing

GUANGZHOU BREWERY, Guangzhou: Double Happiness Guangzhou Beer, Song Hay Double Happiness Beer, Baiyun, Hua Nan

HANGZHOU ZHONGCE BREWERY, Hangzhou: Emperor's Gold, West Lake

Hong Kong Brewery, Hong Kong: Sun Lik
Shenyang Brewery, Shenyang: Snowflake
Zhujiang Brewery, Zhujiang

South and Southeast Asia

Most South and Southeast Asian nations are home to breweries producing light European- or American-style lagers, as well as a few stouts. Many foreign-owned breweries or joint ventures are operating throughout the region. India alone has more than three dozen breweries.

Asia Pacific Breweries
Singapore   Founded 1931

Originally called Malayan Breweries, Asia Pacific Breweries was established as a joint venture of Heineken and a Singapore-based company. Today this large regional brewery has dozens of breweries and joint-ventures throughout Asia, including ones in China, Laos, Cambodia and Vietnam. The main Singapore brewery is a state-of-the-art facility. Its best-known beer is the pale pilsner-style **Tiger Beer**, first brewed in 1932. The classic Tiger Beer advertising slogan of the 1940s inspired the title of British author Anthony Burgess's book Time for a Tiger. **Tiger Classic Beer** is a slight variation that uses crystal malt for a darker and richer character. **ABC Extra Stout**, a strong English-style stout, and the hoppy pilsner-style Anchor Beer were originally brewed by the Archipelago Brewing Company, which joined Malayan Breweries in the 1940s. Asia Pacific also offers the low-alcohol **Raffles Light Beer** and the high-alcohol **Baron's Strong Brew**, the latter based on an old nineteenth century European recipe.

La Fabrica de Cerveza de San Miguel
Manila, Philippines   Founded 1890

When the Philippines was a Spanish colony, La Fabrica de Cerveza de San Miguel obtained a grant from the Spanish government to manufacture beer in the San Miguel district of Manila, establishing the first brewery in Southeast Asia. Built next to the colonial governor's mansion, the San Miguel Brewery later built breweries in Spain, though those are now European-owned. San Miguel is the dominant Filipino beer producer and one of the largest in Asia, operating more than half a dozen breweries in the Philippines and beyond, including in China, Hong Kong and Vietnam. The original **San Miguel Pale Pilsen** is a light lager, but with definite maltiness and hop flavor. The Bavarian-style **San Miguel Dark** is deep reddish-brown in color and has a toasty flavor and aroma with smoky hints. San Miguel also produces a black beer, **Cerveza Negra**; **Super Dry**; **All-Malt**; the pale amber **Gold Eagle** lager; and **Red Horse** malt liquor.

Boon Rawd Brewery Company
Bangkok, Thailand   Founded 1932

As with many of the older breweries in Southeast Asia, Boon Rawd was established with technology and equipment from Germany. **Singha** is the brewery's most widely-known product. It is a gold lager that is hoppier and drier than most Asian interpretations of the pilsner style. The name "Singha" comes from a mythical lion-like creature that appears on the label. There is also a Singha Stout.

Ceylon Brewery
Nuwara Eliya, Sri Lanka FOUNDED 1881

Ceylon Brewery produces a premier Asian stout, **Lion Stout** 🍺🍺. Locally, this rich ale is often mixed with a distilled coconut drink in the tea-planting region in which it is brewed. Ceylon Brewery also brews a bottle-conditioned beer for export and a pilsner.

Cobra
Bangalore, India
FOUNDED 1990

Cobra is brewed in India but only for export. **Cobra Indian Beer** is a light lager that was developed specifically to supply Indian restaurants in England, though it is currently distributed elsewhere in Europe as well.

McCallum Breweries
Colombo, Sri Lanka
FOUNDED 1962

Another classic version of an Asian-produced stout is **Sando Stout** by McCallum, also known as Three Coins Brewery. Sando was the name of a traveling Hungarian strongman of the nineteenth century. McCallum also brews a **Pilsner**.

Mohan Meakin
New Delhi, India FOUNDED 1955

Mohan Meakin's main brewing center is the Solan brewery in northern India, where it produces typical Indian lagers, including **Golden Eagle Lager**, **Lion** and **Gymkhana Pilsner**.

United Breweries
Bangalore, India FOUNDED 1915

A conglomeration of fourteen Indian breweries, the company started with five breweries in southern India, including Castle Breweries, which is the oldest (1857). The lager **Kingfisher** is United Breweries' flagship beer and the top-seller in all of India. The various breweries also offer **Kingfisher Diet**, **UB Premium Ice Beer** and **UB Export Lager,** as well as **Kalyani Black Label Premium Strong Beer**, **Bullet Super Strong** and **Charger Extra Strong**, among others.

OTHER ASIAN BREWERIES

Asia Brewery, Manila, Philippines

Chosun Brewery, Seoul, Korea

Hue Brewery, Hue, Vietnam: Hue Beer

Jinro Coors Brewery, Seoul, Korea

Lao Brewery Company, Laos: Lager Beer, Draft Beer

Muree, Rawalpindi, Pakistan: London Lager

Orang Utan Brewery and Pub, Singapore (proceeds go toward supporting endangered wildlife)

ORIENTAL BREWING COMPANY, Seoul, Korea: OB Lager, OB Dry

PT BINTANG, Tangerang, Indonesia: Bintang Lager

PT DELTA, Jakarta, Indonesia

THAI AMARIT BREWERY, Bangkok, Thailand: Amarit Lager

VIET HA BREWERY, Hanoi, Vietnam

AUSTRALIA AND NEW ZEALAND

Despite Australia's reputation for alcohol consumption, both Australia and neighboring New Zealand experienced significant temperance movements in the early to mid-twentieth century. Laws at the time restricted alcohol consumption by such methods as prohibiting drinking in public establishments after six o'clock in the evening—leading to the practice of the "six o'clock swill," whereby patrons would consume as much beer as they could before closing time. One legacy of this anti-drinking sentiment was industry consolidation in an effort to concentrate forces against the opposition. Today, in each country two companies combine to control more than 90 percent of the beer industry, with the Lion Nathan group having a significant share in both—more than 40 percent of the Australian market and about 55 percent in New Zealand. Dominion Breweries controls nearly 40 percent of the New Zealand market, while the Foster's Brewing Group, which consists of the massive Carlton and United Breweries in addition to other foreign ventures, accounts for more than half of the market in Australia. Needless to say, new microbreweries have had to struggle to survive, although several are thriving, particularly in New Zealand. The major breweries all have operations in other areas of Asia, including many joint ventures.

The Pacific nations of Australia and New Zealand have been brewing beer since the first British settlements were established in the early to mid-nineteenth century, despite limited natural resources and the long distances required for shipping raw ingredients from Europe. The English-influenced ale styles initially defined the beers of the region, but lagers soon became the standard. Few breweries today produce ales, and beers that are labeled "ales" often are in fact bottom-fermented lagers.

AUSTRALIA

Australia saw its first beer brewed at the end of the eighteenth century in Sydney and its first commercial brewery set up in 1804. By the 1820s and 1830s several additional breweries were producing British-style ales, mostly for local consumption. A shift from ales to lagers gradually took place over the decades, partly because the hot temperatures common over much of the country made ale-brewing difficult, and the more stable lagers were more easily produced. Australia has several active barley- and hop-producing regions, including the tiny island of Tasmania, a major producer of the crops and also home to two long-established breweries, Boag and Cascade. Pride of Ringwood hops is the dominant hop in Australian beers.

Throughout the twentieth century the Australian beer industry has been characterized by mergers and consolidation. Carlton and United Breweries is an amalgam of nearly a dozen once-independent breweries, several of which have been around for more than a hundred years. The Australian division of the Lion Nathan group, consisting of five breweries, is the most recent chapter in a long line of mergers: Castlemaine of Victoria and Perkins of Queensland, two breweries dating back to the mid-1800s, merged in 1929; in 1981, Castlemaine Perkins joined up with the Sydney-based Tooheys Brewery, and five years later Castlemaine Tooheys Limited was merged with the Swan Brewery to form the Bond Corporation; within a few years the overextended company began to crumble and Lion Nathan came along in 1991 to pick up the pieces. Lion Nathan soon added the Hahn and South Australian brewing companies to its dominion. Coopers Brewery and J. Boag and Son are the only remaining independent national breweries.

CARLTON AND UNITED BREWERIES

MELBOURNE, VICTORIA   FOUNDED 1907

The largest brewery in Australia today, Carlton and United Breweries began as the Carlton Brewery, founded in Melbourne in 1864. The Foster brothers from America began brewing lager beer in the late 1880s, and in 1907 Carlton and Foster's merged, along with Victoria Brewery, to form Carlton and United Breweries (CUB). Today CUB produces beers under some fifty labels, including the various brands of Carlton, Foster's, Power, Cascade, Matilda Bay and Darwin, among others. Originally brewed by Tooth's Kent Brewery, **Sheaf Stout** 🍺🍺 is one of Carlton and United's premier beers. This dry stout uses roasted barley in addition to a couple of different malts. It has an opaque, deep black color and a coffeeish flavor and aroma. The Kent Brewery also produces **KB Lager** and **Kent Old Brown Ale** 🍺🍺 as well as the Reschs line—**Reschs Pilsner, Reschs DA** (Dinner Ale), **Reschs Draught** and **Reschs Smooth Black Ale.** Matilda Bay Brewing is a specialty brewer that produces **Redback Original** wheat beer, **Redback Light, Redback Hefeweizen,** the powerful **Dogbolter** dark lager, **Brass Monkey Stout, Iron Brew, Freemantle Bitter, Matilda Bay Bitter, Matilda Bay Pils** and **Matilda Bay Premium. Cascade Premium Lager** 🍺, **Cascade Pale Ale, Cascade Stout** 🍺 and **Cascade Draught** 🍺 are brewed by Cascade

Brewery, the oldest brewery in Australia, founded in 1824. The original Carlton Brewery offers **Carlton Crown Lager**, **Carlton Cold**, **Carlton Draught** and **Carlton D-Ale** or **Diamond Draught**. **Foster's Lager** is the leading global brand, and other Foster beers include **Foster's Light**, **Foster's Special Bitter** and **Foster's Ice**. **Victoria Bitter** is the biggest seller in Australia. Among the other beers from CUB are **Melbourne Bitter** and two stouts from the Abbotsford Brewery: **Abbots Extra Double Stout** and **Abbot Invalid Stout**, a creamy bottom-fermented stout.

COOPERS BREWERY

LEABROOK, SOUTH AUSTRALIA   FOUNDED 1862

In the early 1860s, Thomas Cooper brewed an ale based on an old English family recipe in order to help treat his wife's illness. He began selling the ale locally, and this was the origin of Coopers Brewery. More than 130 years later, Coopers is the last family-owned brewery in Australia. It produces its own malt and has been using the same strain of yeast since the early 1900s. Coopers is also one of the few remaining Australian breweries to produce predominantly ales. The brewery's flagship beer is called **Coopers Sparkling Ale** 🍺🍺🍺, although it has a heavy cloudiness from bottle-conditioning. This pale ale has a fruity character. The similar but lighter **Coopers Original Pale Ale** 🍺 has hoppy tones. **Coopers Best Extra Stout** 🍺🍺🍺 uses Coopers' own brand of roasted black malt, imparting the dark color and full body. Coopers also produces **Dark Ale** 🍺🍺 and a line of aged ales, including **Premium Clear Ale**, **Thomas Cooper Finest Export** and the limited-edition **Extra Strong Vintage Ale**. Its lagers are **Coopers Genuine Draught**, **Coopers Dry Beer** (DB), **Coopers Light** and **Birrell Premium**.

J. BOAG & SON BREWING

LAUNCESTON, TASMANIA   FOUNDED 1829

Boag Brewing is one of the oldest Australian breweries and one of the very few independents. It produces the flagship **James Boag's Premium Lager** as well as **Boag's Bitter** 🍺, **Boag's Draught** and **Boag's XXX Ale**, all of which have a definite hoppiness.

Castlemaine Perkins

Brisbane, Queensland — Founded 1929

Established in 1859, Castlemaine was Australia's first truly national beer brand. In 1929 it joined Perkins Brewery, founded in 1866, to form Castlemaine Perkins. The brewery offers several lagers under the XXXX label, such as the dry **XXXX Bitter**, **XXXX Light Bitter**, the low-alcohol **XXXX Gold Lager** and **XXXX Draught**. Additional Castlemaine beers are **DL Lager**, **Castlemaine Extra Dry**, and the roasty, bottom-fermented **Carbine Stout** .

Hahn Brewing Company

Camperdown, New South Wales — Founded 1988

This microbrewery outside of Sydney produces **Premium Lager** and **Premium Light**, **Sydney Bitter**, and the specialty lagers **Gold**, **Dark Ice** and **Cold Cock Bock**. It was purchased by Lion Nathan in 1993.

South Australian Brewing Company

Adelaide, South Australia — Founded 1888

South Australian Brewing has three main brands, mostly lagers: Eagle, including **Eagle Blue Ice** and **Eagle Super**; West End, encompassing **Draught** , **Export**, **Gold** and **Light**; and Southwark's **Bitter**, **Premium**, **Old Black Ale** and **Old Stout** , a rich English-style stout.

Swan Brewery

Perth, Western Australia — Founded 1857

This brewery accounts for more than two-thirds of the Western Australia beer market. Swan's lagers include **Draught**, **Gold**, **Export**, **Premium**, **Stout** and **Special Light**. Its EMU brand comprises **EMU Export**, **EMU Draft** and the hoppy **EMU Bitter** . The 1857 line—**1857 Pilsner** and **1857 Bitter**—is also produced by Swan.

Tooheys

Lidcome, New South Wales — Founded 1869

Tooheys shifted from producing predominantly ales to lagers in the mid-1900s, though it still brews true ales, such as the amber-colored **Old Black Ale** . Its main lagers are **Tooheys New** (formerly Tooheys Draught), **Tooheys Red Bitter**, **Tooheys Amber Bitter**, **Tooheys Gold Bitter**, **Tooheys Extra Dry** and the light, Vienna-style **Blue Label**.

OTHER AUSTRALIAN BREWERIES

Eumundi Brewing, Eumundi, Queensland: Eumundi Premium Beer, Eumundi Light

Geelong Brewing Company, Moolap, Victoria: Dingo Bitter, Geelong Bitter, Cook's Export Lager

Grand Ridge Brewing Company, Mirboo North, Victoria: Brewer's Pilsner, Moonshine, Moonlight

Lord Nelson, Sydney, New South Wales (brewpub): Victory Bitter Ale, Trafalgar Pale Ale, Old Admiral Ale

Pumphouse Brewery, Sydney, New South Wales: Federation Ale, Bull's Head Bitter

Tankstream Brewing Company, Sydney, New South Wales

133

The very man credited with discovering New Zealand for the British Crown, Captain Cook, is also credited with brewing the first beer in the country in the 1770s, when he brewed a concoction from spruce and tea plants mixed with molasses to help stave off scurvy. Despite this beginning, New Zealand has a long history of anti-alcohol sentiment. The New Zealand Breweries (now Lion Nathan) formed in 1923 when ten of the largest breweries merged in resistance to the temperance movement, bringing nearly half of the nation's beer production under a single entity. This concentration encouraged research and development, and an important outcome was Dominion Breweries' invention of the continuous-fermentation system, in which there is a continuous flow of wort and yeast through a series of fermentation vessels. Although Lion Nathan and Dominion Breweries together control more than nine-tenths of New Zealand's beer market, some microbreweries and brewpubs have been able to survive as a result of the loosening of licensing restrictions over the last twenty years.

DOMINION BREWERIES (DB)
AUCKLAND   FOUNDED 1930

Waitemata Brewery was established in Auckland in 1930, and in the late 1960s it acquired Taranaki Brewery, Tui Brewery and Westland and Nelson Breweries to form the Dominion Breweries group. All DB products are lagers. **DB Draught** is the primary brew, and others include the less sweet **DB Bitter** and the paler **DB Gold** and **DB Export Dry**. The malty **Double Brown** is more copper-gold than brown in color. **Tui East India Pale Ale** has been brewed since the 1880s, and this full-bodied beer has a devoted following among the South Island locals. Specialty lagers include **Monteith's Extra Bitter Brown Ale** and **Trapper's Red Beer**, while **Mako** is DB's low-alcohol contribution. **Vita Stout** and **Kiwi Lager** are additional offerings.

LION NATHAN
AUCKLAND   FOUNDED 1923

Although only four of the conglomerate's original ten breweries still exist, Lion Nathan produces more than half of New Zealand's beer. Lion Brewery, the largest, was founded in the 1850s and now has two breweries on North Island; Canterbury Brewery and Speights supply South Island. Founded in 1876, Speights was long New Zealand's largest single brewery. **Steinlager**, the country's most widely exported beer, was first brewed in 1958 in response to the government's request that New Zealand produce a lager of European quality. The biggest-selling beer within New Zealand is **Lion Red**, a malty lager that has been brewed since 1907. The deep amber **Lion Brown** is sweeter than the Red, and additional Lion offerings are the smooth **Lion Ice** and **Light Ice**. Speights' beers are **Speights Gold Medal Ale**, the dark **Speights Distinction Ale** and **Speights Old Dark** porter. **Canterbury Draught** is a malty-sweet brownish lager. Other Lion Nathan lagers are

Rheineck, **Leopard Black Label** and the regional specialties **Waikato Draught** and **Hawkes Bay Draught**.

McCashin's Brewery and Malthouse
Nelson   Founded 1981

New Zealand's first microbrewery was founded by rugby player Terry McCashin, and it has managed to survive the competition from the nation's Big Two. Adhering to the sixteenth-century Reinheitsgebot, McCashin's brews **Mac's Ale**, the dark **Black Mac Ale** and the strong **Mac Extra**—all bottom-fermented lagers.

OTHER NEW ZEALND BREWERIES

EMERSON BREWING COMPANY, Dunedin: London Porter, 1812 India Pale Ale, Old 95, Weissbier, Dunkelweizen, Organic Pilsener, Bookbinder Bitter

HARRINGTON'S, Christchurch: Harrington's Dark Beer, Harrington's Wheat

INDEPENDENT BREWERIES, Auckland: Bighorn Blue, Nighthawk Dark Ale, Panther Premium Lager

MARLBOROUGH BREWING COMPANY, Marlborough: Marlborough Draught

NEWBEGIN BREWERY, Auckland: Silver Fern Lager, Old Thumper Porter

SETTLER'S BREWING COMPANY, Henderson: Stockan Munich Lager, Stockan Draught Ale

SHAKESPEARE TAVERN AND BREWERY, Auckland (brewpub): King Lear Old Ale, Macbeth's Red Ale, Falstaff's Real Ale, Willpower Stout

STRONGCROFT, Wellington

OTHER BREWERIES IN THE PACIFIC REGION

BRASSERIE DE TAHITI, PAPEETE, TAHITI: HINANO TAHITI LAGER

WESTERN SAMOA BREWERIES, APIA, SAMOA

AFRICA AND THE MIDDLE EAST

Brewing has existed in some form in Africa at least since the early civilizations of Egypt and has continued throughout the continent in various forms for thousands of years. Traditionally, native grains and other fermentables such as sorghum, millet and palm sap are the primary ingredients in local beers. These quick-fermenting brews are often characterized by a cloudiness or turbidity or milkiness. Even after the European-style beers were introduced by settlers and colonizers in the nineteenth century, the home-brewed native beers continued to be produced. Most of Africa is too hot and arid for the cultivation of barley and hops, and importing materials from other nations is too expensive for these largely poor, developing nations, and so many have to rely on native grains and other ingredients. Barley-and hop-growing have been introduced in Kenya and South Africa, and the continent's largest brewery, South African Breweries, has its own hop farm. In general, cereals such as maize are often used as adjuncts in malt-based lagers and ales.

The first European commercial brewing operation in Africa was founded in the Cape of Good Hope, South Africa, by a Dutch sailor in the 1650s. Ales predominated during the early period of European colonization, but lagers gradually replaced them. African lagers are generally weak, partly because of cereal adjuncts, although stouts remain popular, especially in Nigeria. A European influence continues as many African breweries have been established as joint ventures with European companies, with Heineken leading the way. Today there are well over a hundred breweries in Africa, the majority concentrated in Nigeria in the west, Kenya in the east and South Africa in the south.

KENYA BREWERIES
NAIROBI, KENYA   FOUNDED 1922

East African Breweries was founded by two brothers and a gold prospector using English equipment and producing, initially, English-style ales and stouts. Eventually changing its name to Kenya Breweries, the company turned to brewing lagers in its second decade, with particular focus on Tusker—named in tribute to one of the two founding brothers who had been killed by an elephant. **Tusker Lager** is a golden, relatively full-bodied, pilsner-style lager that has a hoppier taste than other African lagers. Similar lagers, varying in strength, include **Tusker Premium Lager**, which is brewed for export, and **Pilsner Lager**. Kenya Breweries also produces the fruitier **White Cap Lager**.

NIGERIAN BREWERIES
LAGOS, NIGERIA   FOUNDED 1949

Founded with investment from Dutch-based Heineken, which still owns a substantial share, Nigerian Breweries is the largest in the country, operating four breweries. Its best-known product is **Gulder**, a refreshing, pale lager. **Star** is a deep-golden lager. Nigerian Breweries also offers **Legend Stout**, a rich stout with a roasted malt flavor.

SOUTH AFRICAN BREWERIES (SAB)
JOHANNESBURG, SOUTH AFRICA   FOUNDED 1895

South African Breweries formed from the consolidation of two South African breweries around the turn of the century, and its position as the leading national brewery was solidified when it merged with its main competition, Ohlsson's and Union Breweries. Today SAB has seven breweries in South Africa, plus joint ventures throughout Africa and elsewhere. South African Breweries introduced bottom-fermented beer to Africa in the 1890s with their **Castle Lager**. **Lion Lager** is a darker and fuller-bodied version. The brewery also produces **Ohlsson's Lager** and the dark and rich **Castle Milk Stout** 🍺 🍺, brewed with lactose.

MITCHELL'S BREWERY
KNYSNA, SOUTH AFRICA   FOUNDED 1984

A former brewer for South African Breweries opened the continent's first microbrewery in 1984. Its European-style beers include **Forester's Draught Lager**, **Bosun's Bitter** and the rich **Raven Stout**.

NAMIBIAN BREWERIES
WINDHOEK, NAMIBIA   FOUNDED 1920

Namibian Breweries was founded by German colonial brewers, and it continues to reflect that German influence in its **Windhoek** and **Maibock** lagers.

NESBITT BREWERY
CHIREDI, ZIMBABWE   FOUNDED 1990

A privately owned microbrewery, Nesbitt adheres to the sixteenth-century German beer purity law in brewing its **Hunter's Lager**.

NILE BREWERIES
JINJA, UGANDA   FOUNDED 1992

Re-emerging from an older brewery that had closed during the 1970s, Nile Breweries makes what is reputed to be the strongest lager in Africa, **Extra Strong Brew**, as well as **Nile Special Lager**.

SOLIBRA ABIDJAN
ABIDJAN, CÔTE D'IVOIRE   FOUNDED 1960

The best-known beer produced by this brewery in French West Africa is **Mamba Lager**, a malty lager, but it also produces **Mamba Bock**.

OTHER AFRICAN BREWERIES

ACCRA BREWERY, Accra, Ghana
ARAB BREWERIES COMPANY, Amman, Jordan
ARUSHA BREWERY, Arusha, Tanzania

Asmara Brewery, Asmara, Ethiopia

Bavaria Bräu, Johannesburg, South Africa

Blue Nile Brewery, Khartoum, Sudan: Camel Lager

Brasserie de Brazzaville, Brazzaville, Congo

Brasseries De Guinea, Conakry, Guinea

Brasseries De Logone, Moundou, Chad

Brasseries De Tunisia, Tunis, Tunisia

Brasserie Dle Pellas, Douala, Cameroon

Brasseries du Benin, Lome, Togo: Ngoma Pilsner, Bière Bénin

Brasseries du Maroc, Casablanca: Flag Pilsner, Flag Export Lager

Brasseries Glacieres, Algiers, Algeria

Chibuku Brewery, Harare, Zimbabwe

International Brasserie, Yaounde, Cameroon

Kgalagadi Brewers, Gaberone, Botswana

Meta Brewery, Addis Ababa, Ethiopia

Tanzania Breweries, Dar es Salaam, Tanzania

Tempo Beer Industries, Metanyai, Israel

Zambia Breweries, Lusaka, Zambia

Zimbabwe National Breweries, Harare, Zimbabwe: Zambezi

THE UNITED STATES

Even before the earliest European settlers brought beer to their colonies in the New World, Spanish explorers encountered Native American tribes of the Southwest brewing a form of beer from corn (maize). Archaeological evidence further shows that the indigenous peoples of North America had been brewing for centuries before the first Western contact.

Brewing by European colonists began in the late 1500s, and the first brewery opened in about 1630 in New Amsterdam. Both the Puritans in New England and the Dutch in New York, New Jersey and Pennsylvania built breweries throughout the seventeenth century. The Pilgrims' decision to land at Plymouth Rock in 1620 might have been influenced by beer: A journal from the Mayflower recorded that they could not continue on, for "our victuals are much spent, especially beer."

The favored beers of the colonies were British ales, much of it imported. Following a boycott of British beer and ingredients in the years leading up to the revolution, brewers resorted to corn or wheat and flavorings ranging from nutmeg, molasses or ginger to bark and pumpkin. Many prominent colonial leaders were active homebrewers, including George Washington, Thomas Jefferson and William Penn. More than 120 breweries were operating in the newly formed United States by the beginning of the nineteenth century, when the population was only about seven million, and by the end of the century, there were more than one thousand breweries, including as many as one hundred in Philadelphia alone and another 110 or so in New York City and Brooklyn. By this time, the lager beers introduced by German and Central European immigrants had begun to usurp the tradition of ale-brewing in the United States.

The passing of Prohibition in 1919 forced the major-

An anti-prohibition protest in the 1920s

ity of the nation's breweries to close, and few were able to reopen following its repeal in 1933 in the midst of the Great Depression. (Those breweries that were able to survive Prohibition did so by producing "near-beer" and malt extracts, among other related products.) By the postwar period, a small number of large national and regional breweries dominated. This not only wiped out the smaller breweries, but it also solidified lager brewing as the predominant American style of beer. Anheuser-Busch, Miller and eventually Coors constituted a virtual monopoly, each producing light, nearly flavorless lagers loosely in the pilsner style.

A loosening of home-brewing laws and influences from Britain's Campaign for Real Ale (CAMRA) led to a veritable revolution in brewing in the 1980s and 1990s. Beginning in California and then throughout the Pacific Northwest, microbreweries and brewpubs began producing a range of flavorful beers based on the traditional styles of Europe—in addition to returning to some uniquely American beers, as exemplified by Buffalo Bill's Pumpkin Ale in California. The craftbrewers of the United States have experimented with specialty beers as well, and in general their beers are hoppier than the European progenitors.

The United States now has more breweries than any other nation, surpassing Germany in 1997. By the beginning of 1999, more than 1300 microbreweries, brewpubs and contract breweries were making beer in the United States (there had been fewer than three hundred in 1992). Craft-brewing is a multi-billion-dollar industry, and its share of the national market continues to increase, albeit slowly. Despite this growth, however, over 90 percent of all beer in America is produced by a very small number of national and established regional breweries.

UNITED STATES—NORTHEAST

B rewing has a long tradition in such northeastern cities as Philadelphia and Boston, and a handful of breweries of the region survived Prohibition and industry consolidation during the second half of the twentieth century. The New York breweries Genesee and F. X. Matt even continued to produce popular ales in the face of the dominant lager style.

Although the seeds of the craft-brew revolution were planted in the West, the East Coast was home to significant microbrew pioneers. Several leading craft breweries, such as the Boston Beer Company and the Brooklyn Brewery, began by contract brewing their beers at other larger breweries. In their recipes and techniques, the brewers looked to the historic connections with colonial brewing traditions as well as current British brewing practices. The myriad beer styles of Belgium and Germany are also being adopted by innovative Northeast breweries.

BOSTON BEER COMPANY
BOSTON, MASSACHUSETTS   FOUNDED 1985

The Boston Beer Company was founded by a sixth-generation brewer, and the brewery's first beer was based on an old family recipe from the 1870s. The original **Samuel Adams Boston Lager** 🍺🍺, loosely in the Vienna style, remains the brewery's best-seller. **Samuel Adams Boston Stock Ale** 🍺🍺 is a robust and spicy ale, and **Honey Porter**, **Scotch Ale** and **Cream Stout** 🍺🍺 are other year-round selections derived from the rich ales of England. Belgian-style offerings include

White Ale🍺🍺, **Cherry Wheat** and **Cranberry Lambic**🍺🍺 (not a true lambic), and there is also a **Golden Pilsner**. The roster of Samuel Adams seasonal beers is equally varied: **OctoberFest**; **Winter Lager** weizenbock; **Spring Ale**, based on the German kölsch; and **Summer Ale**, a Belgian-style witbier. In addition to **Samuel Adams Double Bock**🍺🍺, the brewery offers **Triple Bock**🍺🍺🍺, an intensely strong (17% abv), syrupy beer that is more reminiscent of sherry than beer. The low-calorie **Boston Lightship** is a relatively full-bodied and flavorful light beer. The Boston Beer Company brews its beers mostly by contract.

THE BROOKLYN BREWERY
BROOKLYN, NEW YORK
FOUNDED 1987

Located in the once-thriving brewing center of Brooklyn, the Brooklyn Brewery was the area's first commercial brewery in more than two decades and a pioneering microbrewery. **Brooklyn Lager**🍺, based on a nineteenth century recipe, was the brewery's first beer. This award-winning, amber-colored brew is similar to a Vienna-style lager. The winter seasonal **Brooklyn Black Chocolate Stout**🍺🍺 is a heavy but smooth Imperial stout with rich chocolate-malt flavors and aromas; **Brooklyn Dry Stout** is also produced. **Brooklyn Brown Ale**🍺🍺 is hoppier and higher in alcohol than its typical British counterpart. Other English-inspired ales include **Brooklyn Pennant Pale Ale '55**, brewed in tribute to the Brooklyn Dodgers world-champion baseball team; the hoppy **Brooklyn East India Pale Ale**🍺🍺; and **Brooklyn Monster Ale** barley wine, available only on draught. The Brooklyn Brewery also offers two Belgian-influenced seasonal beers: **Blanche de Brooklyn**, a spicy Belgian witbier, and **Breukelen Abbey Ale**. **Brooklyn Pilsner** is a golden lager brewed in the tradition of a German pils, and **Brooklyner Weisse** is an unfiltered Bavarian-style wheat beer.

CATAMOUNT BREWING COMPANY
WHITE RIVER JUNCTION, VERMONT   FOUNDED 1985

The Catamount Brewing Company was the first brewery in the state of Vermont since the 1890s and one of the first modern-day microbreweries on the East Coast. Named for the mountain lion indigenous to the area, Catamount has expanded steadily since its opening. The brewery produces two flavorful pale ales: the malty, copper-colored **Catamount Amber Ale** is brewed in the American interpretation of the style, while the darker and drier **Catamount Pale Ale** is more in the British tradition. **Catamount Porter**, with rich chocolatey and roasty

flavors, is regarded by many as the Northeast's best porter. Introduced in celebration of Catamount's first decade, **Anniversary Ale** is a hoppy and full-bodied India pale ale. Catamount also offers seasonal brews: **Christmas Ale**, a reddish India pale ale; the smooth, coffee-ish **Oatmeal Stout**; **American Wheat**, a refreshing summer brew; and the märzen-style **Octoberfest** lager.

Appalachian Brewing Co.
Harrisburg, Pennsylvania
Founded 1997

The first brewery in the Pennsylvania state capital brews **Purist Pale Ale**, **Water Gap Wheat**, **Jolly Scot Scottish Ale**, **Susquehanna Stout** and seasonal specialties including a hefeweizen and an Oktoberfest.

Atlantic Coast Brewing
Boston, Massachusetts   Founded 1994

The Tremont ales produced by Atlantic Coast Brewing are brewed in the classic British style. **Tremont Ale**, an English pale ale, and **Tremont India Pale Ale** are year-round offerings, while **Tremont Porter**, **Tremont Winter Ale** and **Old Scratch Barley Wine** are seasonal brews.

Dock Street Brewing Company
Philadelphia, Pennsylvania   Founded 1986

This early Philadelphia craft brewery produces **Dock Street Bohemian Pilsner** (brewed true to the traditions of the Czech original), **Dock Street Amber Ale** and **Dock Street Illuminator Double Bock**. The strong and flavorful **Dock Street Barley Wine** is available only on draught.

Elm City Brewing Company/New Haven Brewing Company
New Haven, Connecticut   Founded 1989

Elm City's **Connecticut Ale**, brewed under contract with F. X. Matt, is the only Elm City beer that can be found in bottles. Draught selections include **Blackwell Stout** and the extra special bitter **Broken English Ale**, as well as various seasonal brews.

D. L. Geary Brewing Company
Portland, Maine   Founded 1986

This English-style American microbrewery was the first brewery in Maine since the nineteenth century. Geary currently limits itself to three brews: **Pale Ale**, **London Style Porter** and **Hampshire Special Ale**. The latter is a seasonal strong ale that is available "only when the weather sucks."

GENESEE BREWING COMPANY

ROCHESTER, NEW YORK   FOUNDED 1878

The largest regional brewery in the United States, Genesee continued producing ale when the rest of the nation had switched to light lagers. Today it brews the rare **Cream Ale** as well as **Twelve Horse Ale** and **Genesee Bock**.

MASSACHUSETTS BAY BREWING COMPANY

BOSTON, MASSACHUSETTS   FOUNDED 1987

Massachusetts Bay Brewing produces both ales and lagers. **Harpoon Ale** and **Harpoon India Pale Ale** are based on British styles, while **Harpoon Pilsner** and **Harpoon Munich Dark** reflect Bavarian traditions. **Harpoon Light** and the seasonal **Spring Maibock**, **Summer ESB**, **Oktoberfest** and **Winter Warmer** are also brewed.

F. X. MATT BREWING COMPANY

UTICA, NEW YORK   FOUNDED 1888

This long-established brewery is still run by descendants of founder Francis Xavier Matt. Its Saranac line, introduced in 1985, includes **Adirondack Amber**, **Pale Ale**, **Mountain Berry Ale**, **Golden Pilsner**, **Stout** and **Black & Tan** (stout mixed with lager). Seasonal brews are **Saranac Chocolate Amber**, a Münchner dunkel; **Saranac Season's Best** nut brown ale; and **Saranac Wild Berry Wheat**. F. X. Matt also contract-brews the beers of several notable microbreweries.

NEW AMSTERDAM BREWING COMPANY

NEW YORK, NEW YORK   FOUNDED 1982

A pioneering contract brewery, New Amsterdam beers are brewed by F. X. Matt of Utica, including the original **New Amsterdam Amber**, **New Amsterdam Ale**, **New Amsterdam Blonde Lager** and a winter ale known as **Winter Anniversary New York Beer**.

NEW ENGLAND BREWING COMPANY

NORWALK, CONNECTICUT   FOUNDED 1989

The New England Brewing Company offers **New England Atlantic Amber**, a steam-style or California common beer; **New England Gold Stock Ale**, similar to an English old ale but hoppier; **New England Oatmeal Stout**; **New England Light Lager**; and **New England Holiday Ale**.

NUTFIELD BREWING COMPANY

DERRY, NEW HAMPSHIRE   FOUNDED 1994

Drawing on the Irish heritage of its founder as well as that of the small town of Derry, Nutfield Brewing produces four year-round ales—**Auburn Ale**, **Old Man Ale**, **Black 47 Stout** and **Nor'Easter**—and four seasonal selections: **Hopfest**, **Summer Wheat**, **Harvest Ale** and **Winter Frost**.

OTTER CREEK BREWING COMPANY

MIDDLEBURY, VERMONT   FOUNDED 1991

The leading Vermont brewery, Otter Creek brews in some innovative styles, such as its **Helles Alt Beer** and the seasonal **Hickory Switch Smoked Amber Ale**. Other notable beers are **Copper Ale** and the seasonals **Mud Bock Spring Ale**, **Summer Wheat Ale**, **Stovepipe Porter** and **Oktoberfest**.

143

PENNSYLVANIA BREWING COMPANY
PITTSBURGH, PENNSYLVANIA FOUNDED 1986

Pennsylvania's first modern-day microbrewery was founded by Thomas Pastorius, descendant of the founder of the first German settlement in the United States. Pennsylvania Brewing produces **Penn Pilsner**; **Kaiser Pils**; **Helles Gold** and **Penn Dark**, based on the Münchner helles and dunkel styles, respectively; and the seasonal **Oktoberfest** and **St. Nikolaus Bock Beer**.

SEA DOG BREWING COMPANY
BANGOR, MAINE FOUNDED 1993

Producing beers at both its Camden brewpub and its Bangor brewery, Sea Dog brews English-style ales such as **Windjammer Blonde Ale**, **Old Gollywobber Brown Ale** and **Old East India Pale Ale**. Additional German-style lagers, such as **Jubilator Doppelbock** and **Sea Dog Maibock**, are available at the pub.

SHIPYARD BREWING COMPANY
PORTLAND, MAINE FOUNDED 1992

The Shipyard family of beers consists of **Shipyard Export Ale**, **Blue Fin Stout**, **Brown Ale**, **Fuggles IPA**, **Goat Island Light**, **Old Thumper Extra Special Ale** and a variety of seasonals, including **Longfellow Winter Ale**, **Prelude Holiday Ale** and **Sirius Summer Wheat Ale**. Shipyard Breweries entered into an alliance with Miller Brewing Company in 1995.

SMUTTYNOSE BREWING COMPANY
PORTSMOUTH, NEW HAMPSHIRE FOUNDED 1994

Named for Smuttynose Island off the coast of New Hampshire, Smuttynose Brewing Company is the producer of **Shoals Pale Ale**, an unfiltered pale ale; **Old Brown Dog**, an American-style brown ale; **Smuttynose Portsmouth Lager**; **Chuck Wheat Ale**; and the limited-edition **Winter Porter**, **Imperial Stout**, **Maibock**, **Barley Wine**, **Scotch Ale** and **Oktoberfest**.

SPRING STREET BREWING COMPANY
NEW YORK, NEW YORK FOUNDED 1993

Spring Street Brewing is the rare American microbrewery to focus on Belgian styles, specifically wheat beers. The brewery offers **Wit White Ale**, flavored with orange peel and coriander; **Wit Amber Ale**, a darker version seasoned with a blend of spices; and **Wit Black Ale**, made with dark roasted malts.

STOUDT BREWING COMPANY
ADAMSTOWN, PENNSYLVANIA FOUNDED 1987

The rare woman brewmeister and microbrew pioneer, Carol Stoudt produces beer in accordance with the Bavarian Reinheitsgebot. The brewery's award-winning, German-style beers include **Stoudt's Pils**, **Stoudt's Gold** (a Dortmunder-export style), **Stoudt's Honey Double Mai Bock** and **Stoudt's Fest** (a märzen-style lager), among other ales and lagers.

D. G. Yuengling & Son Brewery

Pottsville, Pennsylvania   Founded 1829

Still run by the Yuengling family, the Yuengling Brewery is the oldest operating brewery in the United States. Its bottom-fermented lagers include **Yuengling Dark Brewed Porter**🍺, **Lord Chesterfield Ale**, **Yuengling Traditional Lager**, **Yuengling Premium Beer**, **Yuengling Premium Light Beer** and **Black & Tan**.

Zip City Brewing Company

New York, New York   Founded 1991

This Manhattan brewpub housed in the old headquarters of the National Temperance Society specializes in German- and Czech-style beers from its Austrian-designed brewhouse. Zip City beers include **Vienna Amber**, **Pilsner**, **Dunkel**, **Altbier**, **Rauchbier**, **Blond Doppelbock**, **Eisbock** and **Hefeweizen**.

Other Northeastern Breweries

Connecticut

Cottrell Brewing Company, Pawcatuck: Old Yankee Ale

Essex Brewing Company, Niantic: S. G. Hooker Pale Ale

Farmington River Brewing Company, Bloomfield: Mahogany Ale, Blond Ale, Brown Ale

Mystic Microbrewery, Mystic

Olde Wyndham Brewery, Willimantic

Delaware

Blue Hen Brewery, Newark: Blue Hen Beer

Rockford Brewing Company, Wilmington: Golden Lager, India Pale Ale, Red Ale

Stewart's Brewing Company, Bear (brewpub): Stewart's Pale Ale, Governor's Golden Ale, Big Bear Amber Ale, Highlander Stout

Maine

Allagash Brewing Company, Portland: Allagash White, Allagash Double Ale, Allagash Grand Cru

Andrew's Brewing Company, Lincolnville: Old English Pale Ale, Old English Brown Ale, old English Porter

Atlantic Brewing Company, Bar Harbor: Bar Harbor Real Ale, Acadia Pale Ale, Acadia Amber Ale, Ginger Wheat, Coal Porter, Lompoc's Ginger Wheat

Bar Harbor Brewing Company, Bar Harbor: Harbor Light Pale Ale, Thunder Hole Ale, Cadillac Mountain Stout

Casco Bay Brewing Company, Portland: Casco Bay Pilsner, Casco

Bay Lager, Katahdin Pale Ale, Katahdin Red Ale, Katahdin
Oatmeal Stout

GRITTY McDUFF'S BREW PUB, Portland: Portland Head Light Pale Ale,
McDuff's Best Bitter, McDuff's Best Brown Ale/Lion's Pride
Brown Ale, Black Fly Stout, Sebago Light Ale

MASSACHUSETTS

BERKSHIRE BREWING COMPANY, South Deerfield: Steel Rail Extra Pale
Ale, Berkshire Ale

COMMONWEALTH BREWING COMPANY, Boston: Amber Ale, Boston's Best
Burton Bitter, Porter

IPSWICH BREWING COMPANY, IPSWICH: Ipswich Ale, Pilgrim, Oatmeal
Stout

MILL CITY/LOWELL BREWING COMPANY, Lowell: Classic Lager, Amber
Ale, Oatmeal Stout, Oktoberfest, Boarding House Ale,
Raspberry Wheat, Spindle Porter, Old Nutcracker Winter Ale

OLD SADDLEBACK BREWING COMPANY, Pittsfield: Half Stock Ale, Honey
Blond Ale, Blackberry Wheat, Scotch Ale

OULD NEWBURY BREWING COMPANY, Newbury: Porter, Spiced Ale,
Belgian Wheat Ale

NEW HAMPSHIRE

NEW HAMPSHIRE CUSTOM BREWERS, Manchester: Loon Pale Ale
PORTSMOUTH BREWERY, Portsmouth: Old Brown Dog

NEW JERSEY

FLYING FISH BREWING COMPANY, Cherry Hill: Porter, Belgian Abbey
Dubbel, ESB Ale, Extra Pale Ale

HOBOKEN BREWING COMPANY, Hoboken: Mile Square Golden Ale, Mile
Square Amber Ale

RIVER HORSE BREWING COMPANY, Lambertville: Lager, Special Ale,
Cream Ale, Dark Harvest Ale

THE SHIP INN/MILFORD BREWING COMPANY, Milford: Ship Inn IPA, Ship
Inn Oatmeal Stout, Milford Best Bitter, Milford Celebration Ale

TRIUMPH BREWING COMPANY, Princeton: Pale Ale, Amber, Honey
Wheat, Irish Stout, Pumpkin Ale

NEW YORK

BREWERY OMMEGANG, Cooperstown: Ommegang Belgian-Style Abbey
Ale, Hennepin Grisette Farmhouse Ale

BUFFALO BREWING COMPANY, Lackawanna: Buffalo Lager, Buffalo
Weisse, Limerick's Irish Style Red Ale

COOPERSTOWN BREWING COMPANY, Cooperstown: Old Slugger Pale Ale, Nine Man Golden Ale, Benchwarmer Porter, Strike Out Stout, Back Yard India Pale Ale

HIGHFALLS BREWING COMPANY, Rochester: Michael Shea's Black & Tan, Michael Shea's Irish Amber, J. W. Dundees Honey Brown, J. W. Dundees Honey Light

NEPTUNE BREWERY, New York: Neptune 66 Premium Ale, Neptune U Premium Ale

PARK SLOPE BREWING COMPANY, Brooklyn

WOODSTOCK BREWING COMPANY, Woodstock: Hudson Lager, St. James Ale, Big Indian Porter, Roundout Stout

PENNSYLVANIA

ARROWHEAD BREWING COMPANY, Chambersburg: Red Feather Pale Ale, Light Feather Golden Ale, Arrowhead Brown Ale

JONES BREWING COMPANY, Smithton: Stoney's Pilsner, Stoney's Light, Esquire Premium Ale, Esquire Extra Dry

LATROBE BREWING COMPANY, Latrobe: Rolling Rock Premium, Rolling Rock Light, Rolling Rock Bock

LION BREWING COMPANY, Wilkes-Barre: Stegmaier 1857 Lager🍺, Stegmaier Porter🍺🍺, Stegmaier Gold Medal, Stegmaier 1857 Light, Liebotschaner Cream Ale

PITTSBURGH BREWING COMPANY, Pittsburgh: Iron City Premium Beer, Iron City Dark, Iron City Golden Lager, J. J. Wainwright's Select Lager

STRAUB BREWERY, St. Mary's: Straub All-Grain Beer, Straub Light Beer

VICTORY BREWING COMPANY, Downingtown: Hop Devil India Pale Ale, Festbier, St. Victorious Doppelbock, Milltown Mild

YARDS BREWING COMPANY, Philadelphia: Yards Porter, Extra Special Ale

RHODE ISLAND

HOPE BREWING COMPANY, Providence: Hope Lager, Hope Red Rooster Ale, Hope Bock, Hope Light

TRINITY BREWING, Providence (brewpub)

UNION STATION BREWERY, Providence (brewpub)

VERMONT

MAGIC HAT BREWING COMPANY, Burlington

MCNEILL'S BREWERY, Brattleboro (brewpub): McNeill's Special Bitter, Dead Horse IPA, Duck's Breath Bitter, Slopbucket Brown, Pale Bock

MOUNTAIN BREWERS, Bridgewater: Long Trail Ale, Long Trail IPA,
Long Trail Kölsch, Long Trail Stout, Long Trail Light
VERMONT PUB & BREWERY, Burlington (brewpub): Vermont Smoked
Porter, Vermont Maple Ale

UNITED STATES—MIDWEST

Led by Anheuser-Busch of St. Louis, Miller of
Milwaukee and Stroh's of Detroit, the Midwest
region was long the brewing center of the United
States. Anheuser-Busch remains the world's largest
brewing conglomerate, controlling nearly half of the U.S.
beer market and producing the single-best-selling beer in
the entire world. Pabst Brewing of Milwaukee and the
Stroh Brewery Company both date back to the mid-
1800s, though they now produce a wide range of light
American-style lagers—as part of the massive S & P
Company, Pabst brews Pabst Blue Ribbon, Olde English
"800," Olympia, Hamm's, Pearl, and Falstaff, while
Stroh's owns the Augsburger, Old Milwaukee, Schaeffer,
and Schlitz brands as well as those under the G. Heileman
Brewing Company, including Old Style, Rheingold,
Schmidt, Carling's, Colt.45, Lone Star, Rainier, Jet City and
Oregon, among many others. The Miller Brewing
Company produces Lowenbräu, Meister Bräu and
Milwaukee's Best, owns the large regional Leinenkugel
brewery, and in early 1999 purchased the old Oregon-
based regional Blitz-Weinhard Brewing Company. All this
is to say that a significant proportion of the weak
American lagers are brewed by a small number of corpo-
rations based in the Midwest.

But the beers of the Midwest were not always limited
to the light golden lagers of those mass-market giants,
and the trend is starting to swing back. When German
and Scandinavian immigrants settled in the area in the
late 1800s they brought with them a range of traditional
styles—bock, dunkel, weisse beer and others—and
Milwaukee alone supported close to one hundred breweries. Although small breweries have had to struggle
against the competition of the large national and regional brands, microbreweries and brewpubs around Chicago,
Cleveland, Minneapolis-St. Paul and even Milwaukee are
returning to the more flavorful and varied styles of
Germany.

GREAT LAKES BREWING COMPANY
CLEVELAND, OHIO   FOUNDED 1988

Cleveland's first modern-day microbrewery and the first post-Prohibition brewpub in the city is located in a historic building that housed breweries of the previous century. The first beer produced by Great Lakes Brewing was **Dortmunder Gold**, then called Heisman. This smooth, balanced lager is true to the brewing tradition of Dortmund, Germany. The brewery has since added the malty **Eliot Ness** Vienna-style lager, **Burning River Pale Ale** and **Edmund Fitzgerald Porter**, a premier American porter. Among the seasonal brews, the **Christmas Ale** is made with malted barley and wheat and is flavored with honey, cinnamon and ginger. **Conway's Irish Ale** is an Irish red ale brewed for winter and early spring. There is also **Rockefeller Bock** and **Commodore Perry India Pale Ale** for spring and early summer, respectively; the fruity summer witbier **Holy Moses**; **Moon Dog Ale**, a bitter-style ale for summer; and the fall-season **Oktoberfest**.

AUGUST SCHELL BREWING COMPANY
NEW ULM, MINNESOTA   FOUNDED 1858

August Schell immigrated to the United States in the 1850s and established a brewery in the Germanic community of New Ulm. Schell Brewing quickly rose to become a major regional brewery producing German-style lagers. Still owned by Schell descendents, the brewery is housed in the family's nineteenth century mansion, which also includes a beer museum and a deer garden. Having survived the era of domination by the mass-market national breweries, Schell produces traditional lagers that are gaining wider attention (and several awards) in the craft-brew revolution. The hoppy **Schell Pils** is brewed in the German tradition of pilsner lagers. **Schell Alt**, though darker than the prototype Düsseldorf altbier, has rich malty flavors. The Bavarian-style **Schell Weizen**, made with 60 percent wheat, has a fruity but dry character. **Schell's Bock** and **Oktoberfest** lagers further exemplify the brewery's strong German heritage.

ANHEUSER-BUSCH BREWING COMPANY
ST. LOUIS, MISSOURI   FOUNDED 1860

Founded as a family brewery by German immigrant Eberhard Anheuser, Anheuser-Busch first introduced its golden Budweiser lager in the 1870s, taking, and subsequently trademarking, the name from the Czech town of Budweis. The Budweiser brand is joined by more than thirty other beers, including **Michelob**, **Busch**, **Red Wolf**, **O'Doul's**, **King Cobra** and others.

SPRECHER BREWING COMPANY
GLENDALE, WISCONSIN   FOUNDED 1985

Randal Sprecher, a native of the microbrew-capital of Oregon and a former brewer for Pabst, made the bold move of opening a small craft-brewing operation in Milwaukee, land of Miller and Pabst. The first beers produced were **Sprecher Special Amber**, a deep gold-colored German-style lager, and **Sprecher Black Bavarian**, a rich and complex dark lager. Sprecher has since added the following year-round brews: the filtered **Hefe Weiss**, the English-style **Pub Brown Ale** and the lighter **Milwaukee Pilsner**, brewed in the Czech-influenced traditions of Milwaukee's old breweries. Available in limited seasons are the alt-style **Fest Bier** for summer; the fall-season **Oktoberfest**; the bock-like **Winter Brew**; **Irish Stout**, produced in a single batch for St. Patrick's Day; and a spring **Mai Bock**. The brewery also brews for limited release **Doppel Bock**, **India Pale Ale**, **Belgian Ale**, **Imperial Stout** and **Anniversary Ale**, a Flanders brown ale flavored with raspberry.

CAPITAL BREWING COMPANY
MIDDLETON, WISCONSIN   FOUNDED 1986

This brewery produces beers with German-sounding names and a German brewing tradition: **Garten Bräu Special** pilsner; the Munich-style **Garten Bräu Dark**; **Garten Bräu Wisconsin Amber**, a märzen lager; **Garten Bräu Weizen**, a Bavarian-style hefeweizen; and **Garten**

150

Bräu Raspberry Wheat. **Garten Bräu Brown Ale** has more of an English influence rather than German.

FRANKENMUTH BREWERY
FRANKENMUTH, MICHIGAN   FOUNDED 1987

Though temporary closed following severe tornado damage, the Frankenmuth Brewery brews quality Bavarian-style beers in accordance with the sixteenth century Reinheitsgebot. **German-Style Pilsner, German-Style Bock, German-Style Dark, Weisse Beer, Extra Light** and **Oktoberfest** are the leading examples.

GOOSE ISLAND BREWING COMPANY
CHICAGO, ILLINOIS   FOUNDED 1988

Named for an island in the Chicago River, Goose Island Brewing brews both English-style ales and German-style lagers, among them the flagship pale ale, **Honker's Ale**; **Hex Nut Brown Ale**; **Oatmeal Stout**; **Kilgubbin Red Ale**, an Irish red (Kilgubbin is Gaelic for "Goose Island"); **India Pale Ale**; **Summertime German-Style Kölsch Bier**; and **Christmas Ale**. **Bourbon Country Stout** is a powerful Imperial stout that is aged in old bourbon barrels.

JACOB LEINENKUGEL BREWING COMPANY
CHIPPEWA FALLS, WISCONSIN   FOUNDED 1867

This longtime regional brewery—affectionately known as "Leinies"—offers many of the same beers from its independent, family-run past, including **Leinenkugel's Original, Red Lager, Northwoods Lager, Auburn Ale, Honey Weiss** 🍺🍺, **Hefeweizen** and the seasonal **Genuine Bock, Big Butt Doppelbock, Autumn Gold** 🍺 and **Winter Lager**.

JAMES PAGE BREWING COMPANY
MINNEAPOLIS, MINNESOTA   FOUNDED 1987

One of the first microbreweries in the Twin Cities, James Page produces six year-round beers: **Iron Range Amber Lager, Boundary Waters Lager** (made with Minnesota wild rice), **Burly Brown Ale, Portage Pilsner, Voyager Pale Ale** and **Klassic Alte Ale**. **Northern Lights Bock, Summer Pale Ale, Oktoberfest** and **Celebration** are the typical seasonal brews.

KALAMAZOO BREWING COMPANY
KALAMAZOO, MICHIGAN   FOUNDED 1985

Kalamazoo Brewing brews unfiltered, unpasteurized, bottle-conditioned ales, including **Bell's Amber Ale, Bell's Pale Ale, Bell's Porter, Bell's Kalamazoo Stout** and the golden pale ale **Third Coast Beer**. In addition to regular seasonals, Kalamazoo periodically offers specialty beers, most notably **Third Coast Old Ale** barley wine.

LAKEFRONT BREWERY
MILWAUKEE, WISCONSIN   FOUNDED 1987

This innovative brewery produces several specialty beers. The ales include **Fuel Cafe Coffee-Flavored Stout** and **Organic Extra Special Bitter**. **Cherry Beer**, flavored with local cherries, **Pumpkin Beer** and **Holiday Spice** are seasonal lagers, while more traditional German-style lagers are **Klisch Pilsner** and **Eastside Dark**. Lakefront's **Riverwest Stein Beer** is a Vienna-style lager, not a true "stone" beer.

Miller Brewing Company
Milwaukee, Wisconsin   FOUNDED 1855

The Miller Brewing Company originated in the 1850s when Frederick Miller purchased a small Milwaukee brewery. The introduction of the first "Lite" beer was key to the company's growth in the 1970s. The Miller line includes **Miller High Life**, **Miller Lite** and **Miller Genuine Draft**. This brewing giant has tried to cash in on the craft-brew market by introducing the "specialty" **Red Dog** beers under the Plank Road Brewery label.

New Glarus Brewing Company
New Glarus, Wisconsin   FOUNDED 1993

This Wisconsin microbrewery was founded by a former brewer with Anheuser-Busch. New Glarus's year-round brews are **Edel Pils**, **Uff-Da Wisconsin Bock** and the wheat-based **Apple Ale**. Seasonal offerings include **Coffee Stout**, **Norski Maibock**, **Solstice Weiss**, **Snowshoe Ale** and **Belgian Red**, a Belgian-style kriek beer.

Pavichevich Brewing Company
Elmhurst, Illinois   FOUNDED 1989

The Pavichevich Brewing Company produces German-style lagers in accordance with the Bavarian Reinheitsgebot. Its brews include **Baderbräu Vienna Style Lager**, **Baderbräu Bock Beer** and **Baderbräu Pilsner Beer**, similar to the original pilsner of Bohemia.

Summit Brewing Company
St. Paul, Minnesota   FOUNDED 1986

Summit Brewing was a trailblazer in the craft-brew phenomenon, though it has not received as much attention as those on the East and West Coasts. Summit offers **Extra Pale Ale** and **Great Northern Porter** regularly, adding **India Pale Ale**, **Winter Ale**, **Heimertingen Maibock**, **Hefe Weizen** and **Düsseldorfer Alt Bier** in various seasons.

Other Midwestern Breweries

Illinois

CHICAGO BREWING COMPANY, Chicago: Legacy Lager, Legacy Red Ale, Big Shoulders Porter, Heartland Weiss.

GOLDEN PRAIRIE BREWING, Chicago: Golden Prairie Ale, Maple Stout

STAR UNION BREWING COMPANY, Hennepin

WEINKELLER BREWERY, Berwyn and Westmont (brewpub): Düsseldorfer Doppelbock, Dublin Stout, Bavarian Weiss, Oktoberfest

WOODSTOCK BREWING AND BOTTLING COMPANY, Woodstock: Arnold's Amber Lager, Herman's Golden Pilsner

INDIANA

BROAD RIPPLE BREWING COMPANY, Indianapolis (brewpub): IPA, ESB, Kölsch, Porter

EVANSVILLE BREWING COMPANY, Evansville

INDIANAPOLIS BREWING COMPANY, Indianapolis: Düsseldorfer Pale Ale, Düsseldorfer Amber Ale, Düsseldorfer Dark Ale

MISHAWAKA BREWING COMPANY, Mishawaka (brewpub): South Shore Amber Ale, Lake Effect Pale Ale, Mishawaka Gold Lager

IOWA

DALLAS COUNTY BREWING COMPANY, Adel: Old Depot Ale, Old Depot Lager, Old Depot Porter

DUBUQUE BREWING COMPANY, Dubuque: Wild Boar Pils, Wild Boar Amber, Wild Boar Wheat, Wild Boar Raspberry Wheat, Wild Boar Winter Spice, Simpatico Golden Lager, Simpatico Amber, Big Muddy Red

MILLSTREAM BREWING COMPANY, Amana: Millstream Lager, Millstream Wheat, Schild Bräu Amber

STONE CITY BREWING, Solon: Hefeweizen, Iowa Pale Ale, Artist Colony Ale

KANSAS

FREE STATE BREWING COMPANY, Lawrence (brewpub): Ad Astra Ale, Copperhead Pale Ale, Wheat State Golden, Invigorator Doppel Bock, Oatmeal Stout

MIRACLE BREWING COMPANY, Wichita

PONY EXPRESS BREWING COMPANY, Olathe: Honey Blonde, Tornado Ale, Nut Brown Ale, Arrowhead Red

MICHIGAN

CANAL STREET BREWING COMPANY, Grand Rapids: Founders Pale Ale, Founders Weizenbier, Founders Red Ale, Founders Porter

DETROIT & MACKINAC BREWERY, Detroit: Detroit & Mackinac IPA, Detroit & Mackinac Irish Red Ale, Mackinac Gold, Mackinac Black

DUSTER'S MICROBREWERY, Lawton

NEW HOLLAND BREWING COMPANY, Holland: Paleooza, Kourage Ale, Ichabod Ale, Mad Hatter Ale

STONEY CREEK BREWING COMPANY, Novi: Stoney Creek Lager, Stoney Creek Vanilla Porter

MINNESOTA

COLD SPRING BREWING COMPANY, Cold Spring: Cold Spring Pale Ale,
   Cold Spring Export Lager, Cold Spring River Road Red
LAKE SUPERIOR BREWING COMPANY, Duluth: Special Ale, Kayak Kölsch
MINNESOTA BREWING COMPANY, St. Paul: Pigs Eye Pilsner, Landmark
   Beer, Landmark Oktoberfest, Grain Belt Premium

MISSOURI

75TH STREET BREWERY, Kansas City (brewpub): Cowtown Wheat,
   Yardbird's Golden Ale, Possom Trot Brown Ale, Muddy Mo'
   Stout
BOULEVARD BREWING COMPANY, Kansas City: Boulevard Pale Ale,
   Boulevard Irish Ale, Bully Porter
FLAT BRANCH BREWING COMPANY, Columbia

NEBRASKA

BARLEY BOYS BREWING COMPANY, Omaha: Phil's Pils, Ed's Red, Jack's
   Black Porter
CRANE RIVER BREWPUB AND CAFE, Lincoln
JONES STREET BREWERY, Omaha (brewpub): Patch Pale Ale, Grand
   Slam Amber, Harvester Wheat Beer, Ryan's Stout

NORTH DAKOTA

DAKOTA BREWING COMPANY, Grand Forks

OHIO

COLUMBUS BREWING COMPANY, Columbus: Columbus Pale Ale,
   Columbus Nut Brown
CROOKED RIVER BREWING COMPANY, Cleveland: Black Forest Lager,
   Settlers Ale, Lighthouse Gold, Cool Mule Porter, Irish Red
HUDEPOHL-SCHOENLING BREWING COMPANY, Cincinnati: Christian
   Moerlein Select ✪, Little Kings Cream Ale, Little Kings Red
   Ale ✪, Schoenling Bock
LIFT BRIDGE BREWING COMPANY, Ashtabula: Amber Lager, India Pale
   Ale, Continental Pilsner, Winter Gale Ale, Oatmeal Stout, Extra
   Special Bitter, Eisbock, Oktoberfest
WESTERN RESERVE BREWING, Cleveland: Western Reserve American
   Wheat Beer, Western Reserve Amber Ale, Western Reserve Nut
   Brown Ale, Lake Effect Winter Ale, Bockzilla, Cloud Nine

154

OKLAHOMA

BRICKTOWN BREWERY, Oklahoma City (brewpub)
TULSA BREWING COMPANY, Tulsa (brewpub)

SOUTH DAKOTA

BLACK HILLS BREWING COMPANY, Deadwood: Deadwood Territorial
Red Lager, Miner's Gold Ale, Holy Terror Ale, Wild Bill Wheat,
Brown Bear Ale, Dakota Maid Mailbock, Highwayman Lager
FIREHOUSE BREWING COMPANY, Rapid City (brewpub): Buffalo Bitter,
Brown Cow Ale, Rushmore Stout
SIOUX FALLS BREWING COMPANY, Sioux Falls (brewpub)

WISCONSIN

CHERRYLAND BREWERY, Sturgeon Bay: Golden Rail, Silver Rail,
Cherry Rail
GRAY BREWING COMPANY, Janesville: American Pale Ale, Gray
Oatmeal Stout
JOSEPH HUBER BREWING COMPANY, Monroe: Original Lager 🍺, Famous
Red Ale, Dark
STEVENS POINT BREWERY, Stevens Point: Point Special, Classic Amber,
Bock, Pale Ale, Maple Wheat, Winter Spice
VIKING BREWING COMPANY, Dallas: HoneyMoon, CopperHead, Sylvan
Springs Bohemian Pilsner,
J. S. BOCK, BLONDE, Big Swede

UNITED STATES—SOUTH

Largely the result of lingering restrictions on home-brewing and other anti-liquor laws, the southern United States was slow to latch onto the microbrew renaissance of the 1980s. The lack of brewing tradition around the region, however, may be one reason for the wide variety of styles currently brewed by southern craft breweries—both British-inspired ales and German lagers, as well as interesting specialty beers. The mid-Atlantic states, such as Maryland and Virginia, can look to the traditions of old colonial-era breweries, and those states have seen several innovative new craft breweries open in the last decade or so.

ABITA BREWING COMPANY
ABITA SPRINGS, LOUISIANA   FOUNDED 1986
Just across Lake Pontchartrain from New Orleans, the indigenous
people of Abita Springs believed that the local water held medicinal

powers, and Abita Brewing prides itself on the purity of the water used in its all-malt ales and lagers. The brewery's first beer was **Abita Amber**, a Munich-style lager, and they followed up that successful brew with eight others, three year-round and five seasonal: the light-bodied **Abita Golden** lager; **Turbodog**, a rich, fairly sweet dark brown ale; **Purple Haze**, an American-style wheat beer made with fresh raspberries; the spring-season **Abita Bock**, similar to a German maibock, and **Abita Red Ale**, a hoppy Irish-style red ale; **Abita Wheat**, a Bavarian-style wheat lager for summer; the märzen **Abita Fallfest**; and **Abita Christmas Ale**, whose recipe changes each winter.

CELIS BREWING COMPANY
AUSTIN, TEXAS
FOUNDED 1991

While many American microbreweries can claim to brew true to the traditions of the great brewers of Belgium, the Celis Brewing Company has a more direct link: its founder, Pierre Celis, ran the De Kluis brewery of Hoegaarden, Belgium, before establishing his Belgian-style brewery in Texas. The brewhouse was brought over to Austin from an abandoned Belgian brewery, and Celis began brewing the distinctive **Celis White** 🍺 🍺 🍺, seasoned with orange peel and coriander according to a traditional Belgian witbier recipe. **Celis Grand Cru** 🍺 🍺 is a well-spiced ale also based on a traditional recipe, and

Celis Dubbel Ale is inspired by Belgium's Trappist ales. Made with malted barley and unmalted wheat, **Celis Raspberry** is flavored with raspberry juice. Influences other than Belgian are found in the top-fermented **Celis Pale Bock** 🍺 and the Czech-style **Celis Golden Ale** 🍺 🍺 pilsner. In 1995 Celis Brewing formed an alliance with a subsidiary of Miller Brewing Company that handles Celis's marketing and distribution.

WILD GOOSE BREWERY
CAMBRIDGE, MARYLAND   FOUNDED 1989

One of the first breweries to open in the mid-Atlantic region, Wild Goose Brewery draws on the classic brewing traditions of England in producing its flavorful ales. Among these, **Wild Goose India Pale Ale** and the brewery's original **Amber Ale** are classics of the British pale ale styles. Other selections crafted in that tradition are Wild Goose Porter and **Wild Goose Oatmeal Stout**. The brewery also offers **Wild Goose Golden Ale** and the seasonal **Spring Wheat Ale**, **Wild Goose Nut Brown Ale** and **Snow Goose Winter Ale**, a flavorful brew similar to an

English old ale. Wild Goose is now a subsidiary of the Frederick Brewing Company, located in Baltimore (see below).

ATLANTA BREWING COMPANY
ATLANTA, GEORGIA
FOUNDED 1994

Atlanta Brewing Company brews a range of distinctive beers. **Red Brick Ale** is similar to an English-style brown ale, **Red Brick Golden Lager** and **Laughing Skull Bohemian Pilsner** are based on the pilsner style, and **Red Brick American Wheat** is an unfiltered Bavarian-style hefeweizen.

BIRMINGHAM BREWING COMPANY
BIRMINGHAM, ALABAMA   FOUNDED 1992

Birmingham Brewing is a modern incarnation of a pre-Prohibition brewery that long ago closed its doors. Today's brewery produces **Red Mountain Red Ale**, which is closer to a brown ale of the English variety, **Red Mountain Golden Ale** and the seasonal **Red Mountain Wheat Beer**.

BLACK BEAR BREWING COMPANY
ATLANTA, GEORGIA   FOUNDED 1996

Black Bear Brewing offers English-style ales: **Black Bear Amber**, a full-bodied ale; the hoppy **Black Bear Pale Ale**; **Black Bear Grizzly Stout**; and the summer-refresher **Black Bear Golden Honey**.

BRIMSTONE BREWING COMPANY
BALTIMORE, MARYLAND   FOUNDED 1993

Brewed in Baltimore's "Brewery Hill," (home to many breweries earlier in the century), Brimstone's line of specialty ales includes **Brimstone Stone Beer**, a rarity for American breweries, as well as **Honey Red**, **Raspberry Porter**, **Big Strong Ale** barley wine and **Amber Ale**, plus **Blueberry Wheat** and various spiced and seasonal beers.

CLIPPER CITY BREWING COMPANY
BALTIMORE, MARYLAND   FOUNDED 1995

Both English-style ales and German-style lagers are brewed at this large Baltimore microbrewery. **Clipper City Pale Ale** and **India Pale Ale** are clearly in the English tradition, while **Clipper City Premium Lager** is a classic of that German style. Clipper City also produces **Märzen** and **Honey Wheat**.

DIXIE BREWING COMPANY
NEW ORLEANS, LOUISIANA   FOUNDED 1907

One of the rare small breweries to survive two world wars, Prohibition, the Depression and big-brewery dominance, Dixie Brewing continues to produce handcrafted beers aged in wood casks. **Blackened Voodoo** 🍺, a dark lager, is the best-known, but the brewery also makes an American-style lager, Dixie Beer, and a relatively tasteful light beer, **Jazz Amber Light**, among others.

FREDERICK BREWING COMPANY
FREDERICK, MARYLAND   FOUNDED 1993
Frederick Brewing's Blue Ridge line includes Golden Ale; the Vienna-style **Amber Lager**; **Porter**; **ESB Red Ale**; **Subliminator Dopplebock**; the honey-fermented **SunRage**; **HopFest**, an unfiltered, dry-hopped brown ale; and the winter ale **Snowball's Chance**. In addition to the occasional specialty beer, Frederick Brewing also brews **Hempen Ale**, which includes hemp seeds with malted barley in the mash, giving this light-brown ale an herbal undertone (though no THC).

HIGHLAND BREWING COMPANY
ASHEVILLE, NORTH CAROLINA
As the name suggests, Highland Brewing produces ales in the Scottish tradition, though with English and Irish influences: **Olde Irish Style Ale**; the amber-colored **Gaelic Ale**; **Oatmeal Porter**; and the robust **Black Mocha Stout**.

OLD DOMINION BREWING COMPANY
ASHBURN, VIRGINIA   FOUNDED 1990
Though mostly limited to the Washington, D.C.–Virginia–Maryland area, Old Dominion brews several successful beers, such as **Dominion Ale**, **Dominion Lager**, **Dominion Stout**, **Dominion Spring Bock**, **Dominion Octoberfest** and **Dominion Millenium** barley wine.

OLDENBERG BREWING COMPANY
FORT MITCHELL, KENTUCKY   FOUNDED 1987
In addition to running a chain of restaurants and a brewpub, Oldenberg Brewing runs a three-day "Beer Camp" twice annually. The brewery's beers include **Oldenberg Premium Verum**, a traditional German lager; **Oldenberg Blonde**, a lighter pilsner-style lager; **Raspberry Wheat**; **Pious Pale Ale**; **Holy Grail Nut Brown Ale**; **Oldenberg Devil's Back Black Oatmeal Stout**; and several seasonal beers, such as **Oldenberg Outrageous Bock**, **Crosley's Red Ale**, **Oldenberg Oktoberfest Lager** and **Oldenberg Winter Ale**.

OXFORD BREWING COMPANY
BALTIMORE, MARYLAND   FOUNDED 1992
Oxford Brewing offers British- and Belgian-inspired ales. **Oxford Class Ale** pale ale, **Oxford IPA**, **Oxford S.O.B. (Special Old Bitter)**, the unfiltered **Oxford Real Ale**, **Oxford Piccadilly Porter** and the holiday-seasonal **Oxford Santa Class** fall in the former category, while **Oxford Raspberry Wheat** and **White Ox Ale** are Belgian-style wheat beers.

ROCK CREEK BREWING COMPANY
RICHMOND, VIRGINIA   FOUNDED 1995
Located near a stretch of the James River once known as **Devil's Elbow**, Rock Creek brews **Devil's Elbow IPA** and other British-style offerings, such as **Rock Creek Red Ale**, **Rock Creek Gold**, **River City ESB**, **Black Raven Porter** and **Nuttrageous Brown Ale**, plus several innovative seasonals: **Pumpkinhead Ale**, **Winter Passion Spiced Ale**, **Irish Honey Cream Ale** and **Wild Summer Passion Wheat Ale**.

SAINT ARNOLD BREWING COMPANY

HOUSTON, TEXAS   FOUNDED 1993

Named in honor of the patron saint of brewers, Saint Arnold Brewing was Houston's first microbrewery. Its year-round brews include **Saint Arnold Amber Ale** and **Saint Arnold Kristall Weizen**, and the seasonals are **Spring Bock, Summerfest, Oktoberfest, Christmas Ale** and **Winter Stout**.

SPOETZL BREWERY

SHINER, TEXAS   FOUNDED 1915

Founded in the Czech-German immigrant town of Shiner, this old regional brewery brews from the original recipes of founder Kosmos Spoetzl. These are **Shiner Blonde** lager; **Shiner Bock**; the citrusy **Shiner Honey Wheat**; **Shiner Kosmos Reserve** lager; and **Shiner Winter Ale** dunkelweizen.

WEEPING RADISH BREWERY

MANTEO, NORTH CAROLINA   FOUNDED 1986

Weeping Radish's traditional lagers and ales adhere to the Bavarian beer purity law of 1516. The brewery currently produces **Corolla Gold**, a Münchner-helles lager; **Fest**, a märzen-style lager; and **Black Radish** dunkel lager. In addition, seasonal brews include **Winter Wheat**, **Spring Bock** and **Christmas Double Bock**.

WILLIAMSVILLE BREWERY

ASHLAND, NORTH CAROLINA,   FOUNDED 1995
AND FERNANDINA BEACH, FLORIDA

Spurred by the success of the flagship North Carolina brewery, Williamsville opened a second operation in Florida and purchased North Carolina's Wilmington Brewing and the Caribbean St. Maarten Breweries. The breweries produce **Amelia Ale, Cabo Pale Ale, Endangered Ale, Studley Ale** brown ale, **Border Porter** and the fruity **Apple and Ale**.

OTHER SOUTHERN BREWERIES

ALABAMA

OXMOOR BREWING COMPANY, Birmingham

PORT CITY BREWERY, Mobile (brewpub): Azalea City Steamer, Gulf Coast Gold, Admiral Semmes Stout

ARKANSAS

OZARK BREWING COMPANY, Fayetteville (brewpub): Ploughman's Pilsner, Friesian Black Lager, India Pale Ale, Lord Freckleberry's Bitter, Long Rein Ale, Whippator Dooplebock, Six in Hand Stout.

WEIDMAN'S OLD FORT BREWERY, Fort Smith (brewpub)

159

FLORIDA

BEACH BREWING COMPANY, Orlando: Magic Brew

DUNEDIN BREWERY, Dunedin: Pale Ale, Gold Ale, Red Ale, Brown Ale, Peach Wheat, Jack O' Lantern Frosty Pumpkin Ale, Dunedin Highland Game Ale

FLORIDA BREWERY, Auburndale: Growlin' Gator Lager, ABC Ale

HOPS GRILL AND BAR, various cities (brewpub chain)

MIAMI BREWING COMPANY, Miami: Hurricane Reef Lager

YBOR CITY BREWING COMPANY, Tampa: Ybor Gold, Ybor Brown Ale, Ybor Calusa Wheat, Ybor Porter

GEORGIA

DOGWOOD BREWING COMPANY, Atlanta: Pale Ale, Wheat Beer, Summer Brew, Stout

MARTHASVILLE BREWING COMPANY, Atlanta

SWEETWATER BREWING COMPANY, Atlanta: Sweetwater Ale, 420 Ale, Sweetwater Blue blueberry wheat

LOUISIANA

CRESCENT CITY BREWHOUSE, New Orleans (brewpub): Crescent City Pilsner, Red Stallion, Black Forest, Crescent City Mardi Gras

RIKENJACKS BREWING COMPANY, Jackson: Rikenjacks ESB, Rikenjacks Select American Ale

MARYLAND

BALTIMORE BREWING COMPANY, Baltimore (brewpub)

OLDE TOWNE TAVERN & BREWERY, Gaithersburg

NORTH CAROLINA

CAROLINA BREWERY, Chapel Hill (brewpub)

DILWORTH MICROBREWERY, Charlotte (brewpub)

WILMINGTON BREWING COMPANY, Wilmington: Dergy's Golden, Dergy's Amber, Dergy Porter, First Coast Light

TENNESSEE

BIG RIVER BREWING, Chattanooga (brewpub)

BOHANNON BREWING COMPANY, Nashville: Market Street Pilsner, Oktoberfest, Wheat Beer, Golden Ale

JACK DANIEL'S BREWERY, Lynchburg

TEXAS

FRIO BREWING COMPANY, San Antonio
HILL COUNTRY BREWING, Austin: Balcones ESB
LIVE OAK BREWING COMPANY, Austin: Pilz, Pale Ale, Hefeweizen, Oaktoberfest
YELLOW ROSE BREWING COMPANY, San Antonio: Yellow Rose Pale Ale, Honcho Grande Brown, Vigilante Porter, Bubba Dog Wheat, Cactus Queen IPA

VIRGINIA

LEGEND BREWING COMPANY, Richmond: Lager, Pilsner, Brown Ale, Porter, seasonal offerings
POTOMAC RIVER BREWING COMPANY, Chantilly: Rappahannock Red Ale, Mount Vernon Porter
RICHBRAU BREWERY, Richmond (brewpub)

WEST VIRGINIA

CARDINAL BREWING COMPANY, Charleston
WEST VIRGINIA BREWING COMPANY, Morgantown

US—WEST

In 1977, the New Albion Brewery of Sonoma, California, began brewing traditional, handcrafted beers, and though this pioneering microbrewery did not survive long, within a few years a wave of new, small breweries opened up along the entire Pacific Coast. Northern California was the leader in the American microbrew revolution, and many quality breweries remain throughout the state; but Oregon and Washington have also cultivated a large number of breweries offering a rich variety of traditional beer styles. Many specialty ales long-abandoned by American breweries were brought back into favor by the region's innovative brewers. The Pacific Northwest is the center of hop-growing in the United States, and the quality varieties grown there are not only used in the local beers (and generously so) but also increasingly in beers brewed in Europe and elsewhere. The American interpretation of the English pale ale style was influenced by the Cascade, Columbus and Cluster varieties of Northwest hops, in addition to the use of paler malts than those used by the

Brits. California's Anchor Brewery and Sierra Nevada were key players in perfecting that American style. In the Rocky Mountain states, while the Golden-based Coors is an established industry giant, many new and creative microbreweries have established themselves in various cities around Colorado. The trend is even hitting the sparsely populated states of Wyoming and Montana.

Today, California has more microbreweries and brewpubs than any other state in the nation, and Colorado, Washington and Oregon all rank near the top as well. Portland, Oregon, has more microbreweries and brewpubs than any other city in the country, earning the title "America's Microbrew Capital"—or, more informally, "Beervana."

ANCHOR BREWING COMPANY

SAN FRANCISCO, CALIFORNIA   FOUNDED 1896

Considered by some the godfather of the modern-day American microbrewery, Anchor Brewing was long a successful regional brewery before it came upon hard times, nearly shutting down in 1965, when Fritz Maytag, heir to the Maytag washing-machine company, bought the fledgling brewery. Anchor has been a trailblazer in craft-brewing ever since. The brewery's most notable beer is its **Anchor Steam Beer**🍺🍺🍺, based on the California common style developed during the gold rush of the nineteenth century—"steam beer" is now an Anchor trademark. A hybrid of ale and lager styles, Anchor Steam is made by the traditional method of using lager yeast in shallow fermenters, but at ale-like fermentation temperatures. The result is a copper-golden beer with a balance of malt flavors and hop dryness. Anchor also produces the dry-hopped **Liberty Ale**🍺🍺🍺, a classi-

cally hoppy American pale ale. **Anchor Porter**🍺🍺 is rich with roasted malt flavors, and **Old Foghorn**🍺🍺🍺 is an excellent barley-wine–style ale, suitable for aging. The slightly fruity **Wheat Beer** and the vintage-dated **Our Special Ale**🍺🍺🍺, brewed for the winter holiday season, are additional Anchor brews.

PYRAMID BREWERIES

SEATTLE, WASHINGTON   FOUNDED 1984

Pyramid ales were first brewed in the small logging town of Kalama, Washington, in the early years of the microbrewery revolution. Originally known as the Hart Brewing Company, it merged with Thomas Kemper Brewery in 1992 and subsequently moved to Seattle. The original **Pyramid Pale Ale** is copper-colored with a nutty-malt flavor along with strong Northwest hops. Pyramid's three wheat beers are the light and dry **Wheaten Ale**; the unfiltered **Hefeweizen**, made with 60 percent wheat malt; and the fruity **Apricot Ale**. Darker, roasty offerings

include **Pyramid Best Brown**, made with dark malts and roasted barley, and the rich **Pyramid Espresso Stout** (formerly Hart Espresso Stout), offering coffee flavors but no actual coffee beans in the recipe. **Snow Cap Ale** is a flavorful winter strong ale, while Sun Fest is a crisp summer brew. Other Pyramid seasonals are **Scotch Ale**, **Porter** and **India Pale Ale**.

Established across the Puget Sound from Seattle on Bainbridge Island in 1985, Thomas Kemper Brewery focuses exclusively on German-style lagers. The wheat lagers include **Weizen Berry**, a Bavarian-style wheat beer flavored with raspberries, and the wheaty **Hefeweizen**. **Thomas Kemper Amber** is a spicy Vienna-style lager, and **Geyser Golden** is more in the pilsner style. Seasonal brews include **Oktoberfest**, **Bock**, **Porter** and **Winter Bräu**.

ROGUE ALES BREWERY
NEWPORT, OREGON
FOUNDED 1989

Located along the dramatic Oregon coast, Rogue Ales Brewery is a premier American craftbrewer, producing a wide range of distinctively flavored, award-winning ales. **Rogue Ale** is an amber-colored, English-style special bitter. The highly regarded **Shakespeare Stout** is a rich, creamy oatmeal stout, while Rogue's **Imperial Stout** is another classic of the style. **Mocha Porter** has definite chocolate notes, **HazelNut Brown Nectar** is flavored with hazelnut extract, and **Rogue-N-Berry** uses locally grown marrionberries that give the beer a purplish tint. **Saint Rogue Red**, **American Amber** and **Oregon Golden Ale** are other British-inspired ales, and Rogue also produces an array of seasonal and limited-edition brews. **Mogul Ale** (or Mogul Madness) is a dark strong ale brewed for winter. The late-fall and winter fruit ale **Cran-N-Cherry** includes actual cherries and cranberries. Rogue's bock beers are **Maierbock**, **Dead Guy Ale**, **Whale Ale** and **Wolf Eel Ale**. **Mo Ale** is a Belgian-style wheat beer. Smoke, known as Welkommen on draught, is a classic top-fermented rauchbier. Aged for months before bottling, **Old Crustacean Barleywine** continues to improve in the bottle. **McRogue Scotch Ale** and the chile-pepper-flavored **Mexicali Rogue** round out Rogue's innovative selection.

ALASKAN BREWING COMPANY
JUNEAU, ALASKA   FOUNDED 1986

The first brewery established in the state, Alaskan Brewing quickly earned praises for its award-winning **Alaskan Amber** 🍺🍺, an altbier based on a nineteenth-century recipe. **Alaskan Pale Ale** 🍺🍺 and the copper-colored **Alaskan Frontier** are flavorful ales, and the brewery recently added **Alaskan Stout**, an oatmeal stout. The premier **Alaskan Smoked Porter** 🍺🍺🍺 is smoked over alder-wood fires.

ANDERSON VALLEY BREWING COMPANY
BOONVILLE, CALIFORNIA   FOUNDED 1987
This northern-California brewery's range of rich ales includes **Boont Amber, Poleeko Gold Pale Ale, Belk's Extra Special Bitter, Hop Otten India Pale Ale, Barney Flats Oatmeal Stout, Deependers Dark Porter** and **High Rollers Wheat Beer**. Specialty brews include **Wee Heavy Scotch Ale** and **Horn of the Beer Barley Wine**.

BRIDGEPORT BREWING COMPANY
PORTLAND, OREGON   FOUNDED 1984
This pioneering Portland microbrewery is styled after the regional breweries of England. In addition to the flagship **Blue Heron Pale Ale** (or **Bridgeport Pale Ale**), named for Portland's official bird, Bridgeport brews the molasses-flavored **Black Strap Stout, BridgePort Amber, ESB** and **Old Knucklehead Barley Wine**. Bridgeport's firkin line of naturally conditioned beers includes **India Pale Ale** and **Porter**.

BUFFALO BILL'S BREWING COMPANY
HAYWARD, CALIFORNIA   FOUNDED 1983
An early California microbrewery, Buffalo Bill's is best known for its **Pumpkin Ale** 🍺🍺, a seasonal made with real pumpkin. In addition, it offers **White Buffalo Ale, Tasmanian Devil Ale, Belle Hop Porter** and the seasonal **Alimony Ale** and **Hearty Ale**.

ADOLPH COORS COMPANY
GOLDEN, COLORADO   FOUNDED 1873
Coors was a longtime regional brewery before joining the ranks of the national giants. Aside from its standard American-style light lagers, Coors produces a line of specialty beers under the Blue Moon label. It also brews **George Killian's Irish Red Lager, Winterfest** 🍺🍺 märzen lager and the clear malt beverage **Zima**.

DESCHUTES BREWING COMPANY
BEND, OREGON   FOUNDED 1988
Deschutes began as a brewpub and has grown steadily to become a leading Northwest microbrewery, producing ales primarily in the English tradition. The rich **Black Butte Porter** is the brewery's best-known beer (and the author's favorite), but Deschutes offers four other quality ales year-round: **Cascade Golden Ale, Mirror Pond Pale Ale, Bachelor Bitter** and **Obsidian Stout**. The winter-warmer **Jubelale** is a flavorful seasonal.

FULL SAIL BREWING COMPANY
HOOD RIVER, OREGON   FOUNDED 1987
Located in the scenic Columbia River Gorge, Full Sail is Oregon's largest bottler of craft beers. Twelve beers are brewed in all, including the flavorful top-fermented **Golden Ale, Amber Ale, Nut Brown Ale** and **India Pale Ale**. Seasonal beers available in bottles are **Oktoberfest, WasSail, Imperial Porter, Equinox E.S.B.** and the limited-edition **Old Boardhead Barleywine Ale**.

Hair of the Dog Brewing Company
Portland, Oregon   Founded 1994

Hair of the Dog's bottle-conditioned ales are produced in small batches and improve with age, for as long as several years. The strong but smooth Adambier has a distinctive garnet-red color from the use of roasted barley. **Fred** is a golden strong ale that incorporates ten varieties of hops and a dose of rye malt. The fruity **Golden Rose** is inspired by the tripel-style ales of Belgium.

Lost Coast Brewery
Eureka, California   Founded 1986

Established by two woman brewers, Lost Coast brews English-style top-fermenting ales, such as **Lost Coast Pale Ale**, **Alley Cat Amber Ale**, **Downtown Brown**, **Eight Ball Stout**, the spring-seasonal **Raspberry Brown Ale** and **Winterbrau Holiday Ale**. It also offers a Belgian-inspired **White Beer**.

McMenamins Brothers Breweries
Various locations in Oregon and Washington
Founded 1990

The innovative McMenamins chain operates more than thirty brewpubs in the Pacific Northwest. Each pub produces its own individual beers in addition to the following company standards: **Bagdad Ale**, **Black Rabbit Porter**, **Cascade Head**, **Crystal Ale**, **Edgefield Wheat**, **Hammerhead Ale**, **Nebraska Bitter**, **Ruby**, **Terminator Stout** and **Transformer Ale**.

Mendocino Brewing Company
Hopland, California   Founded 1983

Mendocino Brewing was founded by former brewers from North America's first modern-day microbrewery, New Albion Brewing. The flagship **Red Tail Ale** is a complex, slightly fruity amber ale, while **Blue Heron Pale Ale** is a hoppier, golden ale. The roasty **Black Hawk Stout** is in the Irish-dry vein.

Mt. Hood Brewing Company
Government Camp, Oregon   Founded 1992

Another Oregon microbrewery to take advantage of the state's striking landscape—it is located at an elevation of 4000 feet on majestic Mount Hood—this brewery offers six English-style ales: **Ice Axe India Pale Ale**, **Pinnacle Extra Special Bitter**, **Cloud Cap Amber Ale**, **Hogsback Oatmeal Stout**, the winter-season **Pittock Wee Heavy** and **Southside Light Session Ale**, a summer-wheat ale.

New Belgium Brewing Company
Fort Collins, Colorado   Founded 1991

Among this brewery's flavorful Belgian-style beers are a traditional witbier known as **Sunshine** and three abbey-style ales: **Abbey** dubbel, **Trippel** and **Porch Swing Single Ale**. The Specialty Release line has included **Old Cherry Ale** and **Frambozen Raspberry Brown Ale**. New Belgium's more American offerings are **Fat Tire Amber Ale** and **Blue Paddle Pilsener**.

North Coast Brewing Company

Fort Bragg, California — Founded 1988

Located in the rich brewing county of Mendocino, North Coast Brewing offers a diversity of award-winning beers, including **Ruedrich's Red Seal Ale**, **Scrimshaw Pilsner Beer**, **Pranqster Belgian-Style Golden Ale** and the unfiltered **Blue Star Wheat Beer**. Its stouts are **Old Rasputin Russian Imperial Stout** and **Old No. 38 Stout**, a highly acclaimed dry stout.

Nor'Wester Brewery

Portland, Oregon — Founded 1995

Publicly owned, Nor'Wester produces both ales and lagers. These include three Bavarian-style wheat ales—**Hefeweizen**, **Dunkel Weizen** and **Raspberry Weizen**—plus **Oregon Pale Ale**, **Oregon Amber**, and **Nor'Wester Best Bitter**. Seasonal offerings are **White Forest** Scotch ale, **Smith Rock Bock** and **Mt. Angel Oktoberfest**, among others.

Oregon Trail Brewery

Corvallis, Oregon — Founded 1987

Oregon Trail utilizes a gravity-fed system of brewing, starting the process on the top floor of the three-story brewhouse. **Oregon Trail White Ale** is a traditional Belgian-style wheat beer, while **Oregon Trail Ale** is similar to a German kölsch. There is also the Irish-style **Oregon Trail Stout** and **Oregon Trail Brown Ale**.

Pete's Brewing Company

Palo Alto, California — Founded 1986

This leading contract-brewer brews a range of craft ales and lagers. The first brew was **Pete's Wicked Ale**, an American-style brown ale, and Pete's has followed that up with **ESP Lager**, **Honey Wheat**, **Signature Pilsner**, **Strawberry Blonde**, **Summer Brew**, **Oktoberfest** and **Winter Brew**.

The Pike Brewery

Seattle, Washington — Founded 1989

Located in the center of the bustling Pike Place Market, the Pike Brewery was founded by renowned beer importer Charles Finkle of Merchant du Vin, and its quality ales have definite European influences. **Pike Pale Ale** is a classic Pike offering, as is **XXXXX Stout** and **Old Bawdy Barley Wine**.

Portland Brewing Company

Portland, Oregon — Founded 1986

Portland Brewing has grown to become a significant regional brewery. Its main brew is the Scottish-style **MacTarnahan's Amber Ale**, but it has also offered **Zig-Zag River Lager**, **Haystack Black Porter**, **Oregon Honey Beer**, **Bavarian-Style Weizen** and **Wheat Berry Beer**, among others.

Redhook Ale Brewery

Seattle, Washington — Founded 1981

A pioneer in the microbrew movement, Redhook is now one of the largest craft breweries—and it is partially owned by Anheuser-Busch. It brews a varied range that includes **Redhook Extra Special Bitter**, **Redhook India Pale Ale** (originally Ballard Bitter), **Redhook Rye Beer**,

Blackhook porter and **Doubleblack Stout,** made with Starbucks coffee. **Winterhook Winter Ale, Blonde Ale** and **Brown Ale** are brewed for limited seasons.

ROCKIES BREWING COMPANY
BOULDER, COLORADO   FOUNDED 1979
Originally known as the Boulder Brewing Company, this is the oldest microbrewery in the United States, though it has had several owners. **Boulder Extra Pale Ale, Boulder Amber Ale, Boulder Porter** and **Boulder Stout** are among the regular brews, in addition to about half a dozen seasonals.

ST. STAN'S BREWERY
MODESTO, CALIFORNIA   FOUNDED 1981
St. Stan's brews several beers in the traditional altbier style of Düsseldorf: the classic **St. Stan's Amber Ale** 🍺 🍺, the dark-malt **St. Stan's Dark** 🍺, the unfiltered **Virgin Amber** and **Virgin Dark** and the seaonal **St. Stan's Fest.** It also produces **Whistle Stop Ale, Red Sky Ale** and **St. Stan's Barley Wine** 🍺 🍺.

SAXER BREWING COMPANY
LAKE OSWEGO, OREGON   FOUNDED 1993
Named for the founder of Oregon's first brewery—Henry Saxer founded Liberty Brewing in 1852—Saxer Brewing is the rare Oregon craft brewery to produce exclusively lagers. Its award-winning offerings include **Three-Finger Jack Roasted Red Hefedunkel,** the märzen-style **Three-Finger Jack Amber,** and **Three-Finger JackFrost Winter Dopplebock.** The brewery also produces **Three-Finger Jack Summer Lager, Saxer's Lemon Lager** and **Three-Finger Jack Stout.**

SIERRA NEVADA BREWING COMPANY
CHICO, CALIFORNIA   FOUNDED 1981
Established by two homebrewers, Sierra Nevada has grown to become an extremely successful and influential microbrewery, with a range of award-winning beers that exemplify American craft-brewing. The deep-amber **Sierra Nevada Pale Ale** 🍺 🍺 🍺 is a premier American pale ale. **Sierra Nevada Porter** 🍺 🍺 🍺 is another classic of ale styles, as is the rich **Sierra Nevada Stout** 🍺 🍺. Among Sierra Nevada's most celebrated brews is its winter-season **Bigfoot Barleywine-Style Ale** 🍺 🍺 🍺. With an alcohol content approaching 11% ABV, it is also one of the strongest American beers and will continue to age well in the bottle. The unfiltered **Wheat, Summerfest** lager, **Pale Bock** and the renowned **Celebration Ale** are Sierra Nevada's other brews.

TABERNASH BREWING COMPANY
DENVER, COLORADO   FOUNDED 1993
Tabernash brews German-style lagers and wheat beers. These include the unfiltered **Tabernash Weiss;** the pilsner-style **Tabernash Golden; Tabernash Amber;** and **Tabernash Munich,** based on a Münchner dunkel. Seasonal beers are **Doppelbock, Dunkel Weiss, Oktoberfest** and **Frostbite** alt.

WIDMER BROTHERS BREWING COMPANY
PORTLAND, OREGON   FOUNDED 1984
This leading craft brewery produced the United States's first hefeweizen, **America's Original Hefeweizen,** the top-selling draught microbrew in the Pacific Northwest. The brewery also produces **Hop**

Jack Pale Ale; the Vienna-style **Ray's Amber Lager**; **Big Ben Porter**, flavored with licorice and molasses; **Widberry Weizen**; and the seasonal **Winternacht**, **Doppelbock**, **Golden Bock**, **Sommerbräu** and **Oktoberfest**. In the spring of 1997, Widmer joined up with Anheuser-Busch to increase national distribution.

YAKIMA BREWING AND MALTING COMPANY
YAKIMA, WASHINGTON   FOUNDED 1982

Having worked in his first brewery at the age of sixteen, Bert Grant began offering his homebrews at this early Washington brewpub. **Bert Grant's Scottish Ale**, hoppier than the classic Scottish version, is the brewery's flagship brand, but the flavorful Bert Grant line also includes **Amber Ale**, **India Pale Ale** 🍺🍺, **HefeWeizen**, **Perfect Porter** and **Imperial Stout** 🍺🍺🍺.

OTHER WESTERN BREWERIES

ALASKA

BIRD CREEK BREWERY, Anchorage: Old 55 Pale Ale, Denali Ale, Anchorage Ale, Illiamna Raspberry Wheat Beer, Alaskafest Winter Ale

MIDNIGHT SUN BREWING COMPANY, Anchorage: Fireweed Honey Wheat Beer, Kodiak Brown Ale, Wolf Spirit Sparkling Ale, Mammoth Extra Stout, Old Whiskers Hefeweizen, Humpy's Sockeye Red Ale

RAILWAY BREWING COMPANY, Anchorage: Railway IPA, Not Brown Ale, Pullman Porter, Steel Rail Chili Ale, Scottish Rail Ale, Trans-Siberian Imperial Stout, Big Stinger Barley Wine

RAVEN RIDGE BREWING COMPANY, Fairbanks

ARIZONA

BANDERSNATCH BREWING, Tempe: Bighorn Premium, Bandersnatch Milk Stout

BLACK MOUNTAIN BREWING COMPANY, Cave Creek: Cave Creek Chili Beer 🍺

MCFARLANE BREWING COMPANY, Phoenix

OAK CREEK BREWING COMPANY, Sedona

CALIFORNIA

BISON BREWING COMPANY, Berkeley: Honey Basil Ale, Lemongrass Wheat, Smoked Scotch Ale, Chocolate Porter, Black Shadow Bock

GOLDEN PACIFIC BREWING COMPANY, Emeryville: Golden Gate Original Ale, Golden Gate Pale Ale, Golden Gate Hefeweizen, Golden

Bear Lager, Black Bear Dry Stout, Black Bear Porter

GORDON BIERSCH BREWING COMPANY, Palo Alto and various locations
(brewpub): Pilsner, Märzen, Dunkles, Blonde Bock

HUMBOLDT BREWING COMPANY, Arcata: Red Nectar Ale, Gold Rush
Pale Ale, Oatmeal Stout

LIND BREWING COMPANY, San Leandro: Drake's Ale, Sir Francis Stout

MAD RIVER BREWING COMPANY, Blue Lake: Steelhead Extra Pale Ale,
Steelhead Extra Stout, Jamaica Red Ale

SUDWERK PRIVATBRAUEREI HÜBSCH, Davis: Hübsch Bräu Pilsner,
Hübsch Bräu Märzen, Hübsch Bräu Hefeweizen, Hübsch Bräu
Dark

COLORADO

AVERY BREWING COMPANY, Boulder: Redpoint Ale, Raspberry Truffale

H. C. BERGER BREWING COMPANY, Fort Collins: Indego Pale Ale,
Whistlepin Wheat

GREAT DIVIDE BREWING COMPANY, Denver

LEFT HAND BREWING COMPANY, Longmont: Sawtooth Ale, Motherlode
Golden Ale, Juju Ginger Ale, Black Jack Porter

ODELL BREWING COMPANY, Fort Collins: 90 Shilling, Cutthroat Porter,
Easy Street Wheat, Levity Ale, Curmudgeon's Nip Barley Wine

PIKE'S PEAK BREWERY, Colorado Springs: Jack Rabbit Pale Ale, Red
Granite Amber Ale

HAWAII

ALI'I BREWING COMPANY, Kalihi

KONA BREWING COMPANY, Kona

IDAHO

BEIER BREWING COMPANY, Boise

COEUR D'ALENE BREWING COMPANY, Coeur D'Alene: T.W. Fisher Pale
Ale, T.W. Fisher Nut Brown

SUN VALLEY BREWING COMPANY, Hailey: White Cloud Ale

THUNDER MOUNTAIN BREWERY, Ketchum

MONTANA BREWERIES

BAYERN BREWING, Missoula

GREAT NORTHERN BREWING COMPANY, Whitefish: Black Star Golden
Lager, Black Star Black Lager, Wheatfish Hefeweizen, Big Fog
Amber Lager

KESSLER BREWING COMPANY, Helena: Ale 7, Oktoberfest, Lorelei,

Weizen, Doppelbock, Nicholas, Wild West

SPANISH PEAKS BREWING COMPANY, Bozeman: Spanish Peaks Porter, Black Dog Bitter

WHITEFISH BREWING COMPANY, Whitefish

NEW MEXICO

ESKE'S: A BREW PUB / SANGRE DE CRISTO BREWING, Taos

RIO GRANDE BREWING COMPANY, Albuquerque

RUSSELL BREWING COMPANY, Santa Fe

SANTA FE BREWING COMPANY, Galisteo: Santa Fe Pale Ale, Porter

OREGON

BANDON BREWING COMPANY, Bandon: Bogwater Wheat Ale, Bogwater Porter

LUCKY LABRADOR BREW PUB, Portland: Black Lab Stout, Hawthorne's Best Bitter

MT. ANGEL BREWING COMPANY, Mt. Angel: Angel Ale, Halo, Holy Grale, Ale Mari

OREGON TRADER BREWING COMPANY, Albany: Hefeweizen, Green Chili Beer, Nut Brown

STEELHEAD BREWING COMPANY, Eugene: Steelhead Amber, Bombay Bomber IPA, Hefeweizen, Porter, Stout

WASHINGTON

ELYSIAN BREWERY, Seattle: Extra Special Bitter, India Pale Ale, Perseus Porter, Dragon's Tooth Oatmeal Stout, Golden Fleece Ale, Loki Lager

FISH BREWING COMPANY, Olympia: Fish Tale Pale Ale, Fish Eye India Pale Ale, Leviathan Barley Wine, Poseidon's Old Scotch Ale

HALE'S ALES, Seattle: Pale Ale, Amber Ale, Moss Bay Extra

MARITIME PACIFIC BREWING COMPANY, Seattle: Islander Pale Ale, Nightwatch Ale, Salmon Bay Bitter, Clipper Gold Wheat Ale

NORTHERN LIGHTS BREWING COMPANY, Airway Heights: Creme Ale, Blueberry Creme Ale, Northern Lights Ale

ONALASKA BREWING COMPANY, Onalaska: Onalaska Ale, Red Dawg Ale, Howlin' Stout

WYOMING

OTTO BROTHERS' BREWING, Wilson: Old Faithful Ale, Teton Ale

SNAKE RIVER BREWING COMPANY, Jackson (brewpub)

CANADA

Although North America's oldest running brewery, Molson, is located in Canada, the nation's beer industry suffered from fifteen years of prohibition (1918–1932), followed by decades of restrictive local laws, many of which remain, and high beer taxes. Molson, Labatt, and Carling long dominated beer production, and only recently has the number of breweries increased, with the emergence of many small craft breweries, particularly in British Columbia, Ontario and Quebec. With the growing popularity of these microbreweries and brewpubs, the big breweries have begun to produce more craft-brew–style beers, such as Labatt's Old Mick's Red and Molson's Rickard's Red.

Canadian beers initially were influenced by the brewing traditions of England, but in the late 1800s Canada, like its neighbor to the south, began focusing primarily on the lager styles. As the industry consolidated under a very small number of breweries in the twentieth century, the lagers took on a lighter, blander character. The new microbreweries have returned to brewing traditional ales, including some specialty Belgian-inspired brews. The beers of western Canada tend toward a maltier, smoother flavor compared to those in the east. Canada can claim its own beer style, though it is infrequently made today. Canadian ales, also known as cream ales, are mild-tasting and golden-colored. The unremarkable "ice beer" was also first introduced by a Canadian brewery, Labatt's, in the early 1990s.

BRASSERIE MCAUSLAN
MONTREAL, QUEBEC
FOUNDED 1989

Similar to many North American microbreweries, McAuslan Brewing began when a longtime homebrewer decided to offer his beers to the public. Peter McAuslan introduced his first beer in 1989, and McAuslan's ales have gone on to earn international attention. **St. Ambroise Pale Ale**—named for the street on which the brasserie is located—is a somewhat hoppy, but well-balanced, reddish-golden ale. **St. Ambroise Oatmeal Stout** uses oatmeal in the mash, while dark malts and roasted barley contribute roasty, coffeeish and chocolatey flavors. McAuslan's Griffon line includes **Griffon Brown Ale**, a complex, mahogany-brown ale brewed according to the English brown ale tradition, and the bright gold **Griffon Extra Pale Ale**. **St. Ambroise Framboise**, a Belgian-style raspberry fruit beer, **McAuslan Strong Ale** and **McAuslan Apricot Wheat Ale** are seasonal brews from McAuslan. A recent draught-only introduction is known as **Cream Ale** in Quebec and **Smooth Ale** in the United States.

GRANVILLE ISLAND BREWING COMPANY
VANCOUVER, BRITISH COLUMBIA   FOUNDED 1984

Granville Island is a picturesque island in the heart of Vancouver, and the brewery of that name is located along the bustling waterfront. It was Canada's first modern-day microbrewery (though it was subsequently acquired by a larger company), and Granville Island Brewing continues to produce quality craft beers in strict accordance with the old Reinheitsgebot purity law. Its inaugural brew was **Island Lager**, a Munich-style helles pilsner, and next came the slightly fruitier, reddish-copper **Lord Granville Pale Ale**. The brewery celebrated its tenth year in operation by releasing **Anniversary Amber Ale**, a full-bodied ale reminiscent of the Irish red style. Among the brewery's most distinctive products, **Island Bock** is rich but smooth, with the sweetness of its dark malts balanced by a variety of hops. **Island Light** beer is another brew.

MOLSON BREWERIES
TORONTO, ONTARIO
FOUNDED 1786

The oldest brewery in North America, Molson has been around longer than Canada has been a nation. It was founded by English immigrant John Molson along the St. Lawrence River. The company solidified its place as Canada's largest brewer when it merged with Carling O'Keefe Brewing in 1989, and today it produces dozens of brands in eight breweries in seven provinces— Molson Breweries accounts for about half of the national beer market. In 1993 Molson formed an alliance with Miller Brewing. The Molson line of beers mostly consists of such light lagers as **Molson Canadian Lager**, **Molson Export**, **Molson Special Dry**, **Molson Light** and **Molson Ice**;

Molson Golden and **Molson Red Jack** are slightly more flavorful. In addition to the **Carling** brand, other Molson-produced labels include **Rickard's Red**, **Calgary Amber** 🍺🍺, **Extra Old Stock Ale** 🍺, **O'Keefe Ale**, **Old Vienna** and the non-alcoholic **Exel NA**.

WELLINGTON COUNTY BREWERY
GUELPH, ONTARIO   FOUNDED 1985

Wellington County Brewery was founded by a group of "real ale" enthusiasts hoping to introduce traditional English-style cask-conditioned ales to Canada. The higher maintenance required with serving cask-conditioned beer initially limited the distribution, but Wellington County now offers a range of cask-conditioned as well as standard ales. **Iron Duke** is a robust but well-balanced English old ale—its success has led Wellington's master brewer to assume the identity "the Iron Duke." The two original cask-conditioned ales are the hoppy, copper-colored

Arkell Best Bitter and the flavorful **County Ale**. **Special Pale Ale**, or SPA, is slightly fruitier than the Best Bitter but more bitter than the County Ale. The brewery also produces **Iron Duke Porter**, **Imperial Stout** and **Black Knight ESB**, as well as two lagers: the Vienna-style **Premium Lager** and **Honey Lager**.

BIG ROCK BREWERY
CALGARY, ALBERTA   FOUNDED 1985

Big Rock Brewery adheres to the Bavarian beer purity law in brewing its traditional ales. These include the dark copper **Traditional Ale**; **Warthog Ale**; the lighter **Buzzard's Breath Ale**; **Grasshöpper** kristallweizen; **McNally's Extra Irish-Style Ale** 🍺🍺; **Magpie Rye Ale**; **Cold Cock Porter** 🍺🍺; **Black Amber Ale** stout; and **Big Rock Light**. Proceeds from the sales of **Chinook Pale Ale** and **Canvasback Golden Ale** are donated to environmental conservation.

BOWEN ISLAND BREWING COMPANY
BOWEN ISLAND, BRITISH COLUMBIA   FOUNDED 1994

Located on a secluded island off Vancouver, Bowen Island Brewing produces filtered, English-style ales, such as **Bowen Island Blonde Ale**, brewed with a portion of wheat malt; the pale ale **Bowen Ale**; and **Bowen Island Special Bitter**. Seasonal brews are the cherry-flavored **Winter Ale** and **Harvest Ale**.

BRASSERIE BRASAL
LASALLE, QUEBEC   FOUNDED 1989

The largest brewery in Quebec Province, Brasserie Brasal brews German-style lagers in accordance with the Reinheitsgebot. It currently produces **Hopps Bräu**, the complex and rich **Brasal Special Amber Lager**, the very flavorful **Brasal Bock** and **Brasal Légère**, a light beer.

BRICK BREWING COMPANY
WATERLOO, ONTARIO   FOUNDED 1984

In a region that has a large German population—and one of the largest Oktoberfest celebrations outside of Germany—Brick Brewing produces European-style lagers and ales following the Reinheitsgebot of 1516. One of Canada's first microbreweries, it offers **Amber Dry**, **Anniversary Bock**, **Brick Premium Lager** and **Brick Red Baron Ale**.

CREEMORE SPRINGS BREWERY
CREEMORE, ONTARIO   FOUNDED 1987

Although Creemore Springs currently brews only two products, it has garnered much attention locally and at various beer tastings and festivals. The pilsner-style **Creemore Springs Premium Lager** was the inaugural brew, joined nearly a decade later by the limited-edition **Creemore urBock**.

HART BREWING COMPANY
CARLETON PLACE, ONTARIO   FOUNDED 1991

The Hart Brewing Company was launched with the release of its English-style **Amber Ale**, developed by microbrew-guru Alan Pugsley. **Hart Cream Ale** is a light, blond-colored ale in the tradition of the Canadian style. Hart also offers **Hardy Stout**, **Finnigan's Red** Irish ale, **Hart Festive Brown** and **Valley Gold** ale.

LABATT BREWING COMPANY

TORONTO, ONTARIO   FOUNDED 1847

Founded by Irish-immigrant John Labatt, the Labatt Brewing Company quickly grew to become a leading national brewer, even surviving Prohibition. Today **Labatt Blue** is Canada's best-selling beer, but the brewery also produces **Labatt Genuine Draft**, **Labatt Ice**, **Labatt "50" Ale**, **Labatt Select**, **John Labatt Classic** and **Labatt Extra Dry**, as well as several regional brands.

MOOSEHEAD BREWERIES

ST. JOHN, NEW BRUNSWICK   FOUNDED 1867

The nation's largest independent, Moosehead brews the smooth **Moosehead Lager Beer**, the slightly drier and darker **Moosehead Pale Ale** and **Moosehead Light**—the latter two available only in the Maritime Provinces of New Brunswick, Nova Scotia and Prince Edwards Island, where the brewery also offers **Alpine Lager** and **Alpine Light**.

NIAGARA FALLS BREWING COMPANY

NIAGARA FALLS, ONTARIO   FOUNDED 1989

This innovative microbrewery produced North America's first eisbock. The strong and malty **Niagara Eisbock** 🍺🍺 was partly inspired by the local eiswein. In addition, Niagara Falls makes **Trapper Premium Lager**, **Gritstone Premium Ale**, **Old Jack Bitter Strong Ale**, **Brock's Extra Stout**, **Maple Wheat** and several fruit beers, including **Cherry Kriek** and **Apple Ale**.

OKANAGAN SPRING BREWERY

VERNON, BRITISH COLUMBIA   FOUNDED 1985

The largest craft brewery in British Columbia was founded by two German immigrants. Okanagan Spring's first brew was the golden **Premium Lager**, though it now produces several quality ales as well, such as the rich **Olde English Porter**, **Pale Ale**, **Classic Brown Ale**, **Spring Wheat** and **St. Patrick's Stout**.

SLEEMAN BREWING AND MALTING COMPANY

GUELPH, ONTARIO   FOUNDED 1988

The original Sleeman family's Silver Creek Brewery was established in the 1830s but closed a century later. In the late 1980s, the family resurrected the brewery in the wake of the craft-brew resurgence. Today its beers include **Silver Creek Lager**, **Sleeman Cream Ale** and **Sleeman Original Dark**.

UNIBROUE

CHAMBLY, QUEBEC   FOUNDED 1990

Unibroue offers bottle-conditioned (*on lees*), Belgian-style ales. **Blanche de Chambly** is a spiced witbier; **Eau Bénite** is a golden ale; **La Fin du Monde** ("the end of the world") is similar to a Belgian strong ale; the abbey-style **La Gaillarde** is based on a medieval recipe; **La Maudite** ("the damned") is a Belgian red ale; the winter-warmer **La Quelque Chose** is cherry-flavored; **Raftman** is a smoky beer made with whiskey malt; and **Trois Pistole** is a dark, strong beer.

UPPER CANADA BREWING COMPANY

TORONTO, ONTARIO   FOUNDED 1985

Relatively large and old for a microbrewery, Upper Canada Brewing has a wide range of all-malt ales and lagers, including **Colonial Stout**

(more of a porter than a stout), **Upper Canada Pale Ale**, **Upper Canada Dark Ale**, **Publican's Special Bitter Ale**, **Point Nine Lager**, **Upper Canada Lager**, **Upper Canada Rebellion Lager**, **Upper Canada True Bock** and the filtered **Upper Canada Wheat**.

OTHER CANADIAN BREWERIES

ALLEY KAT BREWING, Edmonton, Alberta

ARCTIC BREWING COMPANY, Yellowknife, Northwest Territories

BEAR BREWING COMPANY, Kamloops, British Columbia: Black Bear Ale, Brown Bear Ale, Polar Bear Lager

BOW VALLEY BREWING COMPANY, Calgary, Alberta: Bow Valley Premium Lager, Mountain Bock

BRASSERIE PORTNEUVOISE, St. Casimir, Quebec

BRASSEURS DU NORD, St. Jerome, Quebec: Blonde, Rousse, Noire

BRASSEURS GMT, Montreal, Quebec: Belle Guele

BREW BROTHERS BREWING COMPANY, Calgary, Alberta: English Style Amber Ale, Prairie Steam Ale, Black Pilsner

FLANAGAN & SONS BREWING COMPANY, Edmonton, Alberta

FORT GARRY BREWING COMPANY, Winnipeg, Manitoba

GRANITE BREWERY, Halifax, Nova Scotia (brewpub): Best Bitter, Best Bitter Special, Winter IPA, Peculiar Strong Ale, Ringwood Ale, Keefe's Irish Stout, Summer Ale

GREAT LAKES BREWING COMPANY, Toronto, Ontario: Great Lakes Lager

GREAT WESTERN BREWING COMPANY, Saskatoon, Saskatchewan

HORSESHOE BAY BREWING COMPANY, Vancouver, British Columbia: Horseshoe Bay Ale, Marathon Pale Ale, Nut Brown Ale, Triple Frambozen

KAWARTHA LAKES BREWING COMPANY, Peterborough, Ontario: Raspberry Wheat, Premium Pale Ale

KEITH'S BREWERY, Halifax, Nova Scotia

LAKEPORT BREWING COMPANY, Hamilton, Ontario: Around Ontario Lager, Laker Lager, Premium Lager

MARITIME BEER COMPANY, Halifax, Nova Scotia

NORTHERN BREWERIES, Sault Ste. Marie, Ontario: Thunder Bay Lager, Thunder Bay Light, Brew 55, Edelbrau, Northern Ale, Superior Lager

PICAROONS BREWING COMPANY, Fredericton, New Brunswick: Timber Hog Stout, Irish Red Ale

QUIDI VIDI BREWING COMPANY, St. Johns, Newfoundland

SHAFTEBURY BREWING COMPANY, Vancouver, British Columbia: Rainforest Amber Ale, Cream Ale, Honey Pale Ale

STORM BREWING COMPANY, Vancouver, British Columbia: Red Sky Alt Bier, Midnight Porter, Hurricane India Pale Ale

TALL SHIP ALE COMPANY, Squamish, British Columbia: Tall Ship Ale, Black Ship Ale, Tall Ship Raspberry Ale, Smoked Porter

Thames Valley Brewing Company, London, Ontario: Thames Valley Lager

Tin Whistle Brewing Company, Penticton, British Columbia: Coyote Ale, Black Widow Dark, Rattlesnake ESB

Vancouver Island Brewing Company, Victoria, British Columbia: Victoria Lager, Piper's Pale Ale, Hermann's Bavarian Dark Lager

Whistler Brewing Company, Whistler, British Columbia: Whistler's Mother Pale Ale, Whistler Premium Lager, Black Tusk Ale

Latin America and the Caribbean

The indigenous peoples of Central and South America had been brewing various forms of beer for centuries before the first European colonizers established settlements, and European-style breweries, in the sixteenth century. The Aztecs of Mexico brewed a thick beer using maize as a base and tree sap or other plants for flavoring. The indigenous tribes of Brazil produced dark beers from roots and grains roasted over hardwood fires, and a modern version known as Xingu is brewed today by Cervejaria Cacador. Another traditional South American brew was made from corn kernels, which were chewed into a pulp and then spat into brewing pots, where it was mixed with water and left to ferment.

Although the Spanish conquistadors established breweries in the region, beer-making remained secondary to the distilling of spirits such as tequila until the nineteenth century, when Mexico was briefly part of the Austrian Empire. During that time brewers from Austria and Central Europe introduced several lager styles from that region. The amber-colored Vienna-style lager had the most staying power, and today Mexico is a leading producer of beers based on that dark, malty style, though in a slightly lighter version. Mexico is also known for its very light pilsner-style beers, as exemplified by Corona and Sol, among others, which are served ice-cold and often with a wedge of lime. These pale-golden, sweetish lagers were developed as a refreshing, thirst-quenching beverage for manual laborers, and they are brewed with a proportion of rice and corn to be more affordable. The Mexican brewing industry is dominated by two groups: the Mexico City–based Cerveceria Modelo and the Monterrey-based Moctezuma and Cuauhtémoc. Breweries elsewhere in Central America also brew light pilsners, while in South America some of the more traditional beers, such as the Brazilian black beer, as well as German-style dark beers can also be found.

Golden lagers predominate among the Caribbean nations, but a tradition of stout-brewing reflects the influence of the British Empire in the region during the nineteenth century. Guinness Stout has been brewed in the West Indies since the mid-1800s. Often called tropical stouts, the native stouts of the region are sweeter and less-bitter than Irish dry stout, and they also tend to be higher in alcohol—which has given them a mythic association with enhancing male virility.

MEXICO AND CENTRAL AMERICA

CERVECERIA MODELO
MEXICO CITY, MEXICO

One of Mexico's two brewing giants, Modelo brews lagers that reflect an influence from Vienna-style amber and Munich-style dark lagers, and it also offers light beers more indicative of the American trend. Its main export dark lager is **Negra Modelo** 🍺🍺, which has more of a russet-brown color than the black suggested by the name. It is a smooth lager with chocolatey flavors and falls somewhere between the spiciness of a Vienna lager and the richness of a Münchner dunkel. **Negra Leon** 🍺, produced by Modelo's Yucatan brewery, is a regional offering that is similar to Negra Modelo but slightly hoppier. Modelo is also the brewer of **Corona Extra**, a light-bodied, golden lager that is made with a proportion of corn and rice and few hops. Often served with a slice of lime, Corona is widely exported and is popular in the United States.

CERVECERIA MOCTEZUMA-CUAUHTÉMOC
MONTERREY, MEXICO

The Moctezuma and Cuauhtémoc breweries of Monterrey merged to form Mexico's largest brewing group. Cuauhtémoc's popular **Bohemia** is similar to the pilsners of its namesake region and includes Saaz hops from Bohemia. **Tecate** is the light lager offering from Cuauhtémoc. The Moctezuma brewery's best-known lager is **Dos Equis** 🍺, which displays the reddish-amber color and slightly malty flavor of the traditional Vienna-style lager. Also brewed by Moctezuma are **Carta Blanca** lager and the light-bodied **Sol** and **Superior**, the latter being slightly more flavorful. **Noche Buena** 🍺🍺 is a malty, reddish-brown Christmas beer.

CERVECERIA LA CONSTANCIA
SAN SALVADOR, EL SALVADOR

Among the European-style lagers produced by this Central American brewery are the golden **Pilsner of El Salvador Export Beer**, the hoppy **Suprema Special Beer**, and the dark amber and malty **Noche Buena Special Dark Lager**.

OTHER CENTRAL AMERICAN BREWERIES

BELIZE BREWING COMPANY — BELIZE CITY, BELIZE

CERVECERIA CENTROAMERICANA, Guatemala City, Guatemala

CERVECERIA COSTA RICA, San Jose, Costa Rica: Bavaria Gold

CERVECERIA DEL BARU, David, Panama

CERVECERIA HONDUREÑA, San Pedro Sula, Honduras

CERVECERIA NACIONAL DE PANAMA, Panama City, Panama

CERVECERIA PACIFICO, Mazatlan, Mexico: Pacifico

COMPANIA CERVECERIA DE NICARAGUA, Managua, Nicaragua

SOUTH AMERICA

CERVEJARIA CACADOR
CACADOR, BRAZIL

Cacador only offers one beer, but it is one of Latin America's most interesting and best-selling. **Xingu Black Beer**  is a black-colored lager based on an ancient recipe of the Amazonian Indians, though it is also similar in character to the dark lagers of Kulmbach, Germany. Xingu offers complex malt flavors ranging from sweet to coffee-bitter to licorice-spicy; slight hop flavors also show through.

CERVECERIA BIECKERT
BUENOS AIRES,
ARGENTINA

The lagers produced by this Buenos Aires brewery exhibit a Bohemian and German influence. **Bieckert Pilsner Cerveza** and **Bieckert Especial** are malty lagers.

CERVECERIA POLAR
CARACAS, VENEZUELA

The leading beer of Venezuela comes from Cerveceria Polar. **Polar Lager Beer** is a light-bodied, golden lager that has a balanced hop and malt flavor.

COMPANHIA CERVEJARIA BRAHMA
RIO DE JANEIRO, BRAZIL
Operating several breweries throughout Brazil, this brewery produces the hoppy **Brahma Pilsner** and a maltier lager, **Brahma Chopp Export**. It has also produced a strong **Porter**.

OTHER SOUTH AMERICAN BREWERIES

BANKS BREWING COMPANY, Georgetown, Guyana

BAVARIA, Bogota, Colombia

CERVECERIA AGUILA, Barranquilla, Colombia

CERVECERIA BACKUS & JOHNSTON, Lima, Peru

CERVECERIA BOLIVIANA NACIONAL, La Paz, Bolivia

CERVECERIA CORDOBA, Cordoba, Argentina

CERVECERIA DEL SUR DEL PERU, Arequipa, Peru: Cuzco

CERVECERIA NACIONAL, Caracas, Venezuela: Andes, Cardenal

CERVECERIA PARAGUAY, Asuncion, Paraguay

CERVECERIA TAQUINA, Cochabamba, Bolivia

CERVECERIA Y EMBOTELLADORA AUSTRAL, Punta Arenas, Chile

CERVECERIA Y MALTERIA QUILMES, Buenos Aires, Argentina

CERVEJARIA ASTRO, Fortaleza, Brazil: Astro Lager, Astro Draught

CERVEJARIA KAISER, Sao Paulo, Brazil: Kaiser Gold

CERVEJARIAS REUNIDAS SKOL CARACU, Rio de Janeiro, Brazil

COMPANHIA ANTARCTICA PAULISTA, Sao Paulo, Brazil

COMPAÑIA CERVECERIAS UNIDAS, Santiago, Chile

COMPAÑIA DE CERVEJAS NACIONALES, Guayaquil, Ecuador

FABRICA NACIONALES DE CERVEZA, Montevideo, Uruguay

THE CARIBBEAN

DESNOES & GEDDES
KINGSTON, JAMAICA
Desnoes & Geddes brews a classic example of the tropical stout style that developed in the tropical areas of the British Empire, such as the Caribbean and Southeast Asia. D & G's **Dragon Stout** 🍺 is strong and fairly sweet with a slight chocolate-malty flavor. The golden **Red Stripe** is a full-flavored, hoppy lager with a touch of fruitiness; it is also brewed under license in the United Kingdom.

BANKS BREWERIES
ST. MICHAEL, BARBADOS
This leading Caribbean brewery produces the malty, slightly hoppy, and pale **Banks Lager Beer** and the light **Bajan Lager**.

OTHER CARIBBEAN BREWERIES

BRASSERIES NATIONALES D'HAITI, Port-au-Prince, Haiti

CARIBE DEVELOPMENT COMPANY, Port-of-Spain, Trinidad: Caribe Lager,

Royal Extra Stout

Cerveceria Bohemia, Santo Domingo, Dominican Republic

Cerveceria Modelo, Havana, Cuba

Cerveceria Nacional Dominicana, Santo Domingo, Dominican Republic

Commonwealth Brewery, Nassau, the Bahamas: Kalik, Kalik Gold

Compania Cerveceria International, Havana, Cuba

Grenada Breweries, St. George's, Grenada

St. Vincent Brewery, Kingston, St. Vincent

INDEX

A

Aass Amber, 119
Aass Bock, 119
Aass Bryggeri, 119
Abbaye de Notre Dame d'Orval, 91
Abbaye de Notre Dame de Saint-Remy, 90
Abbaye de Notre Dame de Scourmont-Chimay, 89
Abbey, 48; Dubbel, 66; Tripel, 66
Abbey Dubbel, 165
Abbot Ale, 75
Abbot Invalid Stout, 132
Abbots Extra Double Stout, 132
ABC Extra Stout, 128
Abdij der Trappisten van Westmalle, 91
Abdij St. Sixtus, 91
Abdij van Koningshoeven-Trappisten Bierbrouwerij "De Schaapskool", 97
Abita Amber, 156
Abita Bock, 156
Abita Brewing Co., 155
Abita Christmas Ale, 156
Abita Fallfest, 156
Abita Golden, 156
Abita Red Ale, 156
Abita Wheat, 156
Abro Bryggeri, 120
Abt 12, 91
Abts Trunk, 105
Accra Brewery, 137
Adambier, 165
Adambräu, 110
Additives, 23-24
Adelscott Noir, 87
Adelscott, 87
Adironack Amber, 143
Adnams & Co., 75
Adolph Coors Co., 164
Aecht Schlenkerla Rauchbier, 104
Aerts 1900, 93
Affligem Dobbel, 92
Affligem Noël, 92
Affligem Tripel, 92
Africa, 136-138
Aguila, 122
Aguila Pilsner, 122
Aguila Reserve, 122
Akershus Bryggeri, 119
Alaskan Amber, 164
Alaskan Brewing Co., 163
Alaskan Frontier, 164
Alaskan Pale Ale, 164
Alaskan Smoked Porter, 164
Alaskan Stout, 164
Albani Pilsner, 117
Albani Porter, 117
Aldara Baltijas, 114
Aldara Latvijas, 114
Aldara Luksusa, 114
Aldara Pilzenes, 114
Aldara Porter, 114
Aldara Zelta, 114
Aldaris Bryggeri, 114
Aleyard, 36
Alfa Brouwerij, 96
Alfa Edel Oils, 96

Ali'i Brewing Co., 169
Alimony Ale, 164
Alken-Maes Brewery, 91
Allagash Brewing Co., 145
Alley Cat Amber Ale, 165
Alley Kat Brewing, 175
All-Malt, 128
Alloa Brewery Co., 83
Alpine Lager, 174
Alpine Light, 174
Alt, 39, 65
Althairisch Dunkel, 99
Altbier, 39, 65, 145
Ambar, 122
Amber Ale, 156, 157, 164, 168, 173
Amber Dry, 173
Amber Lager, 158
Ambrée, 86
Amelia Ale, 159
American Amber, 163
American Wheat, 142
American's Original Hefeweizen, 167
Amersfoort Wit, 96
Amstel Light, 97
Anchor Brewing Co., 47, 162
Anchor Porter, 162
Anchor Steam Beer, 162
Anderson Valley Brewing Co., 164
Andrew's Brewing Co., 145
Anheuser-Busch Brewing Co., 150
Anker, 108
Anniversary Ale, 73, 142, 150
Anniversary Amber Ale, 172
Anniversary Bock, 173
Ansells Mild, 74
Aperitif, 51, 52
Appalachian Brewing Co., 142
Appearance, 38
Apple Ale, 152, 174
Apple and Ale, 159
Apples, 24
Apricot Ale, 162
Arab Breweries Co., 137
Arabier, 92
Arcen Bierbrouwerij, 96
Archdruid, 80
Arctic Brewing Co., 175
Arkeil Best Bitter, 173
Armada Ale, 71
Arrowhead Brewing Co., 147
Arthur Guiness & Sons, 84
Arusha Brewery, 137
Asahi Breweries, 125
Asahi Stout, 125
Asahi Super Dry, 125
Asia, 123-128
Asia Brewery, 129
Asia Pacific Breweries, 128
Asmara Brewery, 138
Asparagus, 52
Association of Brewers, 8, 64
Athenian Brewery, 123
Atlanta Brewing Co., 157
Atlantic Brewing Co., 145, 157
Atlantic Coast Brewing, 142
Auburn Ale, 143, 153
August Schell Brewing Co., 149
Augustiner Brauerei, 101
Augustiner Dunkel, 102
Augustiner Hell, 102
Australia, 130-133
Austria, 108-110
Autumn Gold, 151

Aventinus, 106
Avery Brewing Co., 169

B

Bacchus, 94
Bachelor Bitter, 164
Back und Bräu, 108
Baderbräu Bock Beer, 152
Baderbräu Vienna Style Lager, 152
Baffo d'Oro, 121
Bagdad Ale, 165
Bajan Lager, 179
Baltic Region, 113-116
Baltika Brewery, 115
Baltimore Brewing Co., 160
Bananas, 24
Bandersnatch Brewing, 168
Bandon Brewing Co., 170
Banks Breweries, 179
Banks Brewing Co., 179
Banks Lager Beer, 179
Bar Harbor Brewing Co., 145
Barbar, 93
Barbecue, 53, 54
Barley, 16, 17
Barley Boys Brewing Co., 154
Barley Mow, 75
Barley Wine, 40, 65, 144
Barney Flats Oatmeal Stout, 164
Baron's Strong Brew, 128
Bass Ale, 21, 74
Bass Brewers, 70, 74
Batham, 75
Bavaria, 179
Bavaria Bräu, 138
Bavaria Breweries, 96
Bavaria Lager, 96
Bavarian-Style Weizen, 166
Bavik-De-Brabandere, 94
Bayer, 119
Bayern Brewing, 169
Bayerische Staatsbrauerei Weihenstephan, 106
Beach Brewing Co., 160
Beamish & Crawford, 84
Beamish Stout, 84
Bear Ale, 82
Bear Brewing Co., 175
Beck's Beer, 102
Beck's Dark, 102
Beck's Oktoberfest, 102
Bederbräu Pilsner Beer, 152
Beer Buster, 61
Beer purity law. See *Reinheitsgebot*
Beier Brewing Co., 169
Beijing Brewery, 127
Beijing Shuanghesheng Brewery, 127
Belgian Ale, 150
Belgian Red, 152
Belgian Strong Ale, 40, 65
Belgium, 87-95
Belhaven Brewery Co., 82
Belize Brewing Co., 178
Belk's Extra Special Bitter, 164
Bell's Amber, 151
Bell's Kalamazoo Stout, 151
Bell's Pale Ale, 151
Bell's Porter, 151
Belle Hop Porter, 164
Belle-Vue, 91
Bering, 117
Berkshire Brewing Co., 146
Berliner Kindl Brauerei, 102
Berliner Kindl Weisse, 102

Bert Grant's Scottish Ale, 168
Best Bitter, 72
Best Mild Ale, 71
Bialystoku Browar, 115
Biddy Early Brewery, 84
Bieckert Especial, 178
Bieckert Pilsner Cerveza, 178
Bierbrouwerij St. Christoffel, 97
Bière Amoureuse, 86
Bière Blanche, 50, 66
Bière de garde, 40, 65
Bière de Mars, 85, 87
Bière de Noël, 85, 86, 87
Bière des Sans Culottes, 86
Bière du Démon, 86
Big Ben Porter, 168
Big Butt Doppelbock, 151
Big Lamp Brewers, 78
Big River Brewing, 160
Big Rock Brewery, 173
Big Rock Light, 173
Big Strong Ale, 157
Bigfoot Barleywine-Style   Ale, 167
Binding Brauerei, 103
Bird Creek Brewery, 168
Birell, 107
Birmingham Brewing Co., 157
Birra Dreher, 123
Birra Forst, 123
Birra Moretti, 121
Birra Peroni, 122
Birra Poretti, 122
Birra Wührer, 123
Bishop's Finger, 72
Bishops Tipple, 73
Bison Brewing Co., 168
Bitburger Brauerei Th. Simon, 103
Bitburger Drive, 103
Bitburger Light, 103
Bitburger Premium Pils, 103
Bitter, 40, 71, 72, 74, 75, 78, 133;
Best, 65; Extra Special, 65; Ordinary,
65; Mild, 71, 75; Special, 65, 71;
Strong, 65
Black & Tan, 143, 145
Black 47 Stout, 143
Black Adder, 71
Black Amber Ale, 173
Black Bear Amber, 157
Black Bear Brewing Co., 157
Black Bear Golden Honey, 157
Black Bear Grizzly Stout, 157
Black Bear Pale Ale, 157
Black Beer, 41, 65
Black Biddy, 84
Black Butte Porter, 164
Black Cap, 91
Black Draft Beer, 125
Black Hawk Stout, 165
Black Hills Brewing Co., 155
Black Knight ESB, 173
Black Mac Ale, 135
Black Mocha Stout, 158
Black Mountain Brewing Co., 168
Black or black patent malt, 19
Black Rabbit Porter, 165
Black Radish, 159
Black Raven Porter, 158
Black Sheep Best Bitter, 77
Black Sheep Brewery, 77
Black Stout Draft, 126
Black Strap Stout, 164
Black Velvet, 61
Blackdown Porter, 72
Blackened Voodoo, 157

Blackhook Porter, 167
Blackwell Stout, 142
Blanche de Brooklyn, 141
Blanche de Chambly, 174
Blanche Wit, 94
Blond, 86
Blonde Ale, 167
Blond Biddy, 84
Blond Dopplebock, 145
Bloody Brew, 61
Blue Fin Stout, 144
Blue Hen Brewery, 145
Blue Heron Pale Ale, 164, 165
Blue Label, 122, 133
Blue Nile, 138
Blue Paddle Pilsener, 165
Blue Star Wheat Beer, 166
Blueberry Wheat, 157
Boag's Bitter, 132
Boag's Draught, 132
Boag's XXX Ale, 132
Bock, 41, 65; 163, Doppel, 65; Eis,
65; Helles, 65; Mai, 65
Bock Damm, 122
Boddingtons, 78
Boddingtons Draught, 78
Bohannon Brewing Co., 160
Bohemia Regent, 112
Bohemia, 177
Boilermaker, 61
Bokbier, 96
Bombadier Premium Bitter, 76
Boon Rawd Brewery Co., 128
Boont Amber, 164
Border Porter, 159
Borsodi Sorgyar, 115
Borve Brew House, 83
Boskeun, 92
Boston Beer Co.,
Boston Lightship, 141
Bosun's Bitter, 137
Bottles, glass, 31
Bottom-fermenting yeast, 23, 39
Boulder Amber Ale, 167
Boulder Extra Pale Ale, 167
Boulder Porter, 167
Boulder Stout, 167
Boulevard Brewing Co., 154
Boundary Waters Lager, 151
Bourbon Country Stout, 151
Bourgogne de Flanders, 94
Bow Valley Brewing Co., 175
Bowen Ale, 173
Bowen Island Blonde Ale, 173
Bowen Island Brewing Co., 173
Bowen Island Special Bitter, 173
Brains Bitter, 80
Brains Dark Smooth, 80
Brains Dark, 80
Brains Smooth, 80
Brand Bierbrouwerij, 96
Brand Dubbelbock, 96
Brand Pils, 96
Brand Urtyp Pilsner, 96
Brandy snifter, 35
Brasal Bock, 173
Brasal Légère, 173
Brasal Special Amber Lager, 173
Brass Monkey Stout, 131
Brasserie de Granges-sur-Baume, 87
Brasserie Amos, 87
Brasserie Annoeullin, 87
Brasserie Artisanale, 87
Brasserie Brasal, 173
Brasserie Cantillon, 92

Brasserie Castelain, 85
Brasserie d'Achouffe, 91
Brasserie De Brazzaville, 138
Brasserie De Guinea, 138
Brasserie De Logone, 138
Brasserie De Pellas, 138
Brasserie de Saverne, 87
Brasserie de Silly, 93
Brasserie de Tahiti, 135
Brasserie De Troch, 95
Brasserie du Cardinal, 108
Brasserie Dubuisson Freres, 92
Brasserie Dupont, 92
Brasserie Duyck, 86
Brasserie Enfants de Gayant, 86
Brasserie Fischer/Pêcheur, 86
Brasserie Friart, 94
Brasserie Jeanne D'Arc, 87
Brasserie La Binchoise, 94
Brasserie La Choulette, 86
Brasserie Lefebvre, 93
Brasserie McAuslan, 171
Brasserie Meteor, 87
Brasserie Palm, 93
Brasserie Pelforth, 87
Brasserie Portneuvoise, 175
Brasserie Schutzenberger, 87
Brasserie St. Sylvestre, 85
Brasserie Tunisia, 138
Brasseries Du Benin, 138
Brasseries Du Maroc, 138
Brasseries Glacieres, 138
Brasseries Kronenbourg, 87
Brasseries Nationales d'Haiti, 179
Brasseurs, 87
Brasseurs GMT, 175
Brauerei Ayinger, 99
Brauerei Bavaria St. Pauli, 106
Brauerei Beck & Co., 102
Brauerei Feldschlösschen, 108
Brauerei Felsenkeller, 106
Brauerei Fischerstube, 108
Brauerei Fohrenburg, 110
Brauerei Gebrüder Maisel, 105
Brauerei Heller-Trum, Schlenkerla,
104
Brauerei Hirter, 110
Brauerei Hürlimann, 107
Brauerei Löwenbräu, 105, 108
Brauerei Pinkus Müller, 105
Brauerei Schwechat, 110
Brauerei Spezial, 106
Brauerei Stiegl, 110
Brauerei Wieselburg, 110
Bräuhaus Nussdorf, 110
Brauherren Pils, 104
Braumeister, 104
Bräu-Weisse, 99
Bread, Sweet Beer, 60
Breukelen Abbey Ale, 141
Brew Brothers Brewing Co., 175
Brew kettle, 16, 26
Brewer's Choice, 122
Brewery De Block, 94
Brewery Ommegang, 146
Brewery works, 16-17
Brewing process, 24-29
Brewmaster's Brown, 118
Brewpubs, 15, 32-34
Brick Brewing Co., 173
Brick Premium Lager, 173
Brick Red Baron Ale, 173
Bricktown Brewery, 155
BridgePort Amber, 164
BridgePort Brewing Co., 164

Bridgeport Pale Ale, 164
Brigand, 94
Brimstone Brewing Co., 157
Brimstone Stone Beer, 157
Brinkhoff's No.1, 104
Broad Ripple Brewing Co., 153
Broadside Ale, 75
Brock's Extra Stout, 174
Broken English Ale, 142
Brooklyn Black Chocolate Stout, 141
Brooklyn Brewery, 141
Brooklyn Brown Ale, 141
Brooklyn Dry Stout, 141
Brooklyn East India Pale Ale, 141
Brooklyn Lager, 141
Brooklyn Monster Ale, 141
Brooklyn Pennant Pale Ale '55, 141
Brooklyn Pilsner, 141
Brooklyner Weisse, 141
Broughton Brewery, 82
Brouwerij 't IJ, 97
Brouwerij Artois, 94
Brouwerij Bockor, 94
Brouwerij Bosteels, 91
Brouwerij Corsendonk, 94
Brouwerij De Gouden Boom, 94
Brouwerij De Kluis, 92
Brouwerij De Koninck, 92
Brouwerij De Ridder, 97
Brouwerij De Smedt, 92
Brouwerij Frank Boon, 93
Brouwerij Haacht, 94
Brouwerij Het Anker, 94
Brouwerij Huyghe, 94
Brouwerij Liefmans, 90
Brouwerij Lindemans, 93
Brouwerij Moortgat, 90
Brouwerij Riva, 94
Brouwerij Rodenbach, 93
Brouwerij Slaghmuylder, 94
Brouwerij St. Bernardus, 94
Brouwerij St. Jozef, 94
Brouwerij Van Honsebrouck, 94
Brown Ale, 41, 144; 167; American, 65; English, 65; Flemish, 65
Brown malt, 19
Brown Velvet, 61
Bruna, 121
Brune Spéciale, 87
Buckley's Best Bitter, 80
Buckley's Dark Mild, 80
Budels Alt, 96
Budels Brouwerij, 96
Budels Pilsner, 96
Budweiser, 7, 150
Budweiser Budvar, 111
Budweiser BudvarCeske, 111
Buffalo Bill's Brewing Co., 164
Buffalo Brewing Co., 146
Bulgarian Breweries, 115
Bulgarska, 115
Bullet Super Strong, 129
Bullmastiff Brewery, 80
Burly Brown Ale, 151
Burning River Pale Ale, 149
Burton Bridge Brewery, 75
Burtonizing, 21
Burton-on-Trent, 21
Burtonwood Brewery, 79
Busch, 150
Butcombe Brewery, 73

Butser Bitter, 73
Buzzard's Breath Ale, 173
Bydgoszczki Browar, 115

C

Cabo Pale Ale, 159
Calanda Haldengut Brauerei, 108
Caledonian Brewing Co., 81
Caledonian Golden pale, 81
Calgary Amber, 172
California Common, 47, 66
Cambrian Best Bitter, 80
Cambrian Brewery Co., 80
Camerons Brewery Co., 78
Campaign for Real Ale, 15, 69-70
Campbell, Hope & King's Double Amber Ale, 81
CAMRA. See *Campaign for Real Ale*
Canada, 171-176
Canal Street Brewing Co., 153
Cannabis, 21
Cans, 31; aluminum, 30
Canterbury Draught, 134
Canvasback Golden Ale, 173
Cap, metal, 31
Capital Brewing Co., 150
Caramel or crystal malt, 19
Carbine Stout, 133
Carbonade Flamande, 59
Cardinal Brewing Co., 161
Cardinal Lager, 108
Caribe Development Co., 179
Caribbean, 179-180
Carling, 172
Carlsberg Brewery, 23, 117
Carlsberg Let, 117
Carlsberg Pilsner, 117
Carlton and United Breweries, 131
Carlton Cold, 132
Carlton Crown Lager, 132
Carlton D-Ale, 132
Carlton Draught, 132
Carolina Brewery, 160
Carolus Doppelbock, 103
Carta Blanca, 177
Cascade Draught, 131
Cascade Golden Ale, 164
Cascade Head, 165
Cascade Pale Ale, 131
Cascade Premium Lager, 131
Cascade Stout, 131
Casco Bay Brewing Co., 145
Castle Eden Ale, 77
Castle Eden Brewery, 77
Castle Lager, 137
Castle Milk Stout, 137
Castlemaine Extra Dry, 133
Castlemaine Perkins, 133
Catamount Amber Ale, 141
Catamount Brewing Co., 141
Catamount Pale Ale, 141
Catamount Porter, 141
Celebration, 151
Celebration Ale, 167
Celebrator, 99
Celis Brewing Co., 156
Celis Dubbel Ale, 156
Celis Golden Ale, 156
Celis Grand Cru, 156
Celis Pale Bock, 156
Celis Raspberry, 156
Celis White, 156
Central America, 178
Central de Cervejas, 121

Ceres Bryggerierne, 117
Ceres Porter, 117
Ceres Royal Export, 117
Ceres Stout, 117
Cerveceria Aguila, 179
Cerveceria Backus & Johnston, 179
Cerveceria Bieckert, 178
Cerveceria Bohemia, 180
Cerveceria Boliviana Nacional, 179
Cerveceria Cacador, 178
Cerveceria Centroamericana, 178
Cerveceria Cordoba, 179
Cerveceria Costa Rica, 178
Cerveceria del Baru, 178
Cerveceria del Sur del Peru, 179
Cerveceria Hondureña, 178
Cerveceria La Constancia, 178
Cerveceria Moctezuma-Cuauhtémoc, 177
Cerveceria Modelo, 177, 180
Cerveceria Nacional, 179
Cerveceria Nacional
de Panama, 178
Cerveceria Nacional
Dominicana, 180
Cerveceria Pacifico, 178
Cerveceria Paraguay, 179
Cerveceria Polar, 178
Cerveceria Taquina, 179
Cerveceria y Embotelladoria
Austral, 179
Cerveceria y Malteria Quilmes, 179
Cervejaria Astro, 179
Cervejaria Kaiser, 179
Cervejarias Reunidas Skol Caracu, 179
Cerveza Negra, 128
Cervezas Alhambra, 123
Ceylon Brewery, 129
Ch'ti Ambrée, 86
Ch'ti Blonde, 86
Ch'ti Brune, 86
Charger Extra Strong, 129
Charles Wells, 76
Cheese, 51, 52
Cherries, 24
Cherry Beer, 151
Cherry Kriek, 174
Cherry Wheat, 141
Cherryland Brewery, 155
Chibuku Brewery, 138
Chicago Brewing Co., 152
Chicken, 52, 53; with Creamy Beer sauce, 58
Chili, Three-bean, 58
Chilies, 24
Chimay Blanche, 89
Chimay Bleu, 89
Chimay Rouge, 89
China, 126-128
Chinook Pale Ale, 173
Chiswick Bitter, 71
Chocolate, 24
Chocolate malt, 19
Chojugura, 126
Chosun Brewery, 129
Chouffe, 91
Christmas Ale, 71, 73, 119, 142, 149, 151, 159
Christmas Double Bock, 159
Christoffel Blond, 97
Christoffel Robertus, 97
Chu Jiang Brewery, 127
Chuck Wheat Ale, 144
Cinq Cents, 89

Clarity, 39
Classic Brown Ale, 174
Classic, 104, 115
Clausthaler, 103
Clipper City Brewing Co., 157
Clipper City Pale Ale, 157
Clipper City Premium Lager, 157
Cloud Cap Amber Ale, 165
Cloudiness, 39
Cluster hops, 21
Coach House, 79
Cobbold's IPA, 76
Cobra, 129
Cobra Indian Beer, 129
Cocker Hoop, 79
Coeur D'Alene Brewing Co., 169
Coffee Stout, 152
Cold Cock Bock, 133
Cold Cock Porter, 173
Cold Spring Brewing Co., 154
Cold-storing, 13
College, 72
Colonial Stout, 174
Columbus, 97
Columbus Brewing Co., 154
Commodore Perry India Pale Ale, 149
Commonwealth Brewery, 180
Commonwealth Brewing Co., 146
Companhia Antarctica Paulista, 179
Companhia Cervejaria Brahma, 179
Compania Cerveceria de Nicaragua, 178
Compania Cerveceria International, 180
Compañía de Cervecerías Unidas, 179
Compañia de Cervejas Nacionales, 179
Connecticut Ale, 142
Conway's Irish Ale, 149
Cooking with beer, 54-60
Coopers Best Extra Stout, 132
Coopers Brewery, 132
Coopers Dry Beer, 132
Coopers Genuine Draught, 132
Coopers Light, 132
Coopers Original Pale Ale, 132
Coopers Sparkling Ale, 132
Cooperstown Brewing Co., 147
Coors, 7, 30. See Also *Adolph Coors Co.*
Cordial, 36
Corn, 18, 23
Corolla Gold, 159
Corona Light, 177
Cotleigh Brewery, 73
Cottage Brewing Co., 73
Cottrell Brewing Co., 145
County Ale, 173
Courage Best Bitter, 82
Craft-brewing, 32-34
Craftsman, 79
Cranberry Lambic, 141
Crane River Brewpub and Cafe, 154
Cran-N-Cherry, 163
Cream Ale, 42, 65, 143, 172
Cream Stout, 140
Creemore Springs Brewery, 173
Creemore Springs Premium Lager, 173
Creemore urBock, 173
Crescent City Brewhouse, 160
Cristal Alken Pils, 91
Crooked river Brewing Co., 154
Crosley's Red Ale, 158

Crouch Vale Brewery, 76
Crown Buckley Brewery, 80
Crown Pale Ale, 80
Cruz del Campo, 123
Crystal Ale, 165
Crystal Lager, 112
Cuivrée, 87
Cumberland Ale, 79
Cuvée de Koninck, 92
Cwrw Castell, 80
Czech Republic, 110-113

D

D.G. Yuengling & Son Brewery, 145
D.L. Geary Brewing Co., 142
DAB Export, 104
DAB Meister Pils, 104
Dahl's Pils, 119
Dakota Brewing Co., 154
Dallas County Brewing Co., 153
Damm, 122
Dampfbier, 105
Daniel Thwaites, 79
Dark 13, 112
Dark Ale, 132
Dark Ice, 133
Dark Island, 82
Dark Mild, 75
DB Bitter, 134
DB Draught, 134
DB Export Dry, 134
DB Gold, 133
De Dolle Brouwers, 92
De Drie Ringen Brouwerij, 96
De Koninck, 92
De Kroon Bierbrouwerij, 98
De Lindeboom Bierbrouwerij, 98
Deacon, 73
Dead Guy Ale, 163
Deependers Dark Porter, 164
Definitions, 64-66
Denmark, 116-117
Depth Charge, 62
Deschutes Brewery's Black Butte Porter, 8
Deschutes Brewing Co., 164
Desnoes & Geddes, 179
Desserts, 53, 54; creamy, 53, 54; Fruit, 53, 54
Detroit & Mackinac Brewery, 153
Deuchar's IPA, 81
Devil's Elbow IPA, 158
Diamond Draught, 132
Diebels Alt, 103
Digestif, 53, 54
Dilworth Microbrewery, 160
Divine, 93
Dixie Brewing Co., 157
DL Lager, 133
Dobbel Palm, 93
Dock Street Amber Ale, 142
Dock Street Barley Wine, 142
Dock Street Brewing Co., 142
Dock Street Illuminator Double Bock, 142
Dogbolter, 131
Dogwood Brewing Co., 160
Dominion Ale, 158
Dominion Breweries, 134
Dominion Lager, 158
Dominion Millenium, 158
Dominion Octoberfest, 158
Dominion Spring Bock, 158
Dominion Stout, 158
Dommelsche Bierbrouwerij, 98

Donnington Brewery, 73
Doppel Bock, 150
Doppelbock, 167, 168
Doppelmalz, 110
Doppo, 126
Dorchester Bitter, 72
Dort, 97
Dortmunder, 42, 65
Dortmunder Actien Alt, 104
Dortmunder Actien Brauerei (DAB), 104
Dortmunder Export, 42, 65
Dortmunder Gold, 149
Dortmunder Hansa Export, 104
Dortmunder Kronen Brauerei, 104
Dortmunder Union Brauerei, 104
Dos Equis, 177
Double Brown, 134
Double Diamond, 74
Double Dragon Ale, 80
Double Enghien Blond, 93
Double Enghien Brune, 93
Doubleblack Stout, 167
Downtown Brown, 165
Dr Johnson's Draught, 80
Dragon Bitter, 80
Dragon Dark, 80
Dragon Stout, 179
Dragonhead Stout, 82
Draught, 133
Draught Bass, 74
Draught Guiness, 84
Dreher Export, 114
Dreher Bak, 114
Dreher Pils, 114
Dreikönigs, 108
Drink recipes, 61-63
Dry hopping, 20
DUB Export, 104
Dubbel, 97
Dubuque Brewing Co., 153
Dunedin Brewery , 160
Dunkel, 42, 145
Dunkel Export, 101
Dunkel Weisen, 166
Dunkel Weiss, 167
Dunkel Weissbier, 104, 106
Dunkle Perle, 108
Düsseldorfer Alt Bier, 152
Duster's Microbrewery, 153
Duvel, 90
Dyffryn Clwyd Brewery, 80

E

E. Smithwick & Sons, 84
Eagle Blue Ice, 133
Eagle Super, 133
East Anglia, 75-76
Eastern Europe, 113-116
Eastside Dark, 151
Eau Bénite, 174
EB Special Pils, 114
Edel Pils, 152
Edelhell, 104
Edelpils, 106
Edgefield Wheat, 165
Edinburgh Strong Ale, 81
Edmund Fitzgerald Porter, 149
Efes Pilsen Breweries, 123
Eggenberg Märzen, 109
Eggenberg Spezial Dunkel, 109
Egyptians, 11, 12
Eichbaum Brauerei, 106
Eichhof, 108
Eight Ball Stout, 165

1857 Bitter, 133
1857 Pilsner, 133
1859 Porter, 71
80/Export Ale, 81, 82
Einbecker Bräuhaus, 104
Eisbock, 145
Elblagu Browar, 114
Eldridge Pope & Co., 72
Elephant Beer, 117
Elgood & Sons, 76
Elizabethan, 71
Elliot Ness, 149
Elm City Brewing Co./New Haven
  Brewing Co., 142
Elysian Brewery, 170
Emerson Brewing Co., 135
Empressa de Cerveja de Madeira,
  123
EMU Bitter, 133
EMU Draft, 133
EMU Export, 133
Endangered Ale, 159
England, 69-79
Enkel, 97
Entire Stout, 73
Equinox E.S.B., 164
Erdinger Pinkantus, 104
Erdinger Weissbräu, 104
ESB Red Ale, 158
ESB, 71, 164
Eske's: A Brew Pub, 170
ESP Lager, 166
Essex Brewing Co., 145
Estrella Damm, 122
Eumundi Brewing, 133
Europa Beer, 121
Evansville Brewing Co., 153
Excel NA, 172
Exmoor Ales, 73
Export, 104, 122, 133
Export Dunkel, 106
Extra, 91
Extra Light, 151
Extra Old Stock Ale, 172
Extra Pale Ale, 151
Extra Strong, 120
Extra Strong Brew, 137
Extra Strong Vintage Ale, 132

F
F.X. Matt Brewing Co., 143
Fabrica de Cerveza de san Miguel,
  128
Fabrica Nacionales de Cerveza, 179
Fair Ale, 82
Falken Bryggeri, 120
Fargo Strong Ale, 76
Farmer's Glory, 73
Farmington River Brewing Co., 145
Faro, 92
Fat Tire Amber Ale, 165
Faxe Bryggeri, 117
Felinfoel Brewing Co., 80
Fermentation tank, 26
Fest, 159
Fest Bier, 150
Festival Ale, 82
Festival Best Mild, 73
Filtration, 30
Finland, 118
Finnigan's Red, 173
Firehouse Brewing Co., 155
First Lady, 124
Fischer Bitter, 86
Fischer Gold, 86

Fish Brewing Co., 170
Fish, 52
Flanagan & Sons Brewing Co., 175
Flanders Winter Ale, 85
Flat Branch Brewing Co., 154
Flekovsky Lezek, 112
Floreffe Dobbel, 93
Floreffe La Meilleure, 93
Floreffe Tripel, 93
Florida Brewery, 160
Flute, stemmed beer, 35
Flying Fish Brewing Co., 146
Food, 51-60
Foreign Extra Stout, 84
Forester's Draught Lager, 137
Foret, 92
Forschungs Brauerei, 106
Fort Garry Brewing Co., 175
Foster's Ice, 132
Foster's Lager, 132
Foster's Light, 132
Foster's Special Bitter, 132
Framboise, 91, 92, 93, 94
Frambozen Raspberry Brown Ale,
  165
Frambozenbier, 90
France, 85-87
Frankenmuth Brewery, 151
Franziskaner Club-Weissbier, 101
Franziskaner Hefe-Weissbier, 101
Franziskaner Hefe-Weissbier
  Dunkel, 101
Fred, 165
Frederic Robinson, 79
Frederick Brewing Co., 158
Free State Brewing Co., 153
Freemantle Bitter, 131
French onion soup, 56
Friesisches Bräuhaus, 106
Frio Brewing Co., 161
Frostbite, 167
Frydenlund Pilsener, 119
Fuel Cafe
  Coffee-Flavored Stout, 151
Fuggles hop, 21
Fuggles Imperial IPA, 77
Fuggles IPA, 144
Full Sail Brewing Co., 164
Fuller, Smith & Turner, 71
Fuller's 1845, 71
Fürstenberg Brauerei, 106
Fürstliche Brauerei Thurn und
  Taxis, 106

G
Gaelic Ale, 158
Gambrinus 12, 112
Gambrinus Brewery, 112
Game, 52, 53
Garten Bräu Brown Ale, 151
Garten Bräu Dark, 150
Garten Bräu Raspberry Wheat, 151
Garten Bräu Special, 150
Garten Bräu Weizen, 150
Garten Bräu Wisconsin Amber,
  150
GB Best Bitter, 73
GB Mild, 79
Geelong Brewing Co., 133
Genesee Bock, 143
Genesee Brewing Co., 143
Genuine Bock, 151
George Bateman & Sons, 75
George Gale & Co., 73
George Killian's Irish Red Lager,

164
German-Style Bock, 151
German-Style Dark, 151
German-Style Pilsner, 151
Germany, 98-107
Geyser Gold, 163
GFB Bitter, 73
Ghillie, 82
Gibbs Mew, 73
Ginger, 24
Ginger Beer, 62
Giraf, 117
Glassware, 35-36
Goat Island Light, 144
Goblets, 36
Godisgood, 22
Gold, 133,
Gold Eagle, 128
Gold Fassl Pils, 109
Gold Fassl Spezial, 109
Gold Roggen, 110
Golden Ale, 158, 164
Golden Bock, 168
Golden Eagle Lager, 129
Golden Pacific Brewing Co., 168
Golden Pilsner, 141, 143
Golden Prairie Brewing, 151
Golden Pride Strong Ale, 71
Golden Rose, 165
Goldings hop, 21
Goose Island Brewing Co., 151
Gordon Biersch Brewing Co., 169
Gösser Brauerei, 109
Gösser Export, 109
Gösser Gold, 109
Gösser Märzen, 109
Gösser Spezial, 109
Gotenba Kohgen Brewery, 126
Goudale, 86
Goudenbrand, 90
Graduate, 72
Granat 12, 112
Grand Cru, 92
Grand Prestige, 96
Grand Réserve, 89
Grand Ridge Brewing Co., 133
Grande Brasserie Moderne, 87
Grandma's Summertime 'Strip Me
  Naked', 62
Granite Brewery, 175
Granville Island Brewing Co., 172
Grasshöpper, 173
Gray Brewing Co., 155
Great Divide Brewing Co., 169
Great Lakes Brewing Co., 149
Great Lakes Brewing Co., 175
Great Northern Brewing Co., 169
Great Northern Porter, 152
Great Western Brewing Co., 175
Greek Brewery, 123
Greeks, 12
Green beer, 29
Green Cap, 90
Green malt, 18
Greene King, 75
Greenmantle Ale, 82
Grenada Breweries, 180
Griffon Brown Ale, 171
Griffon Extra Pale Ale, 172
Grimbergen, 91
Grist, 24
Gritstone premium Ale, 174
Gritty McDuff's Brew Bub, 146
Grolsch Amber Ale, 96
Grolsch Bierbrouwerij, 95

Grolsch Premium Lager, 96
Grolsch Summerblond, 96
Guangzhou Brewery, 127
Gueuze, 92, 93
Gueuze Caveau, 94
Gueuze Cuvée René, 93
Guiness Extra Stout, 84
Guinness Brewery, 22, 26, 28. See also *Arthur Guinness & Sons*
Gulder, 137
Gulpener Bierbrouwerij, 96
Gymkhana Pilsner, 129

H

H. C. Berger Brewing Co., 169
Haake Beck Non-Alcoholic, 102
Hacker-Pschorr Bräu, 104
Hahn Brewing Co., 133
Hair of the Dog Brewing Co., 165
Hale's Ales, 170
Hallertau hop, 21
Hamburgers, 53
Hammerhead Ale, 165
Hampshire Glory, 73
Hampshire Special Ale, 142
Hanby Ales, 75
Hancock Brewery, 80
Hancock's HB, 80
Hangzhou Zhongce Brewery, 127
Hannen Brauereu, 106
Hansa Bayer, 119
Hansa Bryggeri, 119
Hansa Export 01, 119
Hansa Premium Pilsner, 119
Hansen, Emil, 23
Harboes Bryggeri, 117
Hardy Stout, 173
Hardys & Hansons, 75
Harp Export, 84
Harpoon Ale, 143
Harpoon India Pale Ale , 143
Harpoon Light, 143
Harpoon Munich Dark, 143
Harpoon Pilsner, 143
Harrington's, 135
Hart Brewing Co., 173
Hart Cream Ale, 173
Hart Festive Brown, 173
Hartwall Brewery, 118
Harvest Ale, 79, 143, 173
Harvey & Son, 71
Harviestoun Brewery, 83
Hawkes Bay Draught, 135
Haystack Black Porter, 166
HazelNut Brown Nectar, 163
Head, 37
Hearty Ale, 164
Hefe Weiss, 150
Hefe Weissbier, 104
Hefeweissbier, 106
Hefeweizen, 100, 151, 152, 162, 163, 165, 168
Heimertingen Maibock, 152
Heineken, 97
Helles, 42
Helles Alt Beer, 143
Helles Gold, 144
Hempen Ale, 158
Henninger Brauerei, 106
Henry's Original IPA, 73
Hereweizen, 145
Herold Wheat, 112
Hevelius Browar, 116
Hex Nut Brown Ale, 151
Hexen Bräu, 107

Hickory Switch Smoked Amber Ale, 143
High Rollers Wheat Beer, 164
HighFalls Brewing Co., 147
Highgare Brewery, 74
Highgate Dark Mild, 74
Highgate Old Ale, 74
Highland Brewing Co., 158
Hildegarde, 13
Hilden Ale, 84
Hilden Brewery, 84
Hilden Special reserve, 84
Hill Country Brewing, 161
History, 11-15
Hoboken Brewing Compnay, 146
Hoegaarden Witbier, 92
Hogs Back Brewery, 72
Hogsback Oatmeal Stout, 165
Holan 10, 112
Holden's Brewery Co., 75
Holiday Spice, 151
Holsten Brauerei, 104
Holsten Export, 104
Holsten Pils, 104
Holsten Premium Beer, 104
Holy Grail Nut Brown Ale, 158
Holy Moses, 149
Home Bitter, 82
Home-brewing, 15, 32-34
Honey, 24
Honey Dew Spring Ale, 71
Honey Lager, 173
Honey Porter, 140
Honey Red, 157
Honey Weiss, 151
Honey Wheat, 157, 166
Hong Kong Brewery, 128
Honker's Ale, 151
Hook Norton Brewery, 72
Hop Back Brewery, 73
Hop Jack Pale Ale, 168
Hop Leaf, 122
Hop Otten India Pale Ale, 164
Hope Brewing Co., 147
Hopfen König, 109
Hopfenbier, 96
Hopfenperle, 108, 110
Hopfest, 143
HopFest, 158
Hopps Bräu, 173
Hops, 16, 19-21, 26
Hops Grill and Bar, 160
Horn of the Beer Barley Wine, 164
Horseshoe Bay Brewing Co., 175
Hudepohl Schoenling Brewing Co., 154
Hue Brewery, 129
Humboldt Brewing Co., 169
Humulus lupulus. See *Hops*
Hungarian Breweries, 115
Hunter's Lager, 137
Hydes' Anvil Brewery, 79

I

Ice Axe India Pale Ale, 165
Ice Beer, 108
Iceland, 120
Imperator, 96
Imperial, 121
Imperial Porter, 164
Imperial Russian Stout, 77
Imperial Stout, 77, 144, 150, 163, 168, 173
Ind Coope Burton Brewery, 74
Ind Coope's Burton Ale, 74

Independent Breweries, 135
India Pale Ale, 43, 65, 134, 150, 151, 152, 157, 163, 164, 168
Indian food, 53, 54
Indianapolis Brewing Co., 153
Industrial Revolution, 15, 31
International Bitterness Unit, 38, 64
International Brasserie, 138
Internet, 33
Ipswich Brewing Co., 146
Ireland, 83-85
Irish, 43, 65
Irish Honey Cream Ale, 158
Irish Red Ale, 43, 65
Irish Stout, 150
Iron Duke, 172
Iron Duke Porter, 173
Iron Range Amber Lager, 151
Irseer Klosterbräu, 105
Island Bock, 172
Island Lager, 172
Island Light, 172
Italian Breweries, 123

J

J. Boag & Son Brewing, 132
J. W. Lees & Co., 79
Jack Daniel's Brewery, 160
Jacob Leinenkugel Brewing Co., 151
Jacobite Ale, 82
Jade, 86
James Boag's Premium Lager, 132
James Page Brewing Co., 151
Japan, 124-126
Jazz Amber Light, 158
Jean I, Duke of Brabant, 12
Jenlain, 86
Jennings Bitter, 79
Jennings Brothers, 79
Jinro Coors Brewery, 129
John Labatt Classic, 174
John Smith's Brewery, 77
Jolly Jack Tar Porter, 80
Jolly Scot Scottish Ale, 142
Jones Brewing Co., 147
Jones Street Brewery, 154
Joseph Holt, 78
Joseph Huber Brewing Co., 155
Jouloulot, 118
Jubelale, 164
Jubilator, 87
Jubilator Doppelbock, 144
Julius, 92
Julöl, 120
JV Northwest, 8

K

Kaiser Bock, 110
Kaiser Märzen, 110
Kaiser Pils, 144
Kaiser Premium, 110
Kalamazoo Brewing Co., 151
Kalnapilis, 115
Kaltenberg Pils, 105
Kalyani Black Label Premium Strong Beer, 129
Kane's Amber Ale, 82
Kanizsai Sorgyar, 115
Karmen la Bella, 115
Kasteelbier, 94
Kawartha Lakes Brewing Co., 175
KB Lager, 131
Kegs, 32
Keith's Brewery, 175
Kent Old Brown Ale, 131

Kenya Breweries, 136
Kessler Brewing Co., 169
Kgalagadi Brewers, 138
Khan Bräu, 127
Kilgubbin Red Ale, 151
Kilkenny's Irish Beer, 84
Kindl Pils, 102
Kindl Schwarzbier, 102
King & Barnes, 72
King Cobra, 150
Kingfisher, 129
Kingfisher Diet, 129
Kirin Alt, 125
Kirin Beer, 125
Kirin Black, 125
Kirin Brewery Co., 125
Kirin Ichiban, 125
Kirin Light, 125
Kirin Stout, 125
Kirishima Highland Brewery, 126
Kiwi Lager, 134
Klassic Alter Ale, 151
Klisch Pilsner, 151
Kloster Urtunk, 105
Klosterbrauerei Weltenburg, 106
Knights of the Mashing Fork, 12
Knots of May Light Mild, 71
Kobanyai Sorgyar, 114
Koff Export Beer, 118
Koff Extra Strong, 118
Koff Porter, 118
Kölsch, 43, 65
Komaromi Sorgyar, 115
Kona Brewing Co., 169
König Brauerei, 106
König Ludwig Dunkel, 105
Königsbacher Brauerei, 106
Korbinian Dunkels Starkbier, 106
Korenwolf, 97
Kosel Dark, 112
Köstritzer Schwarzbierbrauerei, 106
Kozel Pale, 112
Kozel Premium Lager, 112
Kozel Special Dark Beer, 112
Kräusening, 29
Kreuger Brewing Co., 30
Kriek, 91, 92, 93, 94
Kriekbier, 90
Kristall Weissbier, 104
Kristall Weizen, 105
Kristallweissbier, 106
Kronen Pils, 104
Kronenbourg, 87
Kronenbourg 1664, 87
Kronenbourg 1664 Brune, 87
Küppers Kölsch, 105
Küppers Wiess, 105
Kutscher Alt, 103
Kwak, 91
Kylian, 97

L

La Fin du Monde, 174
La Gaillarde, 174
La Maudite, 174
La Quelque Chose, 174
Labatt "50" Ale, 174
Labatt Blue, 174
Labatt Brewing Co., 174
Labatt Extra Dry, 174
Labatt Genuine Draft, 174
Labatt Ice, 174
Labatt Select, 174
Lacto Milk Stout, 122
Lager, 29; American, 66; American

Amber, 66; American Dark, 66;
American Dry, 66; American Light,
66, American Premium, 66
Lager or pilsner malt, 18
Lager yeast. See *Bottom-fermenting
yeast*
Lagering, 13
Lake Superior Brewing Co., 154
Lakefront Brewery, 151
Lakeport Brewing Co., 175
Lamb, 52
Lambic, 22, 43, 65; Faro, 44;
Framboise, 23, 44; Fruit, 44;
Gueuze, 44, 65; Kriek, 23, 44
Lao Brewery Co., 129
Lapin Kulta, 118
Latrobe Brewing Co., 147
Laughing Skull Bohemian Pilsner,
157
Leann Fraoch, 82
Lees Bitter, 79
Left Hand Brewing Co., 169
Legend Brewing Co., 161
Legend Stout, 137
Leinenkugel's Original, 151
Lemons, 24
Leningrad Cowboy, 118
Lente Bok, 96
Leopard Black Label, 135
Liberty Ale, 162
Licorice, 24
Lift Bridge Brewing Co., 154
Light, 133
Lime and Lager, 62
Lind Brewing Co., 169
Lion, 129
Lion Brewing Co., 147
Lion Brown, 134
Lion Ice, 134
Lion Lager, 137
Lion Light Ice, 134
Lion Nathan, 134
Lion Red, 134
Lion Stout, 129
Live Oak Brewing Co., 161
Lobkowicz Pivovar, 113
Locher, 108
London, 70-72
London Porter, 71
London Pride, 71
London Style Porter, 142
Longfellow Winter Ale, 144
Lord Chesterfield Ale, 145
Lord Granville Pale Ale, 172
Lord Nelson, 133
Lost Coast Brewery, 165
Lost Coast Pale Ale, 165
Lucky Labrador Brew Pub, 170
Lutèce, 86
Luxembourg, 95

M

Maasland Brouwerij, 98
Mac Extra, 135
Mac's Ale, 135
MacAndrew's Stock Ale, 81
Macardle Brewery, 85
Mack Artic Artic Pils, 119
Mack Bayer, 119
Mack Polar Beer, 119
Macks Olbryggeri, 119
Maday & Co., 82
MacQueen's Nessie, 109
MacTarnahan's Amber Ale, 166

Mad River brewing Co., 169
Maes Pils, 91
Magic Hat Brewing Co., 147
Magnet Mild, 77
Magpie Rye Ale, 173
Mahou, 123
Maibock, 99, 137, 144, 150
Maierbock, 163
Maisel's Pilsner, 105
Maisel's Weiss, 105
Makos, 134
Mallasjuoma, 118
Malt, 16, 17-19, 24
Malt and Hops, 73
Malt Liquor, American, 66
Malt producers, 17
Maltezer, 97
Malting process, 18
Malton Brewing Co., 78
Malt's, 126
Mamba Bock, 137
Mamba Lager, 137
Manchester Gold, 78
Mansfield Brewery, 75
Maple Wheat, 174
Maredsous 6, 90
Maredsous 8, 90
Maredsous 10, 90
Mariage Parfait, 93
Maritime Beer Co., 175
Maritime Pacific Brewing Co., 170
Marlborough Brewing Co., 135
Marston, Thompson & Evershed,
74
Martens Brewery, 93
Marthasville Brewing Co., 160
Märzen, 44, 65, 157
Mash, 25
Mash Tun, 16, 25
Master Brew Bitter, 72
Matilda Bay Bitter, 131
Matilda Bay Pils, 131
Matilda Bay Premium, 131
Matthew Brown Dark Mild, 82
Mauldon Special Bitter, 71
Mauldons Brewery, 71
May Day, 75
McAuslan Apricot Wheat Ale, 172
McAuslan Strong Ale, 172
McCallum Breweries, 129
McCashin's Brewery and
Malthouse, 135
McChouffe, 91
McEwan 70/, 82
McEwan 90/, 82
McEwan's 80/, 82
McEwan's Export, 82
McEwan's Scotch Ale, 82
McFarlane Brewing Co., 168
McMenamins Brothers Breweries,
165
McMenamins Brothers'
Hammerhead Ale, 8
McMullen & Sons, 72
McNally's Extra Irish-Style Ale, 173
McNeill's Brewery, 147
McRogue Scotch Ale, 163
Medieval Europe, 12
Meibok, 96, 97
Melbourne Bitter, 132
Mendocino Brewing Co., 165
Merlin's Ale, 82
Merman XXX, 81
Mesopotamia, 16
Mestreechs Aajt, 97

Meta Brewery, 138
Mexicali Rogue, 163
Mexican food, 53, 54
Mexico, 177
Miabock, 104
Miami Brewing Co., 160
Michelob, 150
Microbreweries, 15, 32-34
Middle East, 136-138
Midlands, 73-75
Midnight Sun Brewing Co., 168
Mikrobryggeri, 119
Mild, 72, 78
Mild ale or Vienna malt, 19
Mild Ale, 44; Dark, 65; Pale, 65
Mill City/Lowell Brewing Co., 146
Miller, 7
Miller Brewing Co., 151, 152
Miller Genuine Draft, 152
Miller High Life, 152
Miller Lite, 152
Millstream Brewing Co., 153
Milwaukee Pilsner, 150
Minnesota Brewing Co., 154
Mirade Brewing Co., 153
Mirror Pond Pale Ale, 164
Mishawaka Brewing Co., 153
Mitchell's Brewery, 137
Mitchell's of Lancaster, 79
Mo Ale, 163
Mocha Porter, 163
Mocne, 115
Mogul Ale, 163
Moham Meakin, 129
Moinette Blond, 92
Moinette Brune, 92
Moku Moku, 126
Molasses, 24
Molson Breweries, 172
Molson Canadian Light, 172
Molson Export, 172
Molson Golden, 172
Molson Ice, 172
Molson Light, 172
Molson Red Jack, 172
Molson Special Dry, 172
Monasteries, 13
Monteith's Extra Bitter Brown Ale, 134
Moon Dog Ale, 149
Moonraker, 79
Moorhouse's Brewery, 79
Moosehead Breweries, 174
Moosehead Lager Beer, 174
Moosehead Light, 174
Moosehead Pale Ale, 174
Morland, 72
Morrells Brewery, 71
Mort Subite, 91
Moscovskoye Brewery, 116
Mountain Berry Ale, 143
Mountain Brewers, 148
Moussy, 108
Mt. Angel Brewing Co., 170
Mt. Angel Oktoberfest, 166
Mt. Hood Brewing Co., 165
Mud Bock Spring Ale, 143
Münchner Dunkel, 42, 65, 100, 105
Münchner Helles, 42, 65, 105
Münchner Oktoberfest, 105
Muree, 129
Murphy Brewery, 84
Murphy's Irish Red Beer, 84
Murphy's Irish Stout, 84
Murray's Heavy, 81

Mystic Microbrewery, 145

N
Namibian Breweries, 137
Nastro Azzurro, 122
Natte, 97
Nebraska Bitter, 165
Negra Leon, 177
Negra Modelo, 177
Neptune Brewery, 147
Nesbitt Brewery, 137
Nethergate Brewery Co., 76
Netherlands, 95-98
New Amsterdam Ale, 143
New Amsterdam Amber, 143
New Amsterdam Blonde Lager, 143
New Amsterdam Brewing Co., 143
New Belgian Brewing Co., 165
New England Atlantic Amber, 143
New England Brewing Co., 143
New England Gold Stock Ale, 143
New England Holiday Ale, 143
New England Light Lager, 143
New England Oatmeal Stout, 143
New Glarus Brewing Co., 152
New Hampshire Custom Brewers, 146
New Holland Brewing Co., 153
New Zealand, 130, 134-135
Newbegin Brewery, 135
Newcastle Brown Ale, 82
Niagara Eisbock, 174
Niagara Falls Brewing Co., 174
Nigerian Breweries, 137
Nile Breweries, 137
Nile Special Lager, 137
Ninkasi, 12
Noche Buena Special Dark Lager, 178
Noche Buena, 177
Nor'Easter, 143
Nor'Wester Best Bitter, 166
Nor'Wester Brewery, 166
Norrlands Gold, 120
Norski Maibock, 152
North Coast Brewing Co., 166
Northeast England, 76-78
Northeast US, 140-148
Northern Brewer hop, 21
Northern Breweries, 175
Northern Lights Bock, 151
Northern Lights Brewing Co., 170
Northwest England, 78-79
Northwoods Lager, 151
Norway, 119
Nut Brown Ale, 164
Nutfield Brewing Co., 143
Nuttrageous Brown Ale, 158

O
O'Douls, 150
O'Keefe Ale, 172
Oak Brewing Co., 79
Oak Creek Brewing Co., 168
Oat Malt Stout, 82
Oatmeal Porter, 158
Oatmeal Stout, 71, 77, 82, 142, 151
Oats, 18
OBJ, 71
Obolon Brewery, 116
Obsidian Stout, 164
Octoberfest, 142
Odell Brewing Co., 169
Oerbier, 92
Ohlsson's Lager, 137

Okanagan Spring Brewery, 174
Okocim Browar, 114
Okocim Porter, 115
Okocim Premium Pils, 115
Oktoberfest, 44, 65, 100, 141, 143, 143, 144, 149, 150, 151, 159, 163, 164, 166, 167, 168
Oktober Fest-Märzen, 99
Oktoberfest Märzen, 104
Oktoberfest Ur-Märzen, 101
Old Ale, 44, 65, 75
Old Bawdy Barley Wine, 166
Old Black Ale, 133
Old Boardhead Barleywine Ale, 164
Old Brown Dog, 144
Old Cherry Ale, 165
Old Crustacean Barleywine, 163
Old Dominion Brewing Co., 158
Old East India Pale Ale, 144
Old Foghorn, 162
Old Gold, 120
Old Gollywobber Brown Ale, 144
Old Jack Bitter Strong Ale, 174
Old Jock, 82
Old Knucklehead Barley Wine, 164
Old Man Ale, 143
Old Nick, 71
Old No. 38 Stout, 166
Old Rasputin Russian Imperial Stout, 166
Old Saddleback Brewing Co., 146
Old Scratch Barley Wine, 142
Old Stout, 133
Old Thumper Extra Special Ale, 144
Old Timer, 73
Old Vienna, 172
Old Winter Ale, 71
Olde English Porter, 174
Olde Irish Style Ale, 158
Olde Towne Tavern & Brewery, 160
Olde Wyndham Brewery, 145
Oldenberg Blonde, 158
Oldenberg Brewing Co., 158
Oldenberg Devil's Back Black Oatmeal Stout, 158
Oldenberg Oktoberfest Lager, 158
Oldenberg Outrageous Bock, 158
Oldenberg Premium Verum, 158
Oldenberg Winter Ale, 158
Olvi Brewery, 118
Onalaska Brewing Co., 170
Onix, 121
Op Ale, 92
Optimator, 101
Orang Utan Brewery and Pub, 129
Oranges, 24
Oranjeboom Bierbrouwerij, 97
Oranjeboom Oud Bruin, 97
Oranjeboom Pils, 97
Oregon Amber, 166
Oregon Brewer's Guild, 8
Oregon Brown Ale, 166
Oregon Golden Ale, 163
Oregon Honey Beer, 166
Oregon Pale Ale, 166
Oregon Trader Brewing Co., 170
Oregon Trail Ale, 166
Oregon Trail Brewery, 166
Oregon Trail Stout, 166
Oregon Trail White Ale, 166
Organic Extra Special Bitter, 151
Oriental Brewing Co., 130
Original, 115
Original Draft Black Label, 125
Original Münchner Hell, 100

Original Porter, 72
Orion Breweries, 126
Orkney Brewery, 82
Orval Trappist Ale, 91
Otaru, 126
Ottakringer Bock, 109
Ottakringer Brauerei, 109
Ottakringer Helles Bier, 109
Otter Creek Brewing Co., 143
Otto Brothers' Brewing, 170
Oud Bruin, 90
Ould Newberry Brewing Co., 146
Our Special Ale, 162
Owd Roger, 74
Oxford Brewing Co., 158
Oxford Class Ale, 158
Oxford IPA, 158
Oxford Piccadilly Porter, 158
Oxford Raspberry Wheat, 158
Oxford Real Ale, 158
Oxford S.O.B. (Special Old Bitter), 158
Oxford Santa Claus, 158
Oxmoor Brewing Co., 159
Oyster Stout, 74
Ozark Brewing Co., 159

P

Pale 10, 12, 112
Pale Ale, 44, 142, 143; 174, American, 65; Belgian, 65; English, 65
Pale Ale Malt, 18
Pale Bock, 167
Palm Spéciale, 93
Pancakes, beer-batter, 56
Parel, 96
Park Slope Brewing Co., 147
Pasteur, Louis, 13, 15
Pasteurization, 30
Patriator, 87
Paulaner Salvator Thomas Bräu, 99
Pavichevich Brewing Co., 152
Peche, 93, 94
Pedigree, 74
Pedwar Bawd, 80
Pembroke Brewery Co., 80
Penn Dark, 144
Penn Pilsner, 144
Pennsylvania Brewing Company, 144
Perfect Porter, 168
Pertotale Faro, 93
Pete's Brewing Co., 33, 166
Pete's Wicked Ale, 166
Picaroons Brewing Co., 175
Pike Brewery, 166
Pike Pale Ale, 166
Pike's Pike Brewery, 169
Pilgrim Ales, 72
Pils, 101
Pilsner, 45, 119, 129, 145; American, 65; Czech, 65; German, 65
Pilsner glass, 36
Pilsner Lager, 136
Pilsner of El Salvador Export , 178
Pilsner Urquell, 111
Pilsner Urquell-Plzensky Prazdroj, 111
Pinkus Alt, 105
Pinkus Pils, 105
Pinkus Weizen, 105
Pinnacle Extra Special Bitter, 165
Pint glass, 36; Imperial pint, 36; dimpled pint mug, 36

Pious Pale Ale, 158
Pittock Wee Heavy, 165
Pittsburgh Brewing Co., 30, 147
Pivovar Domazlice, 113
Pivovar Herold, 112
Pivovar Karlovy Vary, 113
Pivovar Nachod, 113
Pivovar Olomouc, 112
Pivovar Ostravar, 113
Pivovar Platan, 113
Pivovar Radegast, 112
Pivovar Regent, 112
Pivovar Samson, 113
Pivovar Velke Popovice, 112
Pivovar Zatec, 113
Pivovare Kosice, 113
Pivovare Martin, 113
Pivovary Branik, 113
Pivovary Krusovice, 113
Pivovary Starobrno, 113
Pizza, 53, 54
Plassey Brewery, 81
Plzen, 15, 21, 45
Point Nine Lager, 175
Polar Lager Beer, 178
Poleeko Gold Pale Ale, 164
Polish Breweries, 115
Pony Express Brewing Co., 153
Porch Swing Single Ale, 165
Poretti Oro, 122
Pork, 52
Port City Brewery, 159
Portage Pilsner, 151
Porter House, 85
Porter Imperial Stout, 117
Porter, 45, 115; 158, 163, 164, Brown, 65; Robust, 65
Portland Brewing Co., 166
Portsmouth Brewery, 146
Portuguese Breweries, 123
Potomac River Brewing Co., 161
Pouring technique, 37
Poznanski Browar, 116
Prangster Belgian-Style Golden Ale, 166
Prelude Holiday Ale, 144
Première, 89
Premium Clear Ale, 132
Premium Lager, 101, 133, 173, 174
Premium Light, 133
Premium Pils, 100
Premium Pilsner, 93, 105
Premium, 133
Printemps, 86
Prinzregent Luitpold Weissbier, 105
Pripps Bla, 120
Pripps Bryggeri, 120
Privatbrauerei Diebels, 103
Privatbrauerei Fritz Egger, 110
Privatbrauerei G. Schneider & Sohn, 105
Privatbrauerei Gaffel, 106
Privatbrauerei Josef Sigl, 109
Privatbrauerei Krombacher, 106
Privatbrauerei Modschiedler, 106
Prize Old Ale, 73
Prohibition, 14
Pschorr Weisse, 104
Pschorr Weisse Dunkel, 104
PT Bintang, 130
PT Delta, 130
Pub Brown Ale, 150
Publican's Special Bitter Ale, 175
Pull-top, 30

Pumphouse Brewery, 133
Pumpkin Ale, 164
Pumpkin Beer, 151
Pumpkinhead Ale, 158
Pure Brewed Lager Beer, 77
Purist Pale Ale, 142
Purple Haze, 156
Pyramid Best Brown, 163
Pyramid Breweries, 162
Pyramid Espresso Stout, 163
Pyramid Pale Ale, 162

Q

Quadrupel, 97
Quidi Vidi Brewing Co., 175

R

Raaf Brouwerij, 98
Radegast Premium Dark, 112
Radegast Premium Light, 112
Raffles Light Beer, 128
Raffo, 122
Raftman, 174
Ragutus, 115
Railway Brewing Co., 168
Ram Rod, 71
Raspberries, 24
Raspberry Brown Ale, 165
Raspberry Porter, 157
Raspberry Weizen, 166
Raspberry Wheat, 158
Rauchbier, 46, 65, 145
Raven Ale, 82
Raven Ridge Brewing Co., 168
Raven Stout, 137
Ray's Amber, 168
Real Biddy, 84
Red Ale, 46; Belgian, 66
Red Biddy Irish Ale, 84
Red Brick Ale, 157
Red Brick American Wheat, 157
Red Brick Golden Lager, 157
Red Cap, 90
Red Dog, 152
Red Horse, 128
Red Lager, 151
Red MacGregor, 82
Red meat, 54
Red Mountain Golden Ale, 157
Red Mountain Red Ale, 157
Red Mountain Wheat Beer, 157
Red Sky Ale, 167
Red Stripe, 179
Red Tail Ale, 165
Red Wolf, 150
Redback Hefeweizen, 131
Redback Light, 131
Redback Original, 131
Redhook Ale Brewery, 166
Redhook Extra Special Bitter, 166
Redhook India Pale Ale, 166
Redhook Rye Beer, 166
Regent Black, 112
Reichelbräu Aktien-Gesellschaft, 105
Reichelbräu Eisbock Bayrisch G'froms, 105
Reinheitsgebot (1516), 14, 16
Reschs DA, 131
Reschs Draught, 131
Reschs Pilsner, 131
Reschs Smooth Black Ale, 131
Reverand James Original Ale, 80
Rheineck, 135
Rice, 18, 23

Richbrau Brewery, 161
Rickard's Red, 172
Riggwelter, 77
Rikenjacks Brewing Co., 160
Ringnes Bryggeri, 119
Ringnes Export, 119
Ringnes Pilsner Beer, 119
Ringwood Brewery, 73
Rio Grande Brewing Co., 170
Ritter First Pils, 104
River City ESB, 158
River Horse Brewing Co., 146
Riverfront Stein Beer, 151
Roast beef, 53, 54
Roasted barley, 19
Roasted meat, 53
Robert Cain & Co., 79
Robespierre, 86
Rochefort 6, 90
Rochefort 8, 90
Rochefort 10, 91
Rock Creek Brewing Co., 158
Rock Creek Gold, 158
Rock Creek Red Ale, 158
Rockefeller Bock, 149
Rockford Brewing Co., 145
Rockies Brewing Co., 167
Rodenbach Belgian Red Ale, 93
Rodenbach Grand Cru, 93
Rogue Ale, 163
Rogue Ale Brewery, 163
Rogue-N-Berry, 163
Roman, Oudenaarde, 94
Romans, 12
Romer Pils, 103
Rossa, 121
Royal Oak Pale Ale, 72
Ruby, 165
Ruedrich's Red Seal Ale, 166
Rugenbräu, 108
Russell Brewing Co., 170
Russian Breweries, 116
Rye, 18
Rye Beer, 46, 65

S
S.A. Brain & Co., 80
SA Best Bitter, 80
Saaz hop, 21
Saccharomyces carlsbergensis. See
Saccharomyces uvarum.
Saccharomyces cerevisiae. See Top-
fermenting yeast
Saccharomyces uvarum, 23
Sagres Dark, 121
Sagres Golden, 121
Saint Arnold Amber Ale, 159
Saint Arnold Brewing Co., 159
Saint Arnold Kristall Weizen, 159
Saint Landelin, 86
Saint Rogue Red, 163
Saison, 46, 66
Saison 1900, 93
Saison de Silly, 93
Saison Dupont, 92
Saku Olletehas Brewery, 114
Saku Original, 114
Saku Pilsner, 114
Saku Porter, 114
Salad, 52
Salem Porter, 75
Salisbury Best Bitter, 73
Salvator, 99
Samichlaus, 107
Samuel Adams, 33

Samuel Adams Boston Lager, 140
Samuel Adams Boston Stock Ale,
140
Samuel Adams Double Bock, 141
Samuel Adams Triple Bock, 141
Samuel Smith Old Brewery, 76
Samuel Smith's Nut Brown Ale, 77
Samuel Smith's Old Brewery Pale
Ale, 77
Samuel Smith's Winter Welcome, 77
San Miguel, 122
San Miguel Dark, 128
San Miguel Pale Pilsen, 128
San Miguel Pale Pilsner, 122
Sando Stout, 129
Sandy Hunter's Ale, 82
Sans Souci, 121
Santa Fe Brewing Co., 170
Sapporo Black Beer, 125
Sapporo Breweries, 125
Sapporo Draft, 125
Saranac Chocolate Amber, 143
Saranac Season's Best, 143
Saranac Wild Berry Wheat, 143
Sausages, 53; Tasty Sausages in
Beer, 60
Saxer Brewing Co., 167
Saxer's Lemon Lager, 167
Scandinavia, 116-120
Schaeffer, 8
Schell Pils, 149
Schell Weizen, 149
Schell's Bock, 149
Schlägel Doppelbock, 110
Schlägel Kristall, 110
Schlägel Märzen, 110
Schlägel Pils, 110
Schlossbrauerei Eggenberg, 109
Schlossbrauerei Kaltenberg, 105
Schlossgold, 108
Schmalt's Alt, 149
Schneider Weisse, 105
Schultheiss Brauerei, 106
Schwarzbier, 41, 65
Schwechater Lager Beer, 110
Scotch Ale, 163
Scotch Ale, 82, 140, 144
Scotland, 81-83
Scottish Ale, 46; Export, 66; Heavy,
66; Light, 66; Strong, 66
Scottish Courage, 70, 82
Scrimshaw Pilsner Beer, 166
Sea Dog Brewing Co., 144
Sea Dog Maibock, 144
Sebourg, 86
Sediment, 39
Sélection Lambic, 91
Septante Cinq, 87
Settler's Brewery, 135
70/Ale, 81, 82
75th Street Brewery, 154
Sezoens, 93
Sezoens Quattro, 93
Sezuen, 46, 66
Shaftebury Brewing Co., 175
Shakespeare Stout, 163
Shakespeare Tavern and Brewery,
135
Shandy Gaff, 62
Sheaf Stout, 131
Shellfish, 52
Shenyang Brewery, 128
Shepherd Neame, 72
Shiner Blonde, 159
Shiner Bock, 159

Shiner Honey Wheat, 159
Shiner Kosmos Reserve, 159
Shiner Winter Ale, 159
Ship Inn/Milford Brewing Co., 146
Shipyard Brewing Co., 144
Shipyard Export Ale, 144
Shoals Pale Ale, 144
Siegel Pilsner, 104
Sierra Nevada Brewing Co., 167
Sierra Nevada Pale Ale, 167
Sierra Nevada Porter, 167
Sierra Nevada Stout, 167
Signature Pilsner, 166
Silver Creek Lager, 174
Simonds-Farsons-Cisk Brewery, 122
Sinebrychoff Brewery, 118
Singha, 128
Sioux Falls Brewing Co., 155
Sirius Summer Wheat Ale, 144
60/Ale, 81, 82
6X, 73
Sjoes, 96
Skull Splitter, 82
Skunky, 34
Sleeman Brewing and Malting Co.,
174
Sleeman Cream Ale, 174
Sleeman Original Dark, 174
Smelling, 37
Smiles Brewing Co., 73
Smith Rock Bock, 166
Smithwick's Ale, 84
Smithwick's Barley Wine, 84
Smoke, 163
Smoked foods, 53
Smooth Ale, 172
Smuttynose Brewing Co., 144
Smuttynose Portsmouth Lager, 144
Snake River Brewing Co., 170
Sneck Lifter, 79
Snow Cap Ale, 163
Snow Goose Winter Ale, 156
Snowball's Chance, 158
Snowshoe Ale, 152
Sol, 177
Solibra Abidjan, 137
Solstice Weiss, 152
Sommerbräu, 168
Soproni Sorgyar, 115
Soup, 51, 52; Midwestern Beer
Cheese Soup, 57
South African Breweries (SAB), 137
South America, 178-179
South Asia, 128-130
South Australia Brewing Co., 133
Southeast Asia, 128-130
Southeast England, 70-72
Southern Europe, 120-123
Southside Light Session Ale, 165
Southwest England, 72-73
Spanish brewers, 123
Spanish Peaks Brewing Co., 170
Sparging, 25
Spaten-Franziskaner-Bräy, 100
Special 6, 91
Special Bitter, 82
Special Bock, 119
Special Dark Lager, 117
Special Light, 133
Special Pale Ale, 173
Special Strong Bitter, 77
Specialty Beers, 50
Speights Distinction Ale, 134
Speights Gold Medal, 134
Speights Old Dark, 134

Spendrups Bryggeri, 120
Spendrups Original, 120
Spitfire, 72
Splügen Bock, 122
Splügen Dry, 122
Spoetzl Brewery, 159
Sprecher Black Bavarian, 150
Sprecher Brewing Co., 150
Sprecher Special Amber,
Spring Ale, 141
Spring Bock, 159
Spring Maibock, 143
Spring Street Brewing Co., 144
Spring Wheat , 174
Spring Wheat Ale, 156
St. Ambroise Framboise, 172
St. Ambroise Oatmeal Stout, 171
St. Ambroise Pale Ale, 171
St. Andrew's Ale, 82
St. Arnoldus, 86
St. Nikolaus Bock Beer, 144
St. Patrick's Stout, 174
St. Pauli Brauerei, 106
St. Stan's Amber Ale, 167
St. Stan's Barley Wine, 167
St. Stan's Brewery, 167
St. Stan's Dark, 167
St. Stan's Fest, 167
St. Vincent Brewery, 180
Staatliches Hofbräuhaus, 106
Stadtbühl, 108
Standard Reference Method, 39, 64
Star, 137
Star Union Brewing Co., 152
Staropramen, 112
Staropramen Brewery, 112
Staropramen Dark, 112
Staub Brewery, 147
Steak, 53, 54
Steam, 47, 66
Steelhead Brewing Co., 170
Steffl Export, 110
Stein, ceramic, 36
Steinbier, 47
Steinlager, 134
Stevens Point Brewery, 155
Stewart's Brewing Co., 145
Stiefel, 36
Stiftsbrauerei Schlägl, 110
Stille Nacht, 92
Stone City Brewing , 153
Stoney Creek Brewing Co., 153
Storage, 34
Storm Brewing Co., 175
Stoudt Brewing Co., 144
Stoudt's Fest, 144
Stoudt's Gold, 144
Stoudt's Honey Double mai Bock, 144
Stoudt's Pils, 144
Stout, 47, 133, 143 ; Dry or Irish
Stout, 47, 66; Foreign-Style, 66;
Oatmeal Stout, 48, 66; 151,
Russian Imperial Stout, 48, 66;
Sweet Stout, 48, 66
Stout Float, 63
Stovepipe Porter, 143
Straffe Hendrik, 94
Strawberry Blonde, 166
Strong Ale, English, 65
Strong Suffolk, 76
Strongcroft, 135
Strubbe Brewery, 94
Struis, 97
Student, 93

Studley Ale, 159
Styles, 39-50, 64-66
Subliminator Dopplebock, 158
Submarino, 63
Sudwerk Privatbrauerei Hübsch, 169
Sugar, 23
Sumerians, 11, 12
Summer Ale, 71, 141
Summer Brew, 166
Summer ESB, 143
Summer Lightening, 73
Summer Pale Ale, 151
Summer Wheat, 143
Summer Wheat Ale, 143
Summerfest, 159, 167
Summersault, 73
Summertime German-Style Kölsch Bier, 151
Summit Brewing Co., 152
Sun Fest, 163
Sun Valley Brewing Co., 169
SunRage, 158
Sunshine, 165
Suntory, 126
Suntory Alt, 126
Suntory Black Beer, 126
Suntory Weizen, 126
Super Dortmunder, 96
Super Dry, 128
Super Hop's, 126
Superior, 177
Suprema Special Beer, 178
Susquehanna Stout, 142
Sussex Best Bitter, 71
Sussex Mild, 71
Sussex Pale Ale, 71
Sussex XXXX Old Ale, 71
Swan Brewery, 133
Sweden, 120
Sweetwater Brewing Co., 160
Swinkel's Export Beer, 96
Switzerland, 107-108
Sydney Bitter, 133
Sylvestor, 96

T

T & R Theakston, 78
T. D. Ridleys & Sons, 76
Tabernash Amber, 167
Tabernash Brewing Co., 167
Tabernash Golden, 167
Tabernash Munich, 167
Tabernash Weiss, 167
Table beer, 13
Taddy Porter, 77
Tall Ship Ale Co., 175
Tally Ho, 75
Tankard, pewter, 36
Tankstream Brewing Co., 133
Tanzania Breweries, 138
Tasmanian Devil Ale, 164
Tasting, 34-39
Tecate, 177
Temperature, serving, 35
Tempo Beer Industries, 138
Terken Blonde, 87
Terken Brune, 87
Terminator Stout, 165
Tetley & Son, 78
Tetley Bitter, 78
Tetley Mild, 78
Tettnang hop, 21
Thai Amarit Brewery, 130
Thai food, 53, 54

Thames Valley Brewing Co., 176
Theakston Best Bitter, 78
Third Coast Beer, 151
Third Coast Old Ale, 151
Thomas Caffrey, 85
Thomas Cooper Finest Export, 132
Thomas Hardy Country Bitter, 72
Thomas Hardy's Ale, 72
Thomas Kemper Amber, 163
Thor Bryggerierne, 117
Three-Finger Jack Amber, 167
Three-Finger Jack Roasted Red Hefedunkel, 167
Three-Finger Jack Stout, 167
Three-Finger Jack Summer Lager, 167
Three-Finger JackFrost Winter Dopplebock, 167
Thunder Valley Brewery, 169
Thunderstorm, 73
Thwaites Best Mild, 79
Thwaites Bitter, 79
Tiger Beer, 128
Tiger Classic Beer, 128
Timmermans, 94
Timothy Taylor & Co., 78
Tin Whistle Brewing Co., 176
Titje, 93
Tollemache & Cobbold Brewery, 76
Tolly's Strong Ale, 76
Tom Paine, 71
Tomintoul Brewery, 83
Tomos Watkin & Sons, 81
Tooheys, 133
Tooheys Amber Bitter, 133
Tooheys Extra Dry, 133
Tooheys Gold Bitter, 133
Tooheys New, 133
Tooheys Red Bitter, 133
Topazio, 121
Top-fermenting yeast, 23, 39
Traditional Ale, 173
Trafalgar Ale, 73
Transformer Ale, 165
Trapper Premium Lager, 174
Trapper's Red Beer, 134
Trappist, 48; Dubbel, 66; Tripel, 66
Traquair House Ale, 82
Traquair House Brewery, 82
Tremont Ale, 142
Tremont India Pale Ale, 142
Tremont Porter, 142
Tremont Winter Ale, 142
Trinity Brewing Co., 147
Tripel, 91, 96, 97
Trippel, 165
Triumph Brewing Co., 146
Trois Monts, 85
Trois Monts Grand Reserve, 85
Trois Pistole, 174
Trumer Pils, 109
Tsingtao (Qingdao) Brewery, 127
Tsingtao Beer, 127
Tsingtao Dark Beer, 127
Tuborg Beer, 117
Tuborg Brewery, 117
Tuborg Gold, 117
Tuborg Groen, 117
Tuborg Porter, 117
Tulip glass, flared, 35
Tulsa Brewing Co., 155
Tumbler, 36; Weizenbier tumbler, 36
Tume, 114
Turbodog, 156

Turkish Brewery, 123
Tusker lage, 136
Tusker Premium Lager, 136
Twelve Horse Ale, 143
Tyskie Browar, 115

U

U Fleku, 112
UB Export Lager, 129
UB Premium Ice Beer, 129
Uehara Shuzo Co., 126
Ueli Lager, 108
Ueli Weizenbier, 108
Uff-Da Wisconsin Dark, 152
Ukrainian Breweries, 116
Unertl Weissbier, 107
Unibroue, 174
Unicer-Uniao Cervejeira, 123
Union Station Brewery, 147
United Breweries, 129
United States, 138-170
Upper Canada Brewing Co., 174
Upper Canada Dark Ale, 175
Upper Canada Lager, 175
Upper Canada Pale Ale, 175
Upper Canada Rebellion Lager, 175
Upper Canada True Bock, 175
Upper Canada Wheat, 175
Urbock 23, 109
Ur-Bock Dunkel, 104
Ur-Bock Hell, 104
Urbock, 104
Ur-Weisse, 99
Ushers, 73

V

Vaclav 12, 112
Valiant, 75
Valley Gold, 173
Van Vollenhoven Stout, 97
Vancouver Island Brewing Co., 176
Vander Linden, 95
Vanilla, 24
Varsity, 72
Vaux Breweries, 78
Vegetables, 52
Verboden Vrucht, 92
Vermont Pub & Brewery, 148
Victoria Bitter, 132
Victory Ale, 75
Victory Brewing Co., 147
Vienna, 49, 66
Vienna Amber, 145
Viet Ha Brewery, 130
Viking Brewing Co., 155
Virgin Amber, 167
Virgin Dark, 167
Vita Stout, 134
Voll Damm, 122
Voyager Pale Ale, 151

W

W.H. Brakspear & Sons, 71
Wadsworth & Co., 73
Waikato Draught, 135
Wales, 79-81
Wallace IPA, 82
Warsteiner Brauerei, 107
Warszawski Browar, 116
Wartek Brewery, 108
Warthog Ale, 173
Wassail Bowl, 63
WasSail, 164
Water, 16, 21-22
Water Gap Wheat, 142
Webster's Yorkshire Bitter, 77, 82
Wee Heavy Scotch Ale , 164

Weeping Radish Brewery, 159
Weidman's Old Fort Brewery, 159
Weinkeller Brewery, 151
Weissbrauerei Hans Hopf, 106
Weisse, 151
Weisse Bock, 106
Weisse Export, 106
Weissbier, 102
Weizen Berry, 163
Weizen Bock, 105
Weizen Gold Champagner, 109
Weizen Gold Dunkel Hefeweizen, 109
Weizenbock, 66
Weizenfest, 118
Wellington County Brewery, 172
West Virginia Brewing Co., 161
Western Reserve Brewing, 154
Western Samoa Breweries, 135
Westmalle Dubbel, 91
Whale Ale, 163
Wheat, 18; 167, American, 66;
  Berliner Weisse, 66; Dunkelweizen,
  66; Hefeweizen, 66; Kristallweizen,
  66
Wheat Beer, 49, 66, 71, 162
Wheat Berry Beer, 166
Wheat malt, 19
Wheaten Ale, 162
Whister Brewing Co., 176
Whistle Stop Ale, 167
Whitbread Beer Co., 70
Whitbread Porter, 77
White Ale, 141
White Beer, 165
White Buffalo Ale, 164
White Cap Lager, 136
White Forest, 166
White Ox Ale, 158
Widberry Weizrn, 168
Widmer Brothers Brewing Co., 167
Wieckse Witte, 97
Wieselburger Gold, 110
Wieselburger Stammbräu, 110
Wilbroe Bryggeri, 117
Wild Goose Brewery, 156
Wild Goose Golden Ale, 156
Wild Goose India Pale Ale, 156
Wild Goose Nut Brown Ale, 156
Wild Goose Oatmeal Stout, 156
Wild Goose Porter, 156
Wild Summer Passion Wheat Ale, 158
Williamsville Brewery, 159
Wilmington Brewing Co., 160
Wiltshire Traditional Bitter, 73
Windhoek, 137
Windjammer Blonde ale, 144
Winter Ale, 76, 152, 173
Winter Anniversary New York Beer, 143
Winter Bräu, 163
Winter Brew, 150, 166
Winter Frost, 143
Winter Lager, 141, 151
Winter Passion Spiced Ale, 158
Winter Porter, 144
Winter Stout, 159
Winter Warmer, 143
Winter Wheat, 159
Winterbrau Holiday Ale, 165
Winterfest, 164
Winterhook Winter Ale, 167
Wintermacht, 168
Wirthington White Shield, 74
Wit Amber Ale, 144
Wit Black Ale, 144

Wit White Ale, 144
Witbier, 50, 66
Wolf Eel Ale, 163
Wolverhampton & Dudley Breweries, 74
Wood Brewery, 75
Woodforde's 76
Woodstock Brewing and Bottling Co., 152
Woodstock Brewing Co., 147
World beers, 67-180
World War I, 15
World War II, 15
Wort, 25, 26
Wort chiller, 16, 26
Wunster, 123

X

XB Best Bitter, 75
XB, 78
Xingu Black Beer, 178
X-Pert, 97
XXXB, 75
XXXX Bitter, 133
XXXX Draught, 133
XXXX Gold Lager, 133
XXXX Light Bitter, 133
XXXXX Stout, 166

Y

Yakima Brewing and Malting Co., 168
Yard-of-ale, 36
Yards Brewing Co., 147
Ybor City Brewing Co., 160
Yeast, 16, 22-23
Yebisu, 126
Yellow Rose Brewing Co., 161
Yorkshire, 76-78
Yorsh, 63
Young & Co.'s Brewery, 70
Younger IPA, 82
Younger No. 3, 82
Younger Scotch Bitter, 82
Yuengling Dark Brewed Porter, 145
Yuengling Premium Beer, 145
Yuengling Premium Light Beer, 145
Yuengling Traditional Lager, 145

Z

Zagorka Brewery, 115
Zambia Breweries, 138
Zaragozana, 122
Zatte, 97
Zhigulevskoye Brewery, 116
Zhujiang Brewery, 128
Zig-Zig River Lager, 166
Zima, 164
Zimbabwe National Breweries, 138
Zip City Brewing Co., 145
Zum Uerige, 107
Zywiec Browar, 115
Zywiec Full Light, 115
Zywiec Porter, 115

Photo Credits
pp.11,13(3),14(3),20(2),22,26,
28(center,bottom),29,31,32,
68(2),83(top),100,102,139 by
agreement with Hulton Getty/
Liaison Agency
p.24 by agreement with Alan Hicks and
Deschutes Brewery
pp.27(top),28(top) by agreement with
Celis Brewing Co.
pp.25,27(bottom) by agreement with
Bitburger Brewery